Advancing
Family
Theories

For my daughter Rebecca and her princess, Kodi.
Thank you both for teaching me about your worlds.

Advancing Family Theories

James M. White
University of British Columbia

SAGE Publications
Thousand Oaks ▪ London ▪ New Delhi

For information:

 Sage Publications, Inc.
2455 Teller Road
Thousand Oaks, California 91320
E-mail: order@sagepub.com

Sage Publications Ltd.
1 Oliver's Yard
55 City Road
London, EC1Y 1SP
United Kingdom

Sage Publications India Pvt. Ltd.
B-42 Panchsheel Enclave
Post Box 4109
New Delhi 110 017 India

Library of Congress Cataloging-in-Publication Data

White, James M., 1946-
Advancing family theories/James M. White.
    p. cm.
Includes bibliographical references and index.
ISBN 0-7619-2905-3 (pbk.)
    1. Family—Philosophy. 2. Family—Research. 3. Sociology—Philosophy.
4. Sociology—Methodology. I. Title.
HQ728.W52 2005
306.85'01—dc22

                                    2004006456

Printed on acid-free paper in the United States of America.

04 05 06 07 08 09 10 9 8 7 6 5 4 3 2 1

Acquiring Editor:	Jim Brace-Thompson
Editorial Assistant:	Karen Ehrmann
Production Editor:	Tracy Alpern
Copy Editor:	Diana Breti
Typesetter:	C&M Digitals (P) Ltd.
Indexer:	Jeanne R. Busemeyer
Cover Designer:	Michelle Kenny

Contents

Preface

This book is the outcome of a series of long-standing difficulties in teaching graduate-level theory courses. Understanding these difficulties is a key to understanding this project. For example, one of the difficulties that consistently plagued me was the absence of any one text that would accomplish all that I would wish. Among those items on my wish list for such a book is that it would grapple with contemporary philosophical challenges to social scientific theory. Certainly there are philosophy books that struggle with these issues, but I wanted a text that would examine these issues from the perspective of the social science theorist. A second item on my wish list is for a book that would give the student a precise notion of what theory is and how theories work in research. A third item on my wish list is that the book would not just stay in the philosophical realms but would examine particular substantive theories that explain and predict family behaviors. Finally, I wanted the book to be complementary to the *Family Theories* book (White & Klein, 2002). The *Family Theories* book provides a useful survey of the major theoretical frameworks. However, I wanted an advanced book that would go into greater detail in specific substantive theories as well as the philosophical foundations. Certainly my wish list is longer, but you can already see that such a book doesn't exist. Hence, as with the first *Family Theories* book, the obvious remedy was to sit down and write it.

Although the principal motivation for this book originated from my graduate teaching, other problems arose through my professional interactions with colleagues. Although these problems are numerous, I can summarize them as a devaluation of theory as a component of research. Many colleagues seem to believe they have attended to theory once they identify what I call a conceptual hypothesis. Indeed, in some areas of endeavor "conceptual hypotheses" are considered theory. This problem is, of course, tied to a resurgence of blind empiricism that assumes all we need are the "facts" and fails to realize that "facts" are theoretical entities created from theoretical propositions and assumptions. Adding this clarification and correction to this perspective would serve graduate students as well as colleagues.

Finally, I see this book as opening up the field of theory to both students and colleagues. I am convinced that once theory and theorizing is seen as actually a very grounded and straightforward process, we might see a resurgence in the building and fortifying of social science theory about families. I feel some urgency for social science to return to a more theoretically oriented stance because I perceive that without theory social science will become a kind of journalism with statistics.

A last word here is on my mistakes and controversy. You can't undertake an ambitious project like this without being prepared to make some mistakes and to stimulate some controversy. No one with any intellectual honesty would ever say that any study or academic project is pristine and without errors and omissions. Certainly that is true of this project. However, it is the nature of the scientific community of scholars to debate and point out these errors. Indeed, I regard the best outcome of this book to be the stimulation of discussion and debate and correction of its errors and omissions. That simply reaffirms for me the perspective on theory and science that this book argues.

James M. White
Vancouver, Canada

Acknowledgments

Although one starts a book alone, as an idea, as a prospectus sent to a publisher, one finishes in the company of a small army of colleagues and supporters. Certainly this book is no different from others, but each project is special and has its own particular cast.

First I would like to thank David Klein, who encouraged me to take on this project years ago. The folks at Sage Publications were their usual marvelous selves. Jim Brace-Thompson's initial enthusiasm for this project and his unswerving support was absolutely essential and so much appreciated. Two anonymous reviewers did a splendid job of reading the first draft, catching major errors, and offering splendid advice. As always, Karen Ehrmann and her crew were there to correct most of my minor errors and bring this book into production. My special thanks to Diana Breti for her excellent copyediting of the manuscript and her ability to keep me moving to meet deadlines.

I also owe a considerable debt of gratitude to my students attending the 2003 fall graduate theory seminar: Alice Balter, Clifton Chow, Theo Elfers, Jassal Surita, Joanna Tang, Laura Templeton, and Lyanne Westie. These students were very patient with me as I tried ideas out on them and exposed them to material used in the book. I also appreciate that the students kindly read the first versions of Chapters 1 through 4 and showed me that this material was not too difficult for these first-year graduate students.

Finally, I owe much gratitude to my family for support, patience, and understanding while I concentrated on writing. Much of the book was written at home, and my family was often neglected and ignored as a result of my concentration on this project. I was also variously assisted by Robin, Amy, Kelly, and Rebecca as they looked up words in the dictionary for me or found missing references.

All of these people supported and assisted me in various capacities. Whatever success this book enjoys is largely due to them. Of course, the errors, omissions, and the more major conceptual problems are ones for which I take full responsibility. And as for me, my rewards have been obtained in the process of writing this book, which was so enriched by all of these people.

1

Introduction

The title of this book, *Advancing Family Theories*, contains a quite intentional double entendre or complex metaphor. On the one hand, this book intends to advance family theory, to push it ahead of where it is today. Part of this project entails explaining where we are today, how we got here, and why the perspectives I propose might move us forward. This means we must look at the history and current practice of family theory. We must gain a good understanding of how and why theory works. The first section of this book deals with these issues.

On the other hand, *Advancing Family Theories* also means placing before you a product I am advancing or promulgating. The second section of this book does exactly that. Two relatively new theories are advanced: rational choice theory and transition theory, both of which deal extensively with families. I regard these two theories as exceptionally promising for family research and understanding. Both theories are relatively underutilized by researchers. Both theories are highly formalized, although in this book I have avoided any reference to their mathematical side. These theories are advanced because I believe they will "travel well" over the cross-cultural and multicultural terrain that family researchers will find themselves traversing in the 21st century.

Finally, *Advancing Family Theories* does not entail certain things. In the third and last section of this book, I examine moral decisions and meta-theory as two elements that are not directly tied to theoretical advancement. In the case of morality and ethics, I argue that we should not expect theories of families to tell us how to act morally or ethically. That is clearly the venue of moral philosophy or religion but not of family theory. Likewise, metatheory may assist us with integrating various family theories, but it is not a family theory in itself. The last chapter of this book seeks to clarify what I have and have not achieved.

What Is Family Theory?

White and Klein (2002) begin their book by addressing the question "what is theory?" and I believe it is an obvious place to begin a book of theory. However, it is also important to explain what makes *family theory* different from other social theories. It is important to explain why family theory, as opposed to other sociological and psychological theories of social groups, is necessary and indeed required if family relationships are to be understood and explained.

As White and Klein (2002) point out, there are many different definitions of theory. However, from the outset it is important that this book focuses on scientific theory as opposed to literary theory or religious theory. The goals of scientific theory are clearly different from the goals of other forms of theory. The goals are to explain and predict observable phenomena. Other forms of theory have other goals; for example, literary theory is more concerned with textual interpretation. Certainly scientific theory may borrow methods and insights from these other forms of theory, but in the final analysis the difference in goals distinguishes these forms of theory.

Scientific theory explains and predicts by subsuming a specific instance of a phenomenon under a more general and inclusive statement regarding all phenomena in the same class. Chapters 2 and 3 examine this process. For the present, however, note that theories must be concerned with producing general statements that "cover" many particular instances. Later in this book I discuss this as the "covering law" model of explanation.

Because scientific theories contain general statements that are capable of covering specific instances, it is clear that among these statements must be propositions that take into consideration the context of the phenomenon. After all, most of us have seen pictures of space travelers floating inside their orbiting craft, seemingly free of gravity. That does not mean the theory of gravity is wrong, but simply that there must be a proposition about the decline of the effects of gravity based on mass and distance from an object. Clearly, theories usually have multiple statements of propositions.

These multiple propositions must be linked together in a systematic and coherent fashion. It is tempting to say they should be logically interconnected, but that might be somewhat limiting. There are many and sundry ways to link propositions besides logic. As we shall see, one of the roles of models can be to formalize and link propositions. Yet there are many types of models, and theory need not be limited to just logic or even to just one of the many types of logic (e.g., Aristotelian, symbolic). So the easiest way to envision how theoretical propositions are linked is to say that they are linked systematically or coherently. The purpose here is to point out that the linkage itself and the coherence of the theory is a topic worthy of consideration.

All of the preceding fails to pinpoint the one critical difference between scientific theories and other forms of theory. That critical difference is that scientific theories can be refuted by empirical evidence. Indeed, most of our theoretical research is concerned with critical tests that would distinguish which of two or more theories would provide a better fit with the data. Other forms of theory (religious or literary) do not demand that theories are empirically testable. This is the *sine qua non* of scientific theory.

The preceding discussion simply lays out what most definitions of scientific theory include as aspects of a definition. Scientific theories are defined by the following:

1. A set of general propositions

2. Scope and boundary statements about the relevant contexts

3. Systematic relations between the propositions that provide intellectual coherence

4. At least some deductions or formulations of the theory can be empirically tested (have the potential to be refuted)

Although this is a minimalist version of a definition of scientific theory, it nonetheless captures the essential elements. Even this minimalist characterization of scientific theory could be interpreted by some to mean that any group of ideas that is called a scientific theory must have each element. This would be totally incorrect, as we shall see later in this book. These essential elements may not always be present in every group of ideas because theories evolve from initial ideas to full-blown deductive theories. There are various stages along the way, and we should not treat the development of theory as a mechanistic "paint by numbers" sort of enterprise. The only element that is absolutely required is that ideas are subject to being empirically refuted. This topic will, of course, receive much more attention later in the book.

Each theory concerns a particular type of phenomenon. The particular phenomenon that we want to explain and understand may require particular types of concepts and may place constraints on the scope of the theory. Nowhere is this more true than in regard to family theory.

Family theory is, of course, concerned with families. This concern provides all family theory with similar scope and boundary assumptions. Furthermore, understanding these assumptions explains why theory about families, rather than theories about generic social groups, is required to explain family relationships. White and Klein (2002) point out four dimensions of families that make them different from other social groups. Families last longer than most social groups. Families have intergenerational relationships unlike other social groups. Families contain two types of social relationships (affinal and consanguineal), whereas most social groups are only based on affinity. Finally, families are part of a larger type of social organization: kinship (pp. 19–21).

These differences are not just differences in quantity or degree from the types of relationships found in other social groups. These differences are so profound as to constitute the need for family theory apart from theories about social groups such as work groups and friendship groups. Indeed, those that would attempt to reduce the study of family to the same concepts and propositions used for theories about friendship or work groups would end up missing the point. As we shall see in Chapter 6, Coleman (1990) attempted to reduce the explanation of family behavior to the same processes that govern other social groups but ended up seeing that this would be impossible. Too many important aspects of the phenomena captured in "family" would be submerged and ignored by such reductionism.

The family is both a biological unit and a social unit, a unit that has a connection with history and a connection with the future. It is a social group where emotions such as loyalty, love, devotion, commitment, and sharing are not only finely expressed but even expected. Seldom do work or friendship groups trace those that preceded them in role or position, yet most families are not only aware of progenitors but consider this as their lineage and heritage.

Unlike other types of social groups, family history is important in understanding behavior. Family relationships are not only present and immediate, as in the home, but some are distant and nonimmediate, as with kin. Family membership is not voluntary in family of orientation (origin) but in many cultures is somewhat more voluntaristic for family of procreation. The recruitment of new family members is totally unlike the recruitment of new members in friendship groups or new members in work groups. All of these differences warrant developing a theory about this form of group that is extremely different from the theory for other social groups.

Theory or Theories?

This book takes an implicit position in regard to whether or not there is the possibility of one unified theory or a diversity of theories. The implicit answer is indicated in the book's title, *Advancing Family Theories*. It is probably wise to make this position more explicit from the start. I do not envision that one encompassing theory about families can, should, or will emerge. Certainly such a unified theory does not emerge in this book, nor is such a unified theory necessarily desirable.

The reason for this position is that I believe the easiest theory to develop in the social sciences is at the macroscopic level. At the macrolevel, classes and categories are easier to construct, and because we deal with aggregations of individuals, the statistical analyses provide more robust findings. For example, dealing with the business cycle or voting behavior or even the survival of organizations, although complex, is not concerned with elements like love and affection. When we move to a relatively small social group such as the family or an even smaller group such as the marital dyad, we find that we move increasingly toward the necessity of incorporating individual and group processes. Categories and classes may seem inadequate to capture the richness and emotion in the relationships. Indeed, only idiographic research may seem up to the task.

I do believe a science of social groups and relationships is possible, which means general nomothetic statements are possible. I see the problems facing the scientific study of the family as not dissimilar to the problems facing the wildlife biologist studying wolf packs. Certainly terrain and context change dramatically from the arctic to the plains. Yet elements of wolf pack social organization and leadership can be understood across these contexts. Likewise, I believe we have generated family theories that truly assist us with understanding families across cultural environments.

Although I believe a nomothetic approach is warranted, I would also argue that the family, marriage, mate selection, and other family relationships are inherently more complex and symbolic. As a result, I believe family theorists initially attempt to understand smaller phenomena and then expand that understanding in an attempt to explain more of family behavior. So, for example, exchange theory may work relatively well when examining voluntaristic mate selection, but as we try to extend it to long-term marriages we may find it less useful. Likewise, several theories, such as feminist theories, use one concept or process in an attempt to explain all family phenomena. The result is that although these single-concept theories are appealingly simple, they fail to assist in explaining a great deal of phenomena; for instance, happy nonegalitarian marriages.

The result of our theorizing to date is to have evolved theory groups or frameworks (see White & Klein, 2002) that largely reflect the limited focus from which they began. In the third section of this book, I discuss using metatheory to help integrate and understand the strengths and weaknesses of these frameworks so that we might better design more complete theories.

For the moment, however, one of the great strengths of family theory is that it is family *theories*. Other areas of the social sciences should be envious of this theoretical richness.

So What?

One of the questions that plague theorists is the "so what?" question. The "so what?" question simply asks, "Why do we need to bother with theory?" Many empiricists believe the data speak for themselves. Even more to the point, some empiricists fear theory, in that they worry that claims will be made that exceed the data and hence present a false impression and grandiose claims to the public. For example, if we know that the birth rate for a country is dropping and that it is below replacement level, why do we need a theory about fertility or a theory about population change? The answer to such questions is far from obvious.

We live in a time where we have tremendous amounts of information available to us. In the empirical sciences, every journal issue contains data and findings that would have represented the output for entire years not more than a couple of decades ago. The challenge this wealth of information provides is the task of turning information into knowledge. To transform this welter of facts and findings into knowledge, it must be integrated so that it forms an internally coherent perspective that can make sense of our world. The only way I can envisage the coherent integration of so much information is by using theories.

Imagine that our data and information is similar to a teenager's closet where clothes are scattered all over the floor of the closet. The rod and hangers above provide a way to hang up the clothes, but they also provide a way to organize the clothes. Blouses on one side, pants, skirts, and so on. Now we can access the clothes we need far more readily, and we know where new skirts or blouses go. Theories are like organizing principles that allow us to not only store and access information but also to recall and understand. Without theory we lack organization of information. Without theory we cannot plan for the future. With an organized closet we know what is clean and available and can see options to combine outfits. Likewise, theories allow us to see information in a particular way and to combine that information with other information to understand our world.

Of course, theories perform many other functions for us besides organizing data and observations. For example, theories explain, interpret, and predict findings. Theories help us accumulate information and guide the direction our research may take. Despite all these varied functions, many researchers and members of the public still ask, "So what?" I can only respond that without theory our world would be a world of sensation and confusion "full of sound and fury, signifying nothing" (*Macbeth*, Act V, Scene 5).

The current status of family theory is somewhat in question (Daly, 2003; Doherty, 1999; Knapp, 1997; Sprey, 1999; Vargus, 1999; White & Mason, 1999a, 1999b). For example, Vargus (1999) offers the following picture of the situation:

> Marriage and family theorists seem, when considered in relation to classical theory, to be those leading a "wander in the wilderness"—a wilderness rooted in biological categories and no concern for individual processes that transcend those categories. Further, the practitioners are wandering with them, without a Moses. (p. 202)

Vargus's concern is further amplified by Doherty (1999) when he identifies the postmodernist challenges to the idea of "family as a phenomenon" and the critiques of positivist family science (p. 209). And for therapists, Hawley and Geske (2000) report that their

> findings raise questions about the role of theory in family therapy research. It may be that researchers need to take a closer look at what purpose theory serves, since a number of studies in this analysis either did not appear to incorporate theory or use it in a way that would be considered traditional "theory" building. Many clinicians today operate from a postpositivist orientation that highlights the uniqueness of each client and they may fail to see the relevance of research that uses theory in a positivist paradigm to evaluate similarities across families instead of focusing on the particular characteristics of each family. (pp. 21–22)

These appraisals raise questions about the degree to which scholars share the view that our major goal is the production of knowledge about the family. As a corollary, there is also a lack of consensus about how our subject matter, our theories, and our research methods are constituted. It is the aim of this book to address these challenges.

Finally, in the concluding chapter of this book I argue that theories are tools we need to assist our understanding and planning. In that same vein, this book aims to assist in organizing the "closet" of theory so that students and scholars of the family can more successfully have access to these marvelous tools.

PART I

Understanding Theory: Product and Process

This book is intended for graduate students and scholars of the family. It necessarily assumes a certain degree of background in family theory and even more so in philosophy and history of science. There are two dominant approaches in philosophy of science. One approach is to cover the schools of thought. For example, Benton and Craig (2001) do an excellent job with this sort of approach in their recent book. Such approaches usually cover schools such as positivism, empiricism, phenomenology, and so on. Although this approach has its merits, it is not the approach I take in the next section. The reason for this is that although such approaches educate the student, they seldom confront the issues except as they are constituted by each school of thought or even ignored by some schools. This can be terribly frustrating for readers. The second approach is to examine issues. Typical issues would be the issue of realism versus subjectivism, the issue of nomothetic versus idiographic knowledge, and so on. For example, Latour (1999) and Potter (1999) use such an approach. Potter uses a Socratic dialogue format to discuss issues such as the compatibility of rationalist and empiricist epistemologies. I am more in favor of such approaches because the reader can readily see the various positions on any given issue. This approach usually faces the problem of biasing the perspectives with the viewpoint of the author. This is virtually unavoidable.

The approach I take in this section, and indeed throughout the book, is more like what might appear in a journal. I assume some passing acquaintanceship with the issue and provide what I believe is the best perspective on this issue at this time. I do take a position. Some will want to label the position as "positivism," others may call it "empiricism," and others still might label it "rationalism." I don't think the labels address the issues, so I consider them irrelevant to any profound academic argument. I am more concerned with the degree to which the science can argue for external knowledge, the degree of uncertainty with which we must live, and the place of morality and ideology in the justification of knowledge. I strongly feel that those studying the family would appreciate the elucidation of positions on such questions. This is the approach that is taken throughout.

A certain level of background is assumed in these discussions. For example, in Chapter 2 the brief history of science is quite distinct from the view Kuhn (1962, 1996) has taken. In fact, Kuhn pays little attention to science before written history, yet ethnobotany certainly shows that classification and taxonomic knowledge was advanced during that time. Furthermore, Kuhn pays great attention to physics and chemistry and little attention to such areas as anthropology and biology during the 1800s. The brief history provided in Chapter 2 attempts to paint a somewhat different and more diverse portrait of science than did Kuhn. So although reading Kuhn's classic work is not necessary to understand the view offered here, it would certainly assist. Indeed, understanding Kuhn's essay is singularly important in order to understand many of the claims made by contextualists. But this is just one example, and I could name other authors, such as Popper and Longino, that would assist in understanding the chapter. In the end, however, I have tried to write for both those familiar with these texts and those who are not familiar. It is my intent in Part I to speak equally well to both audiences, although I realize the threat to such an intention is that I might speak to neither.

The first section of this book could receive many different titles. The section covers a diverse set of issues and subjects, yet I believe it composes a coherent whole. Chapter 2 offers a perspective on the development of family theory within the larger framework of social science. This perspective nicely complements the history contained in the first chapter of White and Klein (2002). It does address the special effects the theory construction movement of the 1960s and 1970s had on the fortunes of theory in family studies. Indeed, I believe the effects of the theory construction movement were so profound as to launch theory into at least a decade of stagnation. I also believe that this stagnation may now have ended and that we are embarked again on a fruitful course for both the social sciences and family theory. In this sense we could title the section "the coming fortunes of family theory."

Chapter 3 deals with the critics of science and theory. This chapter covers some of the most vital arguments about the legitimacy and worth of social science and family theory. These arguments serve to threaten the traditional value placed on logical thinking, rational discourse, and scientific inquiry. Although I believe many of the criticisms are so patently absurd that they do not require answering, I also see from the journals and from my colleagues that I am dead wrong about these criticisms not needing a rejoinder. Indeed, for many the arguments of the postpositivists seem both powerful and appealing. One only has to read the introduction to the 1993 *Sourcebook on Family Theories and Methods* to see that these arguments are attracting adherents. Chapter 3 was a difficult chapter to write because White and Mason (1999a) had previously responded to these critiques. However, with new sources yet again championing the postpositivist perspective (Longino, 2002), it was clear to me that this book must address these issues once again.

I should make it clear that I don't think the critiques are wrong if positivism is as naïve an area of discourse as the critics characterize it as being. For example, many philosophers (e.g., Peirce, Dewey, Husserl, and Popper) have long supported the notion that "objectivity," "community consensus," and "intersubjectivity" are all concerned with the process by which the scientific community agrees on standards of evidence and hence justification. However, hearing that all positivism believes in a simple realist view of the world leads me to wonder if critics exclude these eminent philosophers of science from the "positivist" camp. After a while, the critics list so many absurd characterizations of science and scientific discourse that I don't even know who would be left to hold such naïve and silly positions as are attributed to positivism.

On the other hand, Chapter 3 is not defending the naïve positions that the critics maintain are true of positivism. Science is a social phenomenon. Scientists indeed are human and make mistakes. Truth is consensual. I agree with all of these claims. Who would disagree? However, Chapter 3 endeavors to show that the consequence of these beliefs is not abandoning the scholarly position that truth is tentative and that evidence is necessary for even holding a tentative perspective on the world. I would argue that science is the outcome of these arguments. I believe this discourse to be essential for developing scholars in our field and the social sciences in general.

Chapters 4 and 5 are close companions and serve to provide a transition to the substantive theories that follow in Part II. Chapter 4 focuses more on how social science "does" science and theory. The importance of laws, construction of theory, and models and data are all discussed in this chapter. Perhaps surprising to some will be the accompanying discussion of metaphor. I was convinced early on by Black (1962) of the importance of metaphor in theory and research. After the work by Lakoff and Johnson (1980), I became even more convinced. I believe it is also essential to examine the types of metaphors, including formal mathematical models, and the purpose the metaphor is used to achieve. This perspective is evident in the discussion of the way metaphors or mappings are variously used to achieve the functions that White and Klein (2002) list for theories. In Chapter 5, it is my intention to make our tools for developing theory more easily understood by young scholars, perceived as less rigid, and at the same time more precise. As you can tell, Part I is ambitious, but it does provide the basic tools and understanding for moving into the substantive theories to follow in Part II.

2

Family Theory
and Social Science

Anyone thinking that the current views about social science theory represent a uniform and coherent body of thought is sadly mistaken (see Benton & Craig, 2001; Potter, 1999). Rather, the current thought about social science theory spans a broad gamut from the impossibility of theoretical formulations (Blumer, 1962; Cheal, 1991; Derrida, 1976) to the precise analytic definition of what is and is not a social scientific theory (Burr, 1973). Perhaps the best examples of this are from definitions such as Blumer (1962), where theory is tentative and momentary, to those following Becker (1981) and Coleman (1990), where social science theory is viewed as deductive and formal. Certainly today's students of theory and research must admit to a considerable degree of confusion about the nature of scientific theories of families and the usefulness of formulations that claim scientific credibility. More than any other purpose and focus, this book places these various perspectives within a unitary framework that makes sense of this diversity of perspectives and analyzes the diverse claims. This book ties these divergent themes together by means of the "models and metaphors" originating with Black (1962). However, before we resolve the current dilemma we must first document where we are today in terms of family social science theory.

History is always selective. Selection of one set of events versus some other set obviously involves conscious choice. The choices I have made here are to select the events that I believe give a sense of flow and coherence to what has happened to family theory. Not everyone will agree with these choices because not everyone will agree with my estimation of the current state of family theory. Over a decade ago, Cheal (1991) offered a very different view of this history based on the rise of postmodern influences. In 1993, the editors of the *Sourcebook on Family Theories and Methods* offered a contextual historical interpretation. Even the White and Klein (2002) version of this same history highlights and emphasizes somewhat different events than I have selected here. So although I believe that the following historical account captures many of the most salient events for understanding the current state of family theory, it is certainly not the only interpretation available. I would encourage readers to examine these other histories.

A Retrospective on Family Theory

The First Half of the 20th Century

Prior to the beginning of the 20th century (1900–1999), no theories were devoted solely to the analysis of the family. Adams and Steinmetz (1993) discuss this early theorizing as often being a part of moral and ideological prescriptions about how to live. For example, Comte's often-cited "positivism" is full of moral and ideological discourse. Anthropologists during the late 19th century were intrigued by the origins of marriage, family, and kinship. It was during this time that ethnographies were being completed of New World native groups, and the kinship systems discovered, such as Crow and Omaha, were named after groups (Schusky, 1965). Even Engels (1884/1946) evidenced this early concern with the origins of marriage in the book *The Origin of the Family, Private Property and the State* and prolonged discussion of the now discredited notion of "mother-right."

During the first half of the 20th century (1900–1950), family theory did not develop independently of the theoretical work in social science disciplines such as sociology, anthropology, and economics. Many social scientific theorists, such as Homans and Skinner, paid scant attention to the family, whereas other theorists, such as Parsons and Zimmerman, saw the family as an important theoretical entity within their larger social theory. As White and Klein (2002) note, concerns during this period were often tied to reform movements aimed at the excesses of unfettered capitalism and social Darwinism at the turn of the century.

Christensen (1964) concluded that systematic theory focusing on the family began about midway through the 20th century. The end of World War II and the return of soldiers to civilian life created new demands for housing and schools as these soldiers tried to "catch up" with their civilian lives. During this time Hill (1949) and Bossard and Boll (1950) and others started to focus on the family as a theoretically important group. As White and Klein (2002) note,

> An inspection of the *International Bibliography of Research in Marriage and the Family, 1900–1964* (Aldous & Hill, 1967) shows that of almost 4,000 entries before 1950, only 7 contain theory or a cognate term in their titles. Of the 12,000 entries for the 1950–1964 period, 93 entries contain such terms. By comparison, for the 2-year period from 1991 to 1993, 264 of 7,600 entries in a subsequent inventory (Touliatos, 1994) pertain to family theory. (p. 25)

White and Klein (2002), in their survey of the 50-year period to the turn of the century (1950–1999), envisage three distinct periods: the period of "conceptual frameworks" (1950–1966), the period of "formal theory construction" (1967–1979), and the period they called "pluralism" (1980–1999). Although White and Klein's division into periods is historically defensible, it is just as important to examine this last 50 years of theorizing about families using some of the milestones that demarcate and characterize the changing nature of theorizing. Although I believe White and Klein's analysis to be useful, the analysis I pursue focuses on the "milestones" within this 50-year period.

The Second Half of the 20th Century

Functionalism

Without a doubt, the early work on family theory in the 1950s and 1960s was dominated by the influence of the social theorist Parsons. Parsons's particular style of theorizing was characterized by typologies. As we shall see later, a typology is simply a classification scheme. Even some of today's young scholars may be familiar with the residue of some of Parsons's constructions, such as his "expressive" and "instrumental" dimensions of family roles. Parsons (1943, 1959) will also be remembered for his work on what was known as the "isolated nuclear family hypothesis." His typological thinking led him to identify families as either having extended kinship or being isolated from kin. He launched a compelling yet erroneous argument founded on the belief that at one time most families in the United States had consisted of extended residential kin. The historical argument was later shown to be inaccurate (see, for example, Greenfield, 1961). However, many of the ideas in Parsons's argument survived in the later work of Goode (1963) and the notion of the conjugal-focused family.

Parsons's most lasting influence, however, is the reaction of theorists and researchers to his typological approach. The reaction was to move family theory to a new and more sophisticated level. As scholars became aware of the types of statistical analyses available to them, they were much less enamored of categorical schemes. Basically, categorical schemes could be analyzed by cross-tabulation and nominal level statistics, but the family researchers of the 1960s were discovering the more powerful analysis of relationships afforded by linear regression and correlation. Indeed, categorical thinking was dismissed because it was not concerned with variables and relations between variables. These became the new currency of social science, and any theory that was to gain popularity would have to be amenable to such analyses.

Cross-Cultural Comparisons

During the late 1950s and into the early 1960s, there was a flurry of activity in regard to cross-cultural testing of family theory. Journals such as the *Journal of Comparative Family Studies* emerged to serve as an outlet for this academic activity. Certainly some of this research was encouraged by the accessibility of the Human Relations Area Files and later the World Ethnographic Sample. These data sets allowed researchers to compare across the unit of analysis of societies rather than individuals. Later functionalists such as Zelditch (1956) used such secondary data to test hypotheses such as the function of rites of passage in redefining the mother–son roles.

The work by Blood and Wolfe (1960) on marital power and resources sparked an even broader based cross-cultural concern than did functionalism. Blood and Wolfe's thesis regarding marital resources was the topic of research in many countries, such as Trinidad (Rodman, 1967), Germany (Lupri, 1969), and Greece (Safilios-Rothschild, 1967). The massive multinational study by Rodman examining marital power in France, Greece, Yugoslavia, and the United States in many ways was the apex of the cross-cultural study of the family.

Certainly by the time we entered the 1970s the denouement in cross-cultural activity was being replaced by concerns that were more nationally based, such as race and gender in the United States. As a result, the decades to come showed a considerable concern with intranational comparisons and were not so theoretical driven as driven by social issues surrounding race and gender.

Theory Construction Movement in the 1960s and Early 1970s

In the late 1960s a new wave of theoretical scholarship emerged. These theorists believed theory could be constructed and developed if only researchers knew the "rules" for constructing theories. There are two salient dimensions here. One is that what was previously viewed as a creative act (theorizing) is now being viewed as a mechanical act of following the rules. The second salient dimension to this movement is a new reliance on data analysis as the source of theory. Indeed, many of these scholars produced little in the way of substantive theory but rather were interested in bringing the precision and successes of statistical analysis to the realm of theory.

During the late 1960s through the early 1970s a spate of theory construction books appeared (e.g., Blalock, 1969; Hage, 1972; Stinchcombe, 1968). Interestingly, these books were published almost exclusively within the discipline of sociology. Economics, political science, and other social science disciplines seemed strangely unaffected by the forces that compelled sociologists to develop the rules and techniques of theory construction. Although the books that were published during this time were somewhat diverse in approach, the diversity seemed to be more a matter of the weight that mathematical and statistical formulations were given relative to natural language propositions. The overall thrust of this movement was to argue for systematic sets of theoretical propositions that were sufficiently precise to be modeled mathematically. Although not all of these works set out definite rules to be followed in the course of constructing theories, certainly some of these works did (e.g., Hage, 1972).

Almost two decades later many of these same authors addressed the question "Why did the theory construction movement fail?" The answers provided by these authors are indeed interesting. Some blame the lack of success on resources, whereas others blame the social movements of the 1960s and 1970s as interfering with the program (Hage, 1994). One scholar blames the students. The noted scholar Blalock (1994) states,

> First, sociology does not attract the quality of students needed to support the enterprise. In particular, the overwhelming majority of sociologists are *neither* theoretically nor methodologically inclined or sophisticated. (p. 131)

Later he continues,

> Many indicators suggest that sociology attracts students having low SAT and GRE scores, very poor mathematics and science backgrounds, little or no interest in the philosophy of science, and only a very superficial knowledge of sociological theory. (p. 132)

It is fascinating to note that the retrospective view offered by at least one noted scholar, who was not a party to the original theory construction movement, departs so sharply from those who were part of the movement.

As previously noted, those who were part of the theory construction movement tended to blame people and things that were external to the content of the theory construction movement. However, Turner (1994) argues that the content of the theory construction movement was responsible for its own demise. He argues that the theory construction movement, in its rush to emulate "hard science," adopted the model of physics with its mathematical models and high-level abstractions. He states,

> Thus, theory construction books in sociology presented a vision of theory that is rarely realized in science, especially sciences like biology after which sociology should model itself. Additionally, these theory construction books all communicated a kind of cookbook and mechanical view of theory which was, to say the least, not how theories are created. Theorizing is a creative act, not some lockstep mechanical process. One does not "construct" or "build" a theory like a building. Rather, theories are formalized, when possible, *after* they have been created by intuition and insight. (p. 43)

And later,

> The "theory construction" movement was, therefore, doomed to failure. It communicated an unrealistic and inappropriate ideal; and it sought to reduce theorizing to stilted recipes and protocols. (p. 43)

Included in the theory construction movement were two notable developments in the early 1970s. The first was the creation within the National Council on Family Relations (NCFR) of a group of scholars devoted to theory construction. This group was organized by Hill and Nye in 1970 and was called the Theory Construction and Research Methodology Workshop. The second development was a notable work about theory construction in the area of family studies. The work by Burr (1973), *Theory Construction and the Sociology of the Family,* represented a significant milestone for family theory. Burr, like others in the theory construction movement, affirmed the goal of nomothetic science as being the production of explanations of family phenomena. The principal vehicle carrying researchers to this goal was to be theory. Theory is envisioned as logically linked propositions from which particular phenomena or outcomes can be deduced. Thus it is deductive theory that provides explanation.

So far, nothing I have said about Burr's approach is very different or unique from the movement as a whole. However, Burr's (1973) work contained a dimension that most other theory constructionists did not exploit or explore. Burr attempted to systematize all of the relevant theoretical propositions in the study of the family. This was naturally a mammoth undertaking.

Burr covered the substantive areas: marital satisfaction, mate selection, premarital factors, effects on marriage, role transitions, kinship relations, premarital attitudes and behaviors, marital and family power, family stress, family life cycle, wife employment, and fertility. Although previous handbooks (Christensen, 1964; Hill, 1949; Hill & Hansen, 1960; Nye & Berardo, 1966/1981) devoted to the family had contained the attempts of authors to systematically treat one or another of these areas, the attempt to systematize the entire cluster was audacious and largely successful.

The success of Burr's (1973) project was in no small part due to his departure from a strict and narrow focus on deduction to a more catholic perspective that included induction. Many philosophers of science writing at this time left little room for induction in science and no room for induction as a logical procedure (e.g., Braithwaite, 1953; Popper, 1959). Burr, however, included induction and a combination of induction and deduction in his approach. For instance, Burr states,

> The process of using deduction and induction are vital to theory building and theory testing. One way to illustrate their importance is to explain how both deduction and induction can be used together to expand theoretical knowledge. (p. 21)

Burr provides the following example:

> If a theorist has one or more theoretical propositions, and is able to either find an existing more general proposition that has not been integrated with his proposition or to induce a new proposition that explains the relationship in the first proposition, this is the use of induction and the theory is thereby extended. (p. 21)

In actual fact, Burr's theoretical work relied heavily on empirically generated propositions from researchers, and the interweaving of deduction and induction provided Burr's theory construction project with the success that eluded many others in the theory construction movement. Burr (1973) had the added benefit of predecessors, especially Hill, Katz, and Simpson (1957); Aldous (1970); and Goode, Hopkins, and McClure (1971), who had already designed strategies for combining induction and deduction. The greatest success for Burr's project, however, was the fruit it was to bear in 1979.

Contemporary Theories About the Family (1979)

Without a doubt, the two volumes of *Contemporary Theories About the Family* (Burr, Hill, Nye, & Reiss, 1979) represent the culmination of the theory construction movement in the area of marriage and the family. The great success of these two volumes is that they supplied researchers with a wealth of deductive and inductive conceptual propositions. The great failure of these two volumes was that they divided theory into two solitudes: inductive theories (Volume I) and deductive theories (Volume II). This division would have long-lasting effects on the entire enterprise of family theory for decades to come. Indeed, after this theoretical Humpty Dumpty was broken in two it would take much more than all the king's men to put him back together again.

The reason that the inductive and deductive theories were split into two separate volumes is explained partially by "advances" that Burr had made to the "strategies" (rules) of theory building. Although others (Aldous, 1970; Goode et al., 1971; Hill et al., 1957) had developed strategies for theory construction, it was Burr (1973) who divided strategies into those to be used for inductive theory and those for deductive theory (pp. 278–280). Although the editors of the two volumes (Burr, Hill, Nye, and Reiss) had envisioned an integration of the propositions in the inductive Volume I with the broader deductive theories in Volume II, this goal was never fully realized. As a result, the two volumes presented empirically oriented theories in Volume I and much more abstract and sometimes obtuse theories of grand dimensions in Volume II.

The success of the first volume of *Contemporary Theories About the Family* was that it codified much of the research in 24 areas of marriage and the family into empirical propositions and generalizations. In many cases, such as the chapter on marital quality and marital stability by Lewis and Spanier (1979), these propositions were further synthesized into even more abstract second-order propositions and integrated into deductive theory (e.g., exchange theory). However, the usefulness and integration of deductive theory was easily lost or overlooked by readers because so much of the emphasis was on the empirical studies informing and propelling the development of propositions.

Nothing just said should detract from the enormous advance that these two volumes afforded the study of the family. Indeed, as a result of this project, it could easily be argued that the academic area of marriage and the family was among the leaders in the conscious development of theory.

The Rise of Inductive Empiricism and Its Critics (1980–1992)

After the publication of *Contemporary Theories About the Family*, the field was to undergo upheavals of a very different nature. After the success of the 1979 volumes, Burr and several other colleagues argued that it was time for the area of study to become a discipline with its own identity.

Certainly the theoretical development that occurred in 1979 showed that this area could make a claim to having its own theory apart from what disciplines such as psychology and sociology might provide. Full of their success in the area of theory, several scholars argued about names for the new discipline, such as "familogy" and "family science." These arguments had the effect of alienating some discipline-oriented scholars and leading them to have a greater identity with their disciplines. In contrast, many of the more applied and less theoretical fields such as home economics, nursing, and other types of practices were enamored of this proposal.

One result of these discussions was that little effort was expended on continued theoretical development. Indeed, theoretical progress in general was to languish during this period. This is not to say that there were not isolated pockets of theory development. For example, numerous important developments occurred in regard to the theory of marital quality and marital stability (Gottman & Notarius, 2000). Furthermore, the empirical inductionism in Volume I of *Contemporary Theories About the Family* had demonstrated that inductive empiricism could produce theory. This naturally was at a time when philosophers had largely given up on induction as any form of logic, and European scholars' voices, critical of empiricism and induction, were beginning to be heard in North America.

The "normal" science of the 1980s increasingly became quantitative, empirical studies with little theory development. Indeed, researchers could point to the first volume of *Contemporary Theories About the Family* to demonstrate the "payoff" to their research strategy. In many ways, then, the theory construction movement that culminated in the publication of the 1979 volumes was unintentionally responsible for a return to a form of empiricism that resembled the early inductionism advocated by Francis Bacon (1561–1626) that had been so roundly rejected by Newtonian physics and physical sciences. As Thomas and Wilcox (1987) note,

> The final accomplishment that we note here of this received view of family theory is a faith in the eventual payoff of many research and theory efforts of many social scientists. Building increment on increment of one research project after another in any area of the family field is seen as necessary foundation work that will eventually succeed in creating theory capable of explaining the phenomena under investigation. (p. 93)

During this time, European influences that were critical of attempts at a positivistic science of human behavior entered the full consciousness of North American academic circles. Even before 1979, many North American scholars were aware of the works of phenomenologists such as Husserl, Heidegger, and Merleau-Ponty. Indeed, one of the chapters in Volume II of *Contemporary*

Theories About the Family had been devoted to phenomenological analysis (McLain & Weigert, 1979). But this chapter was careful not to directly attack either the epistemologies undergirding contemporary empiricism or theory. However, such caution evaporated during the 1980s for two distinct reasons. First, feminist theorists found their intuitive distrust of empiricism and quantification to be "justified" by the critiques of positivism launched by some European scholars. Second, many scholars who were coming of age in the 1970s found the European influence an appealing critique of "the establishment."

Neither feminists, disestablishmentarians, nor European critiques, however, could have brought about the doubts and crises perceived in many scientific circles if it had not been for the additional voice of philosophers of science. Recall that the theory constructionists had been reliant on much guidance from philosophy of science. However, in the 1970s and 1980s the agreement between philosophers of science that appeared to exist in the 1950s (Popper, Hempel, Braithwaite, and so on) started to evaporate. Suppe (1977) went so far as to say that positivistic philosophy of science had been reduced to "disagreement and confusion" (p. 618). Indeed, some of the harshest critiques came from philosophers such as Suppes (1960) and Rorty (1979, 1982).

The dissolution of agreement in philosophy of science circles is certainly tied to the influential historical analysis of science by Kuhn (1970). Kuhn's thesis is that science, like other human endeavor, is a social process. Kuhn brought into doubt the common perception that science follows carefully established rules of evidence, thereby protecting its claim to objectivity. Kuhn's historical argument is that although science may have such rules, it is also a social and political organization subject to the same processes of influence, status, and rewards that mark other social organizations. Thus the theories and perspectives that are accepted are as predicted by social politics as by any upholding of pristine standards. The result of Kuhn's analysis was to send philosophers scurrying for an argument that would save science from being just another social organization, with no more veracity to its claims than, say, a political party would have for its claims.

Philosophers attempted to defend science on several fronts, but these were challenged by others. One of these fronts was that the logic of science and scientific formulations was compelling and "true." However, Suppes (1960) showed that scientific, or any other axiomatic systems, could never be complete nor proved to be self-consistent. Rorty (1979, 1982) argued against any epistemological foundation that might allow science to claim special status for its knowledge claims. By the time the European critiques were added to those of North American philosophers and historians, few arguments in favor of the objectivity or the preeminence of scientific claims seemed to be left standing!

Thomas and Wilcox (1987) argue for exactly such a perspective as just outlined. Although the title of their paper is "The Rise of Family Theory," it might well have been the "rise and fall." Thomas and Wilcox are troubled that science has no epistemological foundation assuring that its knowledge is "certain." In the absence of logical and epistemological foundations for science, they feel science is relegated to a "consensus criteria of truth" (p. 98), which would indeed open scientific claims to all of the vagaries of social politics pointed out by Kuhn (1962). In the final analysis, Thomas and Wilcox are not optimistic:

> We await the coming discussion about the nature of family theory with considerable interest. We fully expect family theorists to struggle with questions about the nature of our knowledge about the family as a social order. The decline of certainty has rendered as important the base on which knowledge claims are founded. (p. 99)

Thomas and Wilcox were only to wait three years for the continuation of this discussion.

Family and the State of Theory (1991)

Cheal's (1991) book, *Family and the State of Theory,* came as a surprise to family scholars. Up until this time only a small number of scholars, often those who were on the periphery of the "mainstream," had been cognizant of the critiques launched about positivism and scientific theory. Of course, most North American scholars had read Kuhn (1962), but many saw Kuhn's work as justifying the growth in the "sociology of science" rather than as a major critique of positivism. Furthermore, there had been little coverage of the challenges to positivism in the mainstream journals such as the *Journal of Marriage and the Family.* However, Cheal's 1991 book, and his subsequent appearance as plenary speaker at the National Council on Family Relations Theory Construction and Research Methodology Workshop, gave these discussions a prominence they had not previously enjoyed.

Cheal (1991) argued that a conjunction of feminism, the conclusion in 1970 by Holman and Burr that a unified theory was impossible, and the critiques by postmodern scholars, had the additive effect of leaving the field of family theory in disarray and confusion. In his final chapter, Cheal summarizes the state of theory in the following:

> Since the mid-1970s, a great deal of energy has been expended on the task of tearing down the orthodox consensus about the normal family. That task is now complete. The challenge for us is to renew family theory, in the

aftermath of the Big Bang. Whatever conclusions are drawn about the state of family theory today, they must be made in full knowledge of the situation as it exists now. That situation is complex, and unstable, but it is not random. (p. 153)

Many of Cheal's misgivings about theory in the 1990s would be echoed by the editors of the next major survey of theoretical progress.

Sourcebook of Family Theories and Methods (1993)

The *Sourcebook of Family Theories and Methods* (Doherty, Boss, LaRossa, Schumm, & Steinmetz, 1993) was a prodigious effort. Although it did not necessarily surpass the 1979 *Contemporary Theories About the Family* in regard to coverage of theories, it did add an entirely new dimension in addition to theories. The addition was that it attempted to cover the extant methodologies in the study of families.

The subtitle of the *Sourcebook* was *A Contextual Approach*. This subtitle says a great deal. By the time this work was published, the entire enterprise of family theory was somewhat in question. However, many of the contributors to this volume had conceptualized and, in large part, written their contributions before Cheal (1991) had arrived on the scene. The editors of the volume, however, were especially aware of the disjunction between the recent critical work such as Cheal (1991) and the more normal positivistic approach assumed by the majority of the *Sourcebook*'s contributors. Although most of the theories covered in the *Sourcebook* could be described as "business as normal" positivistic extensions, the last chapters dealt with critiques from feminist and minority scholars as well as phenomenological theorists.

In the first chapter of the *Sourcebook*, the editors attempted to address the changes occurring in the field of family theory. Doherty et al. (1993) identify the following trends in the field:

1. The impact of feminist and ethnic minority theories and perspectives

2. The realization that family forms have changed dramatically

3. The trend toward greater professional inclusiveness

4. The trend toward more theoretical and methodological diversity

5. The trend toward more concern with language and meaning

6. The movement toward more constructivist and contextual approaches

7. An increased concern with ethics, values, and religion

8. A breakdown of the dichotomy between the private and public spheres of family life and between family social science and family interventions

9. Greater recognition by family scholars of the contextual limits of family theory and research knowledge (pp. 15–18)

At the same time as they largely agreed with much of what Cheal (1991) had argued regarding the diversity, instability, and apparent confusion of theoretical approaches, Doherty et al. (1993) also voiced some misgivings about the current state of theory: "Although we support many of the current postpositivist trends in the family field, we also wish to raise concerns about them" (p.18). They list the following seven problem areas:

1. A singular focus on contextualism can blind scholars to "objective" social forces affecting families.

2. A mindless multidisciplinary approach might promote mindless eclecticism and lack of rigorous analysis.

3. The emphasis on pluralism and diversity can blind us to the commonalities among families.

4. The emphasis on acknowledging one's values and context could become a way to avoid critical analysis and dialogue.

5. Skepticism about "big ideas" can lead to an automatic rejection of potentially worthwhile theories.

6. There is the danger that renewed enthusiasm for qualitative methods will become a new orthodoxy that will diminish the usefulness of the remarkable advances in experimental methods and quantitative statistical procedures.

7. Eliminating the dichotomy between science and advocacy creates the danger that important academic values will be lost. (pp. 18–19)

Needless to say, the reservations voiced by Doherty and his colleagues have great significance. Indeed, if even a few of these came to pass the entire project of knowledge production and accumulation that is the output of science could be in jeopardy. Certainly the most radical critiques of post-modernism would leave us in a situation where all knowledge claims are relative and there is no commonly agreed-on method for resolving which knowledge claim is more accurate or "true." Yet Doherty and his associates (1993) remain optimistic.

If we become more inclusive as a field and if we are open to these new perspectives while holding onto the best elements of scholarly rigor and creativity from our social science tradition, then we may be able to generate enlightenment and useful knowledge about families during our time in history. (pp. 27–28)

The problem with this statement is that the two perspectives, positivism and postmodernism, represent largely contradictory claims and epistemologies. In the final analysis, Doherty et al. left us with a "Pollyanna" perspective in the face of what is a desperate quandary for knowledge as we know it. What these authors did achieve was that they recognized the dangers and pitfalls (see the lists above) even though they minimized the degree of actual conflict.

White and Klein (2002) and Klein and White (1996)

One of the remarkable developments during the 1990s was the flourishing of theory books outside the aegis of major projects such as the *Sourcebook* (Sabatelli & Shehan, 1993) or *Contemporary Theories About the Family* (Burr, Hill, et al., 1979). Another milestone was that for the first time, books were developed completely by single authors rather than large teams of scholars specializing in each theoretical school. The Klein and White (1996) volume was well received by scholars and students of family theory. This positive reception was not, however, unanimous because some of the reviewers noted the significant absence of chapters dealing with feminism and postmodern theories (Knapp, 1997). For the most part, though, this book was destined to inform generations of students in the 1990s and the new millennium (White & Klein, 2002).

It would be somewhat inaccurate to characterize the books by these two authors as being conservative. The first edition (1996) contained extensive treatments of postmodern approaches in sections dealing with phenomenology and feminism even though these were considered as part of chapters on symbolic interaction and conflict frameworks. It would not be inaccurate to say that the White and Klein works did little to advance the theoretical thinking in any area. What these books did achieve, however, is much more subtle.

One achievement of these books was that they treated theory and research as coextensive. The *Sourcebook* (1993) had presented theories through the lens of contextualism and, as a result, did not address the interface between theory and research. The methods chapters seldom made reference to the theory chapters, so there was the perception of a disjunction. Certainly this disjunction also existed in *Contemporary Theories About the Family* (1979). In the 1979 inductive volume, theories were inductively constructed from research. Yet the deductive theories were largely abstract and not linked to research (the exception being Nye's exchange theory chapter). Although this was addressed in the first edition of Klein and White (1996), the second edition (White & Klein, 2002) clearly demonstrates how researchers can deduce testable propositions from theory (pp. 12–15). Furthermore, White and Klein begin to introduce some basic rules of logic, such as the distributive rule and *modus tollens* arguments, into the discussion of theory. This was not previously attempted in either the *Sourcebook* or *Contemporary Theories About the Family*.

A second contribution that these authors made was to develop theoretical propositions to characterize each theoretical framework. Naturally, predecessors such as *Contemporary Theories About the Family* had dealt with propositions, but in the *Sourcebook* only the chapters on family development (Rodgers & White, 1993) and life course (Bengtson & Allen, 1993) attempted formalization into propositions. Hence the production of theoretical propositions had not been witnessed for almost two decades (1979–1996).

The third contribution these authors made was to make the notion of "frameworks" a heuristic and organizing device by which the theories clustered within the framework, it was argued, shared theoretical assumptions with other theories within the cluster. Certainly previous scholars had invoked such organizational devices (see, for example, Christensen, 1964). Although scholars may argue about the relative merits of this scheme, the success of this heuristic is to make a large number of theories accessible to students.

Despite the successes of the White and Klein books, they also had two glaring omissions. The first of these omissions is that White and Klein left the many questions for science and theory raised by postmodern scholars largely unaddressed. Although some of these issues are touched on in sections on feminist theory and phenomenology, they nowhere receive the sustained and direct scholarly response they warrant. This was indeed somewhat strange because White (1998; White & Klein, 2002; White & Mason 1999a, 1999b) had demonstrated an obvious concern with addressing these issues directly. It can only be said that White and Klein seemed content to assume the attitude of many positivists: if they wait long enough the postmodern threat will simply expire, whereas the tangible successes of positivistic science in the modern world is sufficiently compelling argument alone.

The second major omission of the White and Klein books was that they did not "push" or further develop existing theory. There are few designated outlets for theoretical work when it is unattached to empirical data. However, theories that can be empirically tested are already very well developed. So theory development principally has publication problems because it most often has a "half-baked" character. However, the goal of White and Klein was to introduce advanced undergraduates and graduate students to theory, not to use their book to advance family theory.

The place to advance family theory should have been the *Sourcebook*. However, a perhaps unintended consequence of the contextual approach was that authors focused on the history and context of theory to the exclusion of advancing theoretical thinking. It will be interesting to see if the new *Sourcebook* currently in the writing stage will address such issues as the logical analysis and formalization of family theory. The fact that the new project is modeled on the 1993 "success" leads to some pessimism in this regard. So it is with these two omissions in mind that we now turn to an overall assessment of the current state of family theory.

The Current State of Family Theory

The retrospective on family theory provides a list of largely unaddressed questions and uncompleted agendas. Two things will be achieved by reviewing these questions and agendas. First, the major shortcomings of family theory in the last century will become obvious. Second, by pointing out these problem areas, the agenda is set for the remainder of this book. Indeed, it is the audacious intention of this book to place family theory on a firm footing for developing and growing in this new century.

Family theory in the 1950s was dominated by Parsonian functionalism. One of the major criticisms of this school was its use of typological constructs rather than variables and relations. Certainly this criticism made sense at the time; however, the methodological progress enjoyed over the last 40 years suggests that we might take another look at the status of typologies and typological constructs in family theory.

The 1960s were marked by cross-cultural testing of theoretical propositions. Since that time, family theory and research has concentrated on theory mainly within the cultural context of the United States. The question remains, however, whether theoretical progress is best served by this orientation to the variation within one specific culture.

The theory construction era culminated in family studies with the two-volume *Contemporary Theories About the Family* (Burr, Hill, et al., 1979). The volumes were divided into inductive and deductive family theories. However, there has been little discussion about whether this bifurcation was helpful or productive. Even Burr (1973) acknowledged that there existed theory construction techniques combining both processes. It is time to reexamine these approaches, induction and deduction, and ask if the separation is warranted and fruitful for developing and advancing theory.

The emergence of postmodern critiques has led Cheal (1991) and Doherty et al. (1993), as well as White and Klein (2002), to conclude that these criticisms of science and theory are problematic. Yet to date, family theorists have largely been quiet in addressing and answering these criticisms. Certainly it is time to end over two decades of reluctance in this regard.

Finally, the advancement of existing theory needs to be addressed. This goal is not, however, achieved by adding new or more prescriptions and rules about theory construction. (Clearly this statement needs to be justified.) Even more important, theory is only advanced by an in-depth understanding of both theoretical and substantive issues. In the final section of this book I examine two theories that are ripe for further refinement and development and have great promise for enhancing our understanding of families.

It is the purpose of this book to address these issues. To address each of these adequately, however, larger issues that provide the context for either the question or answer must also be given consideration. For example, to address the role of typologies in scientific theory, we must place this question in the broader framework of the architecture of scientific theories in general. In regard to the issue of induction and deduction, the discussion must be broadened to general questions of logic, proof, and fallibility. In confronting these many issues, it is the breadth and depth of these discussions that provide the basis for an understanding of advanced family theory.

3

Science and Its Critics

A few years ago I served as an examiner for a doctoral dissertation. The student had done an excellent job of collecting qualitative data to support a conceptual model. Indeed, the dissertation was both theoretically and methodologically sophisticated. One examiner asked what seemed a relatively unproblematic question: "What is the major knowledge claim your thesis makes?" The student, however, assumed this was more of a philosophical question and launched into a discussion regarding the relativity and plurality of knowledge claims. After hearing the student argue that knowledge was relative and there was no way of deciding which claim might be more adequate, the examiner paused and reflected. The next question was "Are you telling me that there is no difference between the data and theory that you took three years to develop and, for example, the opinions of a local taxi driver?" The student, pleased that the postpositivist argument had been correctly understood, said, "Yes!" The examiner's next question was obvious: "Why then do we not award the taxi driver the doctoral degree?"

This anecdote points out the importance of the issues that I discuss in this chapter. At the core of these issues is a most fundamental question regarding the nature of human knowledge and its production and accumulation. After all, if the student in this anecdote is correct, then there is no need to maintain great universities at taxpayers' expense. Likewise, the very foundation of education and knowledge is put into question.

This chapter addresses the criticisms of theory and science launched by postmodern critics. It would be very easy to address these criticisms with a sweeping dismissal, such as by citing the success of science in providing us a better life. Such a response seems, however, to be overly defensive on the part of scientific theorists and might very well dismissively throw out valuable insights that are the basis of these criticisms. Rather, the strategy I pursue here is first to address some of the basic notions in traditional philosophy of science so that when we move to the analysis of the criticisms, the basic concepts and distinctions will already be in hand. This will also have the additional benefit of avoiding the impression that distinctions are being introduced *ex nihilo* simply in order to obviate a criticism.

Basic Philosophy of Science

Caveat

Before we begin this discussion, one caveat should be forwarded. Philosophy of science, like its close relative history of science, is first and foremost an after the fact (*ex post facto*) reconstruction. I cannot sufficiently stress the importance of this fact. Science developed over centuries, refining its methods and logic to more adequately address empirical problems. Long after the success of science, philosophy of science evolved as a way to study this apparently successful and influential body of knowledge and methodology. Somewhere, somehow, students and colleagues seem to have gotten the impression that science was based on this or that epistemology (theory of knowledge) or this or that ontology (theory of being), but this is far from the case. For the most part, scientists have not been very profound thinkers in either philosophy of knowledge or philosophy of being. As we shall see, one of the great strengths of scientific thinking has been to fold two contradictory epistemologies (rationalism and empiricism) into the basis of scientific methodology. This has been the grounds for great philosophical consternation (Norris, 1989) while providing relatively few problems for scientists. The point that philosophy of science is "reconstructive" will need to be revisited several times during the course of this book.

Science and Diversity

Critics and defenders alike often refer to "science" as representing a certain unity of disciplines. One of the most interesting observations about science is that it is anything but a unity. In some areas, such as the physics of time, science is much closer to literary metaphor than to "hard" measurement. Certainly the methods of contemporary wildlife biology, microchemistry, and geology defy common representation by the most glaring generalities. If we take a more historical perspective, science has used many different methodologies.

Indeed, in Chapter 1 I hinted at this fact by stating that there was a return to Baconian inductionism. Bacon (1561–1626) focused on observation and the accrual of observations as the foundation of scientific method. Since that time, his perspective has been largely rejected by several other views of science. Finally, there is always the argument within the sciences about which disciplines are sciences. Is physics the model to which every other science should be compared? To what extent is science unified by a common method? Are the social sciences to be considered sciences? Is history a science or one of the humanities? The point is, however, that science is not easily treated as one monolithic codified and unified whole.

This insight might seem relatively unimportant until criticisms are launched at all of "science" or until one wants to glorify one's discipline by stating that it is a "science" or increase the legitimacy of one's theory by calling it "scientific" theory. The successes of some of the physical and natural sciences have created the common perception that "science" is responsible for such progress rather than a particular theory or method or instrumentation. This glorified perception of "science" is perhaps tied to the reason some family researchers preferred the term family "science" over the term family "studies" during the discussions of the name for the new discipline in the 1980s. Clearly the "science" name would be viewed as more serious and worthwhile. Simultaneously, critics have wanted to paint all of the sciences with the same brush regardless of epistemological and methodological differences between these disciplines.

Defining "Science"

When we turn to lexical definitions of science found in most dictionaries, a terrible and uncomfortable generality leaves us knowing less than we did before we availed ourselves of the dictionary definition. I have performed these searches over several decades and remain undeterred by the results. It is always my first line of analysis even though it has been uniformly unrewarding. "Science" is equated with a body of knowledge achieved through scientific methods. "Scientific methods" are illuminatingly defined as the methods of observation and experimentation commonly used in the sciences. Although this does somewhat determine the meaning, it is less than revealing or informative for our purposes.

Another way to proceed is to use some of the myriad characterizations of science offered in the diverse discourse known as philosophy of science. The inherent danger in this approach is that these interpretations might tell us as much about the philosophical commitments of the philosopher as they do about science. Yet another danger is that philosophers of science have tended to take one discipline, often physics, as representing the pinnacle of how science exists in its most sophisticated form. Interestingly, such judgments expose dubious assumptions but also clearly fail to see "science" in historical perspective. If we were to define science by its "pinnacle discipline," will such a characterization capture the meaning of science as studied by the historian? And, of course, as I stated earlier, there may be multiple models of science rather than one unifying solitary pinnacle discipline.

Kaplan (1964) uses a metaphorical story to capture both the fact that philosophy of science "reconstructs" science and the manner in which biases enter such reconstructions. He first states that philosophers seem drawn to fields, such as physics, that have elegant mathematical formulae and a relatively unambiguous, unproblematic use of deductive theory. He states,

> But the crucial question concerns, not the intrinsic values of the reconstructed logic taken in itself, but rather its usefulness in illuminating the logic-in-use. There is a story of a drunkhard searching under a street lamp for his house key, which had dropped some distance away. Asked why he didn't look where he had dropped it, he replied, "It's lighter here!" Much effort, not only in the logic of behavioral science, but also in behavioral science itself, is vitiated, in my opinion, by the principle of *the drunkhard's search*. (p. 11)

I believe Kaplan's parable to be a useful one, and I will freely cite *the drunkhard's search* as standing for examinations that choose to avoid the difficult and messy in favor of the clear and obvious, even though it fails to address the issue.

Yet another distinction that plagues our quest to define "science" is the distinction between science as "product" and science as "process." I don't remember where I first came across this distinction, but it has been useful in sorting out approaches to science. As an example, the reader may turn to almost any lexical (dictionary) definition of "science" and find definitions that refer to (1) science as a body of systematic knowledge, and (2) science as knowledge arrived at by means of the scientific method (induction, deduction, or both). Certainly science as a product is "systematized knowledge." Later in this book, I will argue that this systematizing is largely a function of theory. Science is also that product produced by a specific method. The trick here is whether there is consensus on the exact nature of scientific method or methods. Certainly over the history of science the understanding of the nature of the scientific method has changed. Naturally, disciplines (e.g., physics, biology, archaeology) of inquiry may emphasize certain methods and exclude others. So defining science as any body of knowledge achieved by means of the scientific method does not supply us with an unambiguous definition.

Although I have not defined science nor solved how to define science, I have noted some of the problems in arriving at such a definition. The failure to arrive at a definition may not seem particularly instructive, yet when we eventually examine the criticisms of science we may find that what is a complex, diverse, and difficult issue may be uncritically viewed by critics of science as a monolithic and uniform endeavor.

History and Science

Many readers may know about the history of science mainly through reading or being informed of the effects of Kuhn's (1962, 1996) *The Structure of Scientific Revolutions.* Later in this chapter we will need to address the constructionist perspective attributed to Kuhn's work as well as Kuhn's concept of "paradigm." Of course, the history of science is much broader than just the work of this single author. For our purpose in this section, however, we are not so interested in the interpretive elements of the history of science as encountered in works such as Kuhn's. Rather, we turn to the descriptive and accounting aspects of the history of science to provide us with a great deal of illumination about science.

Hellemans and Bunch (1988) discuss science across the sweep of human history. It is instructive that these authors do not expend much energy on finding a definition of science so much as listing scientific discoveries and advances. Of course, their list of these discoveries must be at least unconsciously driven by a definition of science even if it is not explicit. As we review some of these discoveries, this implicit definition will be increasingly clear.

Hellemans and Bunch (1988) state from the outset that science is anything but a consistent and coherent monolithic endeavor.

> Historians of science have abandoned the idea that science develops linearly, according to rules. Instead, the growth of science is much like a stream, growing slowly from its source, meandering through plains, and fed by other small streams until it becomes a river. (Preface, p. v.)

This analogy of science finally becoming a "river" is further qualified by the authors' perspective that sometimes the main channel of the river is dominated by one discipline, such as physics in the 20th century, but at other times other disciplines might be dominant or the river could spread into several channels.

We can only guess at the first scientific advance because these discoveries had to be made in human prehistory. For example, prehistoric humans had to have made substantial advances in regard to fire, seasons, animal behavior, and climate. Even in the most elementary forms, such as food, we can see that they had to have some categorization about which plants were poisonous to eat and which were edible. These basic categorical dimensions have been discussed by Levi-Strauss (1966) in his book *The Savage Mind*. Today, ethnobotanists study the wealth of natural science information that was represented by these prehistorical groups in some of the well-preserved medicine bundles for healing. We believe that many elaborate systems of categorization (taxonomies) were developed so this information could be passed from one generation to another. By the time civilization started, about 10,000 years ago, there was already an abundance of information stored in these taxonomic silos. The full-fledged blossoming of civilization showed further developments such as the performance of brain surgeries and mummification of the dead in ancient Egypt. So although the rudimentary beginnings of science were first and foremost tied to taxonomies, early discoveries were also attempting to explain and understand so that interventions could mitigate effects (e.g., medicine, alchemy, and climatology) (Hellemans & Bunch, 1988).

Certainly most of us would equate the advances in science during early civilization with the cultures that flourished in ancient Greece and Egypt. However, other cultures such as the Mayans and Chinese were also flourishing during this time. Although there were advances in almost every area, the major advance came from the developments in mathematics. Not only did these advances include Euclidean geometry, but in Mesopotamia mathematics developed to the point of being able to solve quadratic equations (Hellemans & Bunch, 1988, p. 3). The mathematical advances, especially geometry, made it possible for forms of engineering to develop that would create edifices that remain impressive to this day. It was just as important for our understanding of science that during this time the notion of science developed.

> Scientific thinking originated in Greece with the Ionian philosophers Thales, Anaximander, and Anaximenes. . . . [T]he Ionian philosophers were the first to believe that people could understand the universe using reason alone rather than mythology and religion. They searched for a prime cause for all natural phenomena. No personal forces of gods were involved, only impersonal, natural processes. (Hellemans & Bunch, 1988, p. 21)

One of the first tenets of science that developed, then, was a faith in human reason over superstition, myth, and religion. This faith in reason seemed justified by the great progress many cultures had made in mathematics during this period. Interestingly, this faith in reason changed the very way phenomena were defined. For example, Anaximander put forth the opinion that the rainbow was a natural occurrence rather than a divine act of the gods (Hellemans & Bunch, 1988, p. 21). Indeed, the faith in reason was destined to redefine the phenomena around us because, rather than look to the gods, humans turned to observation and reason.

The themes we see for science as we approach the Christian era were (1) that by observation and taxonomy we can organize phenomena in a consistent and stable way, and (2) that by applying reason and mathematics to our observations we can explain phenomena without the use of explanations based on myth or divine interdiction. However, these two tenets did not occur uniformly throughout all cultures.

> The attitude of Chinese society toward nature was quite different from the attitude that developed in Europe during the Renaissance. The Chinese never separated the material from the sacred world, and did not have the conviction that people can dominate nature. They were not interested in developing a scientific method; thus their theories often remained divorced from observation and experimentation. (Hellemans & Bunch, 1988, p. 59)

This is not to say, however, that European science continued to make uniform progress. During the Roman cultural dominance there was little interest in science. Indeed, if it had not been for the rise of Islamic scholarship and the fact that many Greek and Indian works were saved in the libraries and universities of Islam, much of the knowledge acquired might have been wiped out. In addition, Arabs were responsible for major advances in number systems and the invention of algebra and optics (Hellemans & Bunch, 1988, pp. 58–59).

The lack of development in science during the period after the birth of Christ is extremely important because it shows that despite the obvious progress and material advances that could be tied to scientific thinking it was easily dampened if not extinguished for almost a thousand years. Although the causes are complex, Hellemans and Bunch (1988) put one critical aspect succinctly:

> Several reasons for the decline of science in Europe between 530 and 100 have been put forward by historians. For one, European culture was still strongly influenced by the Romans, who were notoriously little interested in theoretical science. (p. 58)

It must also be recalled that Christianity itself originated from a largely nonscientific culture and so did not offer supports for the development of science. In addition, the Black Death that swept Europe in several waves created a huge distraction. But what is instructive about this era is that without cultural and social support and value for scientific theory, the activity of science can be lost.

With the Renaissance in the 1400s, science once again began to flourish. Most readers are familiar with the Copernican revolution in astronomy (1543) and the acceptance of this position by Galileo until the Inquisition of Pope Urban VIII led to his recanting the Copernican theory (1633). The position of the church was that a literal interpretation of the Bible states that Earth is the center of the universe. Although Copernicus had developed a theory that allowed for better prediction of planetary motion, at the time of the Inquisition it was still one among many theories. It is, however, much more revealing that the church did not change its denial of Copernican theory until well into the 20th century (1922) (Hellemans & Bunch, 1988, p. 134).

The Renaissance was also marked by a flurry of explorations and demands for better navigational systems. Universities were founded throughout Europe, although this process began in the 1200s. Leonardo da Vinci developed the notions of capillary action, pendulum clocks, and drawings for a flying machine. In some ways the late Renaissance also gave birth to the philosophy of science. Bacon's *Novum Organum* (1620) argued that induction is the basis of the scientific method. Bacon's logic of induction would serve as counterpoint to the writings of rationalist philosophers such as Descartes (b. 1596) and would later be pilloried by the success of Newton (b. 1642).

Hellemans and Bunch (1988) state that the period 1660 to 1734 provides a fundamental revolution in the thinking within science. Newton's *Principia* (1687) described the three laws of motion and the universal law of gravity. The great advances of Newton were in part due to the mathematical advances in calculus prompted by both Newton and Leibniz. In relation to the scientific methods, Newton provided a combination of the pure rationalism of Descartes and the inductive empiricism of Bacon. Indeed, it might be impossible to separate his empirical observations such as musing on falling bodies (apple and moon) from his rationalistic deductive approach using mathematical equations to predict observations. Newton's great success was to cement the perspective that rational empiricism and theory are necessary components of science.

It is interesting that after the theoretical work by Newton, physics, astronomy, geography, and earth sciences made great strides. However, chemistry was mired in adherence to a theoretical dead end with Stahl's (1723) theory of phlogiston and did not emerge from the intellectual doldrums until the 18th century (Hellemans & Bunch, 1988, p. 191). The inductive taxonomic work of Linnaeus (*Systema Naturae*, 1707) positioned biology to become theoretical; however, Linnaeus dampened such moves with his dismissal of the notion of evolution in 1751 (Hellemans & Bunch, 1988, p. 206).

By the 1800s, however, chemistry was on its way to atomic theory (Dalton) and the biological sciences were to develop evolutionary theory (Darwin) and genetics (Mendel). Indeed, although science in the 1700s was clearly dominated by physics, the 1800s were dominated by chemistry and even more so by biological sciences. Although Adam Smith (1723–1790) had laid the foundation for economics, this was expanded to population dynamics in the work of Malthus (1798/1872). Throughout the 1800s, the embryonic social sciences struggled to separate moral philosophy and religion from scientific observation and theory. This was, of course, the same gauntlet through which physics and astronomy had passed (Galileo and the church) and through which evolutionary theory would have to pass in the 19th century. Even before Wallace or Darwin published any influential works on evolution, the public had rejected the notion put forth by geologists that Earth was much older than indicated in the Bible. This was, of course, only a mild prelude to the public response the theory of evolution was to receive. With the spread of evolutionary theory and natural history during the 1800s, the social sciences of archaeology and anthropology also developed (Hellemans & Bunch, 1988, p. 272).

The 20th century was marked by enormous technological change in addition to scientific progress. The development of the theory of chemical bonding (Pauling) finally cemented theory in chemistry. In physics, of course, Einstein's theories of relativity and the resulting technological implications (nuclear bomb) showed that Newtonian theory had been eclipsed. In addition, the development of quantum physics (Planck, Bohr) threatened to split physics into two disparate areas: microphysics and macrophysics. In medicine, Fleming's discovery of penicillin saved millions of lives. Some of the social sciences, especially anthropology and economics, made significant advances. And at the close of the century, geneticists completely mapped the human genome. Physicists and astronomers were wrestling with one of the most basic notions in physical sciences, the concept of time and how it might be measured. In many ways, science in the 20th century is still too close for us to gain a perspective of which of these developments, if any, is the main channel of the river.

What we can summarize from this very brief historical perspective on science is that physics alone does not represent science. Second, sciences seem to advance on the basis of foundational observation and categorization followed by theoretical advances. Third, the public has continually been annoyed with the fact that science proceeds without the assistance of commonly held myths and religious beliefs, and explains events without invoking gods. Finally, the methods of science seem much more a mixture of induction and deduction combined with generous amounts of creativity and intuition than any philosopher of science would want to admit.

Critics and Postpositivism

Thomas and Wilcox (1987) use the term "postpositivism" to refer to the cluster of criticisms about positivistic science that have emerged in the last 50 years. Gross and Levitt (1994) see postpositivist claims as threatening to return science to the "dark ages." In general, what are viewed with such dismay are claims about the "relativity" of knowledge, whether or not there is an underlying reality, and the objectivity of a knowledge claim. Although these issues and arguments are not new to many social scientists, they have taken on new and formidable statements in the hands of current postpositivists.[1]

Positivism

Before we find out about the nature of "postpositivism" it is useful to depict the character of "positivism." The term "positivism" is associated with one of the fathers of social science, August Comte, rather than a scholar from the physical sciences. Comte (1798–1857) imagined a pantheon of sciences with sociology occupying its highest rung. The details regarding "positive" methods of knowledge are somewhat sketchy. Comte believed that observation by the physical senses was the foundation of positivism. He stressed that observation could only be useful when it was guided by theory. It was not his emphasis on theory that marked Comte's work but his emphasis on observation. Until and including Comte, social theory had been infused with large amounts of ideology, utopianism, and moralistic banter. Comte's "positivism" emphasized sense data and scientific principles. In large part, the radical contribution of Comte was his argument that the methods of science used in the physical sciences could and should be adopted in the social sciences.

After Comte, the social sciences in general headed down the road of positivism. Contributions by Durkheim, Burgess, and many others drove the social sciences into a headlong imitation of the methodological techniques used by the physical sciences. That is not to say that there were not some sidetracks, such as the Weberian method of *verstehen*. But the early analytic positivism of sociology led by Durkheim and Tönnies moved forcefully into the 20th century. Throughout the 20th century, scholars such as Merton and Parsons (for general sociology) and Burgess and Hill (in the area of family) emphasized a moderate view of positivism. (A more extreme view is represented in the work of Lundberg (1942).)

As White and Mason (1999a) observe,

> Even though positivism has been inextricably linked with quantification by some of its critics, this is not a necessary criteria for a discipline being positivistic. For example, much of contemporary biology, geology and geography developed without the formal mathematics found in chemistry and physics. So quantification is not one of the defining factors of positivism. Martindale (1960) identifies positivism as ". . . the view that the methods which had proved their worth in the physical sciences were appropriate to the study of social phenomena. . . ." (1960, p. 73). This view then presents us with an historically diverse picture since scientific methods and our understanding of them have changed over time. For example, Bacon's *Novum Organum* (1620) presented an inductivist's view of science where all knowledge was gained by observation. By the time of Newton, this notion that by classifying and organizing our findings scientists will "find" laws and theory, has been overwhelmingly rejected. As Martindale notes "Sir Isaac Newton's *Principia* (1687) fused the two major elements of science—rational proof and experimental-observational evidence" (1960, p. 24). The inductivists' emphasis on observation, measurement and data lacked the creative ingredients of science which are the rational and mathematical. Today's science can be characterized as "rational empiricism." (p. 4)

Today, most philosophers of science would characterize science as a combination of two disparate epistemologies: rationalism and empiricism. On the one hand, empiricists such as Hume (1711–1776) argue that all our knowledge comes from experience of sense data and associations. The empiricist perspective is very much focused on induction and would assume that knowledge is "discovered" from observations. On the other hand, rationalists such as Descartes (1596–1650) or Kant (1724–1804) posit that the associations and connections formed are based on *a priori* structures or forms of thinking that ground formal reasoning, such as mathematics. Indeed, the newer versions of rationalism might be represented in structural works such as those by Chomsky and Levi-Strauss.

The argument between these two epistemologies is an old one (see, for example, Plato's *Meno*). The basic argument is whether our knowledge is "out there" and "discovered" or is already in our heads and is "constructed" or "*a priori*" to experience. Fortunately, we do not have to get into this debate because contemporary science is quite ecumenical (though philosophically incoherent) in this regard. Contemporary science has largely adopted criteria from both epistemologies. From the rationalists, science has adopted the criteria that knowledge must be in a logical or systematic form. This is not as restrictive as it might sound because there are a great many ways to think "logically." At the base of all of these various logical systems, however, is the assumption that our thinking should at least be internally consistent and not contradictory with what we are saying. One might debate whether this is a criteria for a knowledge claim or a criteria for the "comprehension" of a knowledge claim because I am not sure how humans would understand a proposition (a = a) is simultaneously true and false.

Empiricism, on the other hand, has a long history in science. Certainly early philosophers of science, such as Bacon (1561–1626), believed that observational inductionism was the *sine qua non* of science. After the advances in physics by Newton, sheer unadulterated inductionism was de-emphasized in science. However, the criteria persist that any knowledge claim must be judged and scrutinized by comparison to sense data. Indeed, science without empiricism would be only speculative philosophy or theory. The notion of measurement is especially tied to the criteria of subjecting claims to sense data validation. In the next chapter we will need to explore the nature of measurement and sense data to better understand how theory works. For the moment, all we need is to understand that the empirical criteria is essential to contemporary science.

Even though these two epistemological positions may be at odds, contemporary science is catholic in its use of both. Contemporary science would like knowledge claims to be both rational and empirical. That is, science would like a knowledge claim to be logically coherent (within a system) and to be empirically valid. The characterization of positivism as rational-empiricism would not pertain to the entire history of science because at times science has been dominated by observationalism, inductionism, and rationalism. At the present, however, any discussion of positivism (meaning contemporary science) must take this dual character into account.

These two perspectives on science were fused together by the positivist philosophers (especially Braithwaite, 1953; Carnap, 1966; Hempel, 1966; Popper, 1959; Reichenbach, 1958; Rudner, 1966) into a picture of science commonly known as the "hypothetico-deductive" model. This model of science sees empirical induction building general propositions, which are then tested by deducing predictions that are either "true" or "false." It is this model of science that is the principal subject of criticism.

Three Critiques of Positivism

The philosopher of science Frederick Suppe noted in 1977 that critiques of the positivistic view of science had been so devastating that by the end of the 1960s science was in a state of disarray and confusion (p. 618). Among the many critics are Feyerabend (1975), Gadamer (1982), Habermas (1971), Knapp (1997), and Longino (2002). Although there are many critiques from diverse sets of background assumptions (see Knapp, 1997; White, 1997; White & Mason, 1999a), three principal areas of criticism seem to emerge: constructionism, relativism, and the impossibility of a science of human behavior. A few years ago, White and Mason summarized the many and varied arguments against positivism in two overarching questions. Since White and Mason (1999a, 1999b), important arguments, such as those raised by Longino (2002), have been launched that clarify and focus the questions to a much greater extent than previous discussions. In this section I will discuss each of the following three critiques of positivism: contextual arguments, decidability arguments, and arguments about the possibility of science of human subjects.

Contextualism

The contextual argument is most properly identified with Kuhn (1962, 1996). Kuhn argues that the history of science is characterized by political upheavals rather than scientific discoveries. The most radical interpretation of Kuhn is that knowledge claims are accepted by the scientific world according to the same political principles of greed, career enhancement, and fame that drive many other political agendas. Thus replication and certitude are illusory compared to the desire for scientists to conform to the expectations of colleagues or to be on the "winning" side.

Positivism is a social construction that is a product of its time and place. Critics point out that science itself, as all knowledge, is a social construction. Scientists are convinced of measures and findings on the basis of status and rewards within the historical context or period, rather than any kind of objectivity. As a result, the notion that science is objective is suspect. Because science proceeds as a political process, the accumulation of knowledge that science supposedly holds as a goal may be illusory and unreachable.

Relativism and Decidability

Decidability arguments focus on whether any knowledge claim from science can actually be proven to be true or false. Clearly, if knowledge claims cannot be verified then science becomes speculative philosophy at best. There are several components of this argument.

One important component of this argument comes from logicians. Scientific rationalists often held up deductive systems as offering science the power to predict and accumulate knowledge across contexts. However, mathematicians such as Godel brought such assumptions into question. Later, Suppes (1960) in his work on axiomatic set theory demonstrated that not all assumptions could be generated for any logical deductive system. As a result, deduction becomes less than the definitive and certain tool envisioned by rationalists.

In addition, the analytic philosopher Wittgenstein (1958b) suggested that the natural language we use to compose knowledge claims and propositions is incomplete. Other scholars, such as Derrida (1976), continued to discuss the vagueness in language systems (propositions) that make any knowledge claim inherently ambiguous. As a result, every scientific proposition is viewed as so ambiguous that it will not afford definitive tests for its truth or falsity.

The second closely related component and extension of the preceding criticism is the argument that science lacks any "foundation" that would assure that its knowledge is objective. This criticism is often called "antifoundationalism." The antifoundational argument assails the assumption that science has any epistemological claim to objectivity. Certainly the arguments about deduction and vagueness feed into this argument, but the crux of the argument focuses on objectivity and the fact that all knowledge is a social construction. It often is pointed out that objectivity is an illusion since it would mean curtailing normal human valuations and perceptions colored by time and place. Certainly Kuhn's (1962, 1996) work establishes that measurement is tied to the scientist's time and place. In addition, anti-foundationalists argue that evolutionary theory in both biology and physics predicates a changing world of existences, such as an expanding universe. What we observe today may be different the next day, not because of measurement error but because change is endemic to the world.

Science of Human Behavior

Many scholars have expressed doubts as to the possibility of a science of human behavior. Certainly Weber (*Gesammelte Aufsätze zur Wissenschaftslehre*, Gerth & Mills, 1958) expressed concerns, and more recently so did such scholars as the philosopher Winch (1958) and the sociologist Blumer (1962, 1969). The criticism is that humans and their activities are more complex in their meanings than can possibly be captured by quantitative measures. Although this is often a complex series of arguments, it can be summarized as the argument that human activity is a meaning construction activity of the actor developed by the actor's manipulation of symbols and meanings in the actor's social world. A "behavior," therefore, does not have the same uniform meaning across actors and situations. But counting a "behavior" assumes a uniformity of meaning of the activity, one that for

Blumer does not exist except in the mind of the quantitative social scientist (Turner, 1991, p. 400). This critique, popular among ethnomethodologists, suggests a more qualitative and interactive type of research process. Turner (1991) notes that for Blumer,

> the research act itself must be viewed as a process of symbolic interaction in which the researchers take the role of those individuals whom they are studying. To do such role taking effectively, researchers must study interaction with a set of concepts that, rather than prematurely structuring the social world for investigators, sensitize them to interactive processes. (p. 401)

An important element in this criticism is that positivistic science does not incorporate the reflexive nature of humans into its perspective. Since humans learn and change, they modify their behavior and actions based on the very knowledge gained by science. White and Mason (1999a) use the following example:

> Twenty years ago it was relatively uncommon to hear people discussing *social roles,* however, this is common today. The social science concept of "role" has entered the vernacular of the social world and is now used by the general public to explain and interpret their behavior. The social scientist now finds herself interviewing respondents who describe and explain their behavior in what was just a short time ago regarded as the "arcane jargon" of sociology. Knowledge is reflexive in the sense that it becomes formative of human behavior. Science in general and the social sciences in particular have failed to incorporate the reflexive nature of knowledge into their picture of knowledge construction. (p. 16)

Certainty, Relativity, and Knowledge Claims

One of the notions I developed in the previous history of science is that science is not a monolithic institution following prescribed sets of rules. Rather, science has changed over time, and as a result of these changes it is very difficult to define. Critics of science often focus on the philosophers of science in the 1950s and 1960s that viewed science as being characterized by the hypothetico-deductive model. This particular focus, however, assumes that physics is the model of science to which other sciences should be compared. This assumption is particularly problematic for the social sciences and life sciences. The relevance of this observation will become more clear as we address the issues raised by the critiques of science. This section deals with one among many possible responses to each of the criticisms discussed in the previous section.

Contextualism

I see the realization that science is subject to political and status-driven behaviors as akin to the observation that "science is a human activity." Kuhn's discussion of these processes is quite correct, and anyone who has been a working member of the scientific community can supply examples to further elaborate this point. The problem, however, arises when critics believe that these so typically human foibles compose the totality of science and hence doom science to be nothing more than a political process. Even more important, some critics might take this further and argue that scientific knowledge is not to be trusted.

Some very important points within this critique provide keys to addressing the problem. First, science is a human activity, but it also is a selective human activity that is organized in a particular way with particular membership criteria. Some human activities, such as eating and sleeping, are universal, but science is not of this kind. Rather, science, as we have seen from our brief history, evolved over several centuries and was organized along certain principles. Foremost were the following principles:

1. Science would not look to gods, metaphysics, or other worldly forces to explain what is observed. (principle of metaphysics)

2. Science would not appeal to authority (church, peer, or state) to resolve disputes or supply explanations. (principle of authority)

3. Science was founded on sense observations of our world that could be repeated by any other observer. (principle of replication)

4. Accounts of the way things work must be buttressed by observations. (principle of empiricism)

These four principles forced those interested in science to form a community of scholars that were assailed by kings and princes, bishops and vicars, to see the world in ways that conformed to religion, metaphysics, or the "common sense" of peers. So, for example, the argument that the world was flat received great force from a deeply rooted "common sense." It was this same common sense that believed Earth to be the center of the universe or skin color to be related to intelligence. Each of these beliefs slowly gave way to the observation and arguments of science.

Clearly the community of scientists irritated church, state, and commoner because they used criteria for knowledge and argument not based on the appeals to authority. Indeed, scientific skepticism of knowledge based on such appeals to authority garnered rejection and persecution of scientists. To protect themselves and the knowledge they acquired, scientists tended to discuss and exchange ideas within their community. Thus the scientific community became identified with certain beliefs and methodological criteria necessary for the continuation of inquisitiveness.

Like many organized human activities, the development of a scientific community enabled scholars to elucidate certain ideals. One of these ideals, for which science is currently pilloried, is the ideal of "objectivity." Objectivity was a term that captured what the four aforementioned principles were attempting to achieve. That is, knowledge that was founded on replicable observations rather than authority and metaphysics. However, this "objectivity" could only be approached and was an ideal, rather than a claim regarding knowledge as some critics contend. As an ideal it was tantamount to not allowing influence from peers, church, or state dictate observations and knowledge. Of course, scientists are human, and even Galileo had to recant the Copernican view of the universe when threatened by the papacy.

So I believe Kuhn and others are correct that science is a human activity with all the normal failings of humans. I find it even less problematic to agree with contextualists that science is constrained by the historical period and place. This agreement with the contextualist view, however, should be complemented by the realization that the great strength of science has been the particular ideals and principles around which these humans are organized. The fact that scientific associations and organizations allow relatively unfettered discussion and argumentation regarding observations and theories is testimony to the evolution of these principles and ideals within this community.

Relativism and Decidability

If all knowledge is a social construction and the "objectivity" of science is simply an unattainable ideal, doesn't that suggest scientific knowledge is no different from any other form of knowledge? Furthermore, if there is no epistemological foundation to ensure that scientific knowledge is "superior" or "objective," then scientific knowledge claims should be judged as all other knowledge claims. Critics of positivism might argue, however, because there is no agreement as to how to decide the superiority of a knowledge claim, that all knowledge claims are either equally true or equally false. This perspective ends up in what Cheal (1991) has termed a "paralogy" of theory and leads the philosopher of science Longino (2002) to conclude,

> Knowledge is plural. There may be multiple sets of practices, each capable of producing knowledge of the same process or phenomenon. Different knowers

differently situated and motivated by different cognitive goals may have different and nonreconcilable knowledge of the same phenomenon. There may be multiple epistemically acceptable correct (i.e., conforming) representations of a given phenomenon or process. Which among these counts as knowledge on which to act depends on the cognitive goals and particular cognitive resources of a given context. (p. 207)

Longino, however, fails to address whether this relativism of knowledge is indeed the state of knowledge within science.[2]

As we have seen in our discussion of the development of the scientific community in the previous section, scientists would not be particularly upset if the church, state, or peers failed to accept their theories and claims. However, if knowledge claims and theories were rejected by the scientific community, this would have far greater meaning. The reason for this, as pointed out by Peirce (1955), is simply that the scientific community has developed ways of resolving disputed knowledge claims. Certainly the religions can resolve disputes by means of excommunication, and the state may resolve disputes by wars, but these avenues were neither preferred nor open to scientists. The community of scientists developed criteria for resolving disputed knowledge. First and foremost, scientists would ask which theory or account would best fit with what was observed. If two accounts were equally capable of accounting for observations then logical criteria such as noncontradiction or extralogical criteria such as simplicity (Occam's razor) were invoked.

Some scholars, such as Knapp (1997), have argued that science relies on a "representational" epistemology. That is, science views adequate knowledge as where our knowledge construction corresponds to an independent reality. Certainly the history of philosophy, from Plato's allegory of the cave to the infamous fight between George Berkeley and Lord David Hume,[3] is replete with arguments about the degree of independence between the knower and known. Although I believe this is an important area for continued philosophical speculation, I do not regard it as central to science. Certainly the core of science is that there should be a correspondence between knowledge and observations, but that does not necessarily entail a metaphysical position so much as long-standing methodological criteria. Certainly the correspondence between the "shadow" of an electron and nuclear theory goes way beyond a simple version of representationalism, as does the theory regarding a parallel universe. The important point here is not which criteria are used but is the fact that the community of scientists invoke shared, agreed-on criteria to resolve knowledge disputes. Over time, these criteria will change and evolve as new methodological rules come into vogue and old ones vanish.

Decidability of the superiority of knowledge claims within science will be decided by the criteria commonly agreed on within science. Of course within particular sciences, such as biology, sociology, and physics, the criteria will vary. Science has, for the most part, been uncomfortable with simultaneously maintaining competing claims such as light particles and rays, or quantum and macrophysics. As Kuhn (1962) has pointed out, however, several schools of thought might develop around particular disputes until they are eventually resolved. But this is not evidence in favor of relativism so much as the normal process of scientific accumulation, thought, and testing.

Relativism is the doctrine that assumes that there is no independent "truth" to knowledge. It assumes that knowledge is relative to the knower and is commonly tied to "subjectivism." Certainly the quote we used earlier from Longino (2002) could be used as an example of such a position. However, the notion that there is some permanent, epistemologically privileged objective truth is equally noxious. It would be especially upsetting to scientists because it would probably entail a strong metaphysical element. The problem is that world, reality, or whatever, is somewhere between these two positions. As I have argued elsewhere (White, 1997), we only have knowledge that is relatively superior for some purposes over other knowledge. This is the position I equate with the writing of Peirce (1905, 1955, 1958) and more recently the epistemologist Haack (1993, 1998).

Basically, scientific knowledge has proved superior to many other forms of knowledge for certain purposes but not others. If one desires *feelings* of unity, perhaps religion or other forms of mysticism are superior to science. However, if one deals with the social, organic, or physical world for certain purposes, science seems clearly superior. This "superiority" is of course relative to the use and the further caveat that it is fallible. Indeed, Peirce's "fallibilism" is the hallmark of today's science. Indeed, the history of science is rich with disproved and discredited theories. Science proceeds by tentatively holding a theory until it is revised, disproved, or simply surpassed. To hold a theory as "true" would turn science (the tentative) into religion (the true). Hatcher (1991) argues this pragmatist perspective.

The same kind of argument applies to the diagnoses and treatment in modern medicine versus those of the witch doctors. Each employs different methods, each has a different conceptual scheme, and perhaps each was considered rational for their particular culture or historical context. It does not follow, however, that the methods of modern medicine are no closer to the truth concerning the causes and treatment of disease that those of the witch doctor. The fact is, I believe, we understand a lot more about how the human body works than our preceding generations, and the burden of proof is on whomever endorses a position that claims otherwise. We should, in the spirit of fallibilism, conclude that our present understanding is limited and subject to change, but it is superior to prior understanding because it is more effective in restoring health to sick patients. (p. 11)

Thus the problem for many scholars is that the actual situation in which we find our knowledge is not well described by the oppositions of absolute objectivism or subjective relativism. We live in a scientific world of tentative hypotheses and theories, not absolutes at either end of the continuum.

Science of Human Behavior

From the outset, the term "behavior" creates problems. "Behavior" often denotes unintentional acts and "action" is seen as denoting intentional acts. The intentionality of acts is viewed as critical in certain social sciences (see, for example, Parsons & Shils, 1952). But what I am trying to get at by using "behavior" is the entire pantheon of human activity, including species-specific behavior (ontogenetic), habit (sociogenic), and action (intentional).

The single question that most critics pose is in regard to the reflexive nature of human action. However, reflexivity is a potential and not necessarily an attribute. For example, we still do not fully understand nor can we accurately predict individual fertility. We do not know at this time which behaviors are better analyzed as aggregate behaviors and which as individual behaviors. But the question of whether a social science is possible (rather than desirable) can certainly be answered.

Many scholars contend that studying humans is not the same as studying subatomic particles or geological strata. The scientific study of the physical world is somehow seen as appropriate since these inanimate objects do not direct themselves as do humans. However, if we change the model of science from physics or geology to biology or zoology we have an entirely different argument. Now the question becomes "Can we study human behavior in the same way we study primate behavior?" The answer to this question would seem to be affirmative. So, in large part, many of the objections come from assuming the physical science model as determining what is and is not a "science."

This is not to say that this perspective addresses many of the important issues raised by such scholars as Winch (1958). In the next chapter we will need to address the use of teleological explanations and intentionality, issues about predicting aggregates rather than individual behavior, and the notion of rule-governed behavior. But for the moment it would seem that a social science is at least as possible as any other life science.

Theory and Its Critics

One of the glaring omissions in this chapter is an adequate discussion of social science theory. This is intentional. Before we can move to an understanding of how and why scientific theory works, we needed to first have a foundation in science. This chapter has tried to develop such a foundation. I have not pursued the traditional philosophy of science approaches emphasizing various scientific epistemologies because I feel that although such approaches might be philosophically accurate, they are often responsible for some of the confusion social scientists experience in dealing with postpositivist thinking. Rather, this chapter has tried to maintain a larger historical picture and to keep issues as straightforward as possible. If I have erred it will not be in terms of generality but in terms of detail.

The next chapter will, however, make up for many of these oversights. Theory is indeed the driving force behind any science. Science will always be concerned with how we make sense of our world, and it is theory that performs that function. So it is my expectation that the next chapter will address any grievous oversights contained in the discussion of science and its critics.

Notes

1. This section builds on the discussion of this topic in a previous paper by myself and Lisa Mason (White & Mason, 1999a, 1999b).

2. I remain unconvinced by Longino's (2002) examples from the history of science.

3. I was told about this as an undergraduate in philosophy. Hume the empiricist is rumored to have thrown a book at Berkeley the idealist to awaken him to a world independent of his cognitions.

4

Theory, Models, and Metaphors

This chapter is devoted to an examination of theory and theoretical method in the study of the family. It addresses many of the details about explanation, logical form, and propositional statements left unaddressed in the previous chapter. However, the structure of this chapter needs a little explanation.

This chapter begins with a discussion of models and metaphors based on and extending the work by Black (1962). The principal reason for beginning with this is that I believe the key to understanding theory and its diverse functions in family studies is to view it through the bifocal lens of models and metaphors. Recall that in Chapter 1 of this book I agreed with Turner's assessment that the theory constructionists of the 1960s and 1970s became too mechanistic about theory. The one purpose of introducing the functions of models and metaphors is to loosen this mechanistic grip on theory.

The second section of this chapter examines the definition of theory and data. It raises questions about the extent to which "data" are in actuality very dependent on theory. Interestingly, the theory that is the foundation for data may be independent from the substantive theory in which we are interested. This second section seeks to clarify the issues and definitions that distinguish data from theory.

The third section of this chapter introduces a discussion of theory and propositions. The complex relations that theoretical propositions and methodology enjoy are presented with the help of a diagram originally proposed by Leik and Meeker (1975). The theory-model-data diagram introduces some of the complex relationships between theory and research.

Models and Metaphors

For centuries, philosophers and logicians regarded metaphor as being the poor cousin of literal meaning. Indeed, metaphor was viewed as hazy, vague, and imprecise compared to literal language formulations. Black (1962) challenged some of this "wisdom" in his examination of metaphors and models.

Black (1962) loosely defines a metaphor as a group of words or phrase that relates the literal aspects of the sentence or phrase to some other frame or context. One example would be to say one "plows through a report." Certainly the term "report" is a literal reference to an object. However, the verb "plowing" clearly means more than just "reading." "Plowing" suggests a farmer's hard work, toil, and digging through the surface of the terrain. Black suggests that these connotations from another context (farming) enrich and construct the meaning of how the report is treated over and above the literal statement "reading the report."

Black (1962) suggests three different interpretations of the way metaphors work: substitutional, transformational, and interactional. In the substitutional view, the metaphor simply substitutes for some other word or phrase. For example, if one says that "this argument is a trap," the word "trap" connotes that this argument "places us in a closed place without means of escape." Thus the word "trap" is simply shorthand for a phrase. It is obvious, however, that the connotations of "trap" may go beyond the literal substitution. However, words like "orange" were undoubtedly literal metaphorical connections between the fruit and the color and eventually became applied to both (p. 33).

The second way in which metaphors function is transformationally, as an analogy or simile. For example, "I was trapped by her argument" treats the argument as a mobile object capable of following a path or falling into a hole. Furthermore, the connotation that we do not like being trapped, and that this is a circumstance we would not prefer, adds to and transforms the meaning beyond what a literal term could achieve. Indeed, this is not replacement but is enrichment and embellishment of meaning, in the sense Black (1962, p. 35) calls transformative.

The third way that Black sees metaphors working is interactionally. In this sense the juxtaposition of the literal part of the phrase with the figurative parts creates a new meaning that goes beyond either singular meaning. For example, a "wolf of a vegetarian" goes beyond just replacing the literal meaning of "voracious vegetarian" and goes beyond saying the person eats like a wolf. The juxtaposition between a carnivore that rips and tears its meat with a browsing vegetarian suggests a contradiction for humans as vegetarians and a mismatch of ideas (vegetarianism) and nature (carnivore). This use of metaphor produces new and unusual images and thoughts.

Black (1962) identifies several general components of metaphor. First, metaphors must contain two elements: a major and a minor component. The major component is often the literal component, whereas the minor is the figurative element. The figurative element is usually a commonly understood element (farming, animals, traps) that relates to some other group of meanings and connotations than the literal component. Finally, Black (1962, p. 46) argues that explication of a metaphor's meanings is extremely valuable for understanding the meanings that are intended. As we will see later, following this particular suggestion resulted in enormous payoffs in linguistics and neuroscience and later in philosophy of science (see Lakoff & Johnson, 1980, 1999).

In a separate chapter from metaphor, Black (1962) discusses models. He begins by stating "scientists often speak of using models but seldom pause to consider the presuppositions and the implications of their practice." He continues that "to speak of 'models' in connection with scientific theory already smacks of the metaphorical" (p. 219). Indeed, at the conclusion of his chapter Black focuses on models as a form of metaphor. This in part explains why we began this section with a discussion of metaphor rather than with models.

Black (1962) details three principal types of models: physical or scale models, analog models, and theoretical models (pp. 219–243). Because all three of these are used in science, it is useful to follow his discussion. Scale (or physical) models always are models of an object rather than of ideas. For example, a scale model of an F-18 fighter jet would bear a physical resemblance to the airplane but would be on a different scale. Usually it would be smaller and would neglect certain aspects of the original airplane and emphasize others. So, for example, the ratio of wing length to fuselage length might be accurate but the missiles would not function because details such as wiring and explosives are deemphasized. Scale models always bear resemblance or degrees of isomorphism to that which they take as an object.

Analog models replicate the systems of relationships or structure in one object in another and different type of object. For example, if the system relationships in a heating system with a thermostat were used as a model for a "family system" (see "Systems Theory" in White & Klein, 2002), then such a replication would be an analog model. Analog models often use one object's structure to assist in understanding the relationships in another.

One particular set of analog models is mathematical models. The same is true for mathematical models as for all analog models; that is, the mathematical model specifies some of the structural or relational components in the object. Later in this chapter I will discuss in detail the double use of mathematical models in science. One use of mathematical models in science is as an analog of data or observations. In this sense, the relationship between variables is described in terms of the mathematical model. For example, the data might be said to be linear or to be a logistic function. In addition, mathematical models may be used as models of theory. In this case, the object to be modeled would be the relationships between concepts proposed in the theory and the mathematical model would capture this structure and express it as a system of relations. It is extremely important to note Black's (1962) warning:

> Especially important it is to remember that the mathematical treatment furnishes no *explanations*. Mathematics can be expected to do no more than draw consequences from the original empirical assumptions. (p. 225)

To add to this admonition, I would note that a mathematical model of theoretical statements only exposes the logic that is already there. As we shall see, both of these uses of mathematical models can provide useful elucidation of what is already there in the theory or data. Furthermore, this elucidation may sometimes force both researcher and theorist to see the subject differently.

The last type is what Black (1962) termed theoretical models. Theoretical models are most often described as supplying a picture of a scientific theory. It is interesting to note that in some cases the picture may be a speculative model that is on its way to being a theory. For example, Black discusses Maxwell's initial discussion of electrical fields using the metaphor of "the motion of fluids." Black is quick to note that to make good use of a theoretical model it must be "intuitively grasped" in order to draw novel inferences and lines of inquiry (p. 232). In this last sense, theoretical models perform in a very similar way to metaphor.

The importance of Black's distinctions will gradually become clear in this chapter. For the present, it is important to note that models and metaphors can both be explicated in terms of rules of correspondence and analogy. It is also important that models and metaphors be understood as corresponding to the most creative and intuitive aspects of science. It is obvious that science without ideas such as those afforded by models and metaphors is simply description.

Theory

It is very tempting to simply quote one or even a few of the many definitions of theory that are current. Certainly such discussions are abundantly available (see White & Klein, 2002, Chapter 1) and, I think, offer a fruitful approach. However, such definitions usually have hidden assumptions regarding the nature of science, the nature of human thought, and even the nature of reality. It is, of course, impossible to say very much of interest without making some of these assumptions; however, these assumptions account for the diversity of definitions and some of the disagreements about theory.

If we start with a lexical definition of theory from a common dictionary we find something like "a set of ideas put forward to explain something" or "principles of a subject rather than its practice." Indeed, most of the common definitions of theory focus on either the function of explanation or the identification of basic principles. This perspective can be traced to early Greek philosophy and especially the perspective found in Plato. However, the original Greek term *theoria* was equated with thinking about a subject or considering something. In this broader perspective, theory would include both product and process.

Many definitions emphasizing theory as a set of explanatory propositions have failed to capture the process component in the original Greek term. As a result, theory has come to represent a product that somehow explains rather than a process of consideration. Even when the process is considered, it is often within fairly confining discussions of induction and deduction. Inductive and deductive methods (as opposed to logic) are often thought of as an exhaustive list of the methods used in science. Even though I believe that inductive and deductive methods do not represent the totality of approaches used in science, it is impossible to go beyond these two methods without first understanding their importance and function.

Induction

Inductive arguments proceed from specific instances to generalizations. It is certainly the first part of building taxonomic categories in science and may have represented the earliest form of science in many cultures (Hellemans & Bunch, 1988). Bacon is perhaps one of the most widely cited champions of a purely inductive method in science. For centuries, induction was thought to be not just a method in science but also to be a form of logic. Induction as a logical form has been regaled with criticism since the writings of Hume (see, for example, Black, 1962; Braithwaite, 1953).

As I have stated, induction proceeds from specific observations to general statements. The procedure may not just create taxonomic categories but generalizations that constitute lawlike statements. Indeed, one of the major ingredients in many definitions of scientific theory is that at least some of the propositions in the theory are generalizations of such empirical uniformity that they constitute empirical laws (see Rudner, 1966). When science is championed for being nomothetic, it is precisely these lawlike statements that support that attribution.

However, when the claim is that induction is a form of *logic* rather than *method,* the criticisms are overwhelming. Foremost among these is the relatively simple criticism that the number of observations to entail a certifiable (valid) generalization is impossible to determine. For example, observe the following pattern of x's and o's: xxxxoooxxxxoooxxxxoooxxxxooo. It might seem relatively clear cut that four x's are followed by three o's. However, we have only observed a set of four groups of x's and o's and the very next observation might change the pattern. So the question becomes, how many observations are required in order to make a valid generalization? That no number can be determined is obvious because it could be argued that we are interested in patterns "in the long run" and that time frame is clearly unspecified. A second criticism is how such generalizations can be refuted. For example, if there is a generalization that "four x's are invariably followed by three o's that in turn are followed by four x's," then the occurrence of one extra o would cast the law as a contingency rather than a law. In general, the biggest single criticism of induction as logic is that there are no rules by which certifiable (valid) laws may be produced.

Induction as a method, however, is simply observation and leaps to generalization with no claims for certifiability or validity. This is what Kaplan (1964) described as part of the "context of discovery." Indeed, the justification for induction is that it may produce generalizations. However, these generalizations are not produced by anyone making the observation but only by those with proper training in the subject matter, or with creative intuitive insight, or both. In other words, the method of observing individual instances and producing generalizations may produce either profound or trivial generalizations based not on the method but on the individual scientist. The inductive method by itself is much more a description of the elements that might go into the making of a generalization, but these elements lack the necessary condition of creative insight that comes from the theorist or researcher.

One consequence of this view of induction is that we cannot judge the validity of a general proposition on the basis of how it was discovered. Indeed, a research scientist could study a phenomenon for a considerable time, whereas a novice might produce a generalization based on one observation. Once a proposition is produced, however, it is the role of induction to develop further supporting observations that move the proposition toward the status of a lawlike statement. These "laws" can then be used as the empirical propositions within deductive theory.

Deduction

Although Kaplan (1964) views induction as being located within the "context of discovery," it is very important to note that discoveries in science only produce propositions for theories. The interweaving of empirical law-like statements with analytic propositions is also a creative endeavor. Once a theory is proposed, however, we then move to the "context of justification." According to Kaplan (1964), the context of justification is where theories are "judged" for their validity, coherence, and empirical relevance. Many philosophers and scholars of science emphasize the processes of judging the validity and coherence of a theory, whereas historians of science might emphasize the process of judging the relevance of the theory.

In discussions of the coherence and validity of a theory, the focus is usually on what is commonly but diversely called either the "hypothetico-deductive" or "deductive-nomological" or "covering law" model of science (see, for example, Hempel, 1966; Homans, 1967). As with induction, the term "deduction" might have two meanings; it might mean either the logical form or the method. Most scholars, such as Hempel (1966), emphasize the logical form. Deductive theory is organized so that the theoretical propositions form "logically valid" deductions that can then be empirically verified. In its simplest model of argument (*modus ponens* and *modus tollens*), if the premises are true then the conclusion must necessarily be true. However, it should be pointed out that "true" in this context means that the sequence of propositions follows certain rules of logical implication. Usually scientific researchers use the second of these logical forms (*modus tollens*) because it proposes the negation of the consequent. The *modus tollens* logic goes as follows:

If H is true, then so is I
I is not true
Therefore H is not true. (Hempel, 1966, p. 7)

To affirm the consequent (I is true) in this example would be to commit the "fallacy of affirming the consequent" and not be a valid form of argument. The reason for this is that there are many other possible accounts for "I" being true. However, if "I" is not true then "H" cannot be true.

The logic of implication and entailment can be expressed in many different forms; however, one of the most visual and simple ways of explaining this is by means of Venn diagrams (also known as Euler circles). Let's take the case just given. If "I" is necessarily contained in "H" then we can express this as a proper subset of "H" as shown in Figure 4.1.

Now from this diagram it is clear that not all of "H" is "I". It is also clear that if "I" is false then "H" is false because "I" is a proper subset.

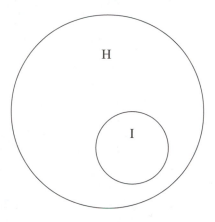

Figure 4.1   Venn Diagram

There are many examples of deductive theory in the family. One example is found in Burr, Hill, et al. (1979, p. 83). Burr, Hill, et al. state that "the greater the diversification of a person's roles, the less consensus the person will perceive in the expectations about those roles" (p. 80). Consensus of expectations is then negatively linked to role strain as in Diagram 4.1.

Degree of diversification → consensus → role strain

Diagram 4.1   Path of Effects

However, to apply the rules of implication to the relations between these concepts, certain conditions must prevail. These relations need to be asymmetric and transitive. When relations are of this type, we can deduce new propositions for testing. For example,

Degree of diversification "is negatively related to" consensus

Consensus "is negatively related to" role strain

Therefore,

Degree of diversification "is positively related to" role strain

In this example, it is proposed that as a person gains more roles, the consensus on each role is reduced. As consensus about enacting any role is reduced, role strain becomes more likely. It is an interesting deduction to

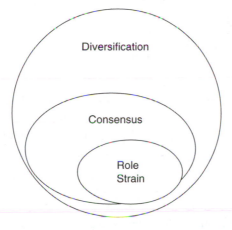

Figure 4.2   Venn Diagrams and Implication

propose that the more diversified the role set a person has, the greater the role strain. Such propositional statements are often seen as good examples of deductive family theory.

It is worth pursuing this example a little further. If we visualize the implication in terms of Venn diagrams we find some problems.

We must admit that the propositions about roles are not similar to propositions about classes of things, such as "Cats are mammals, mammals bear live young, therefore cats bear live young." The propositions about role diversification are different, because the relation is not class inclusion but one of implication. In the case of implication, however, regarding degree of role diversification and consensus and role strain, determination will only be partial. We are really saying these are causally related, such that when diversification occurs consensus is necessarily reduced, leading in turn to the production of more role strain "net of all other relevant causal variables" (*ceteris paribus*). The problem is, of course, that we may never be able to specify all the relevant causal variables. This case of not being able to specify the relevant causal variables is known as "specification error." There are other forms of error that keep us from attaining perfect determination of changes in role strain, but those will be discussed later.

That we may not be able to specify all other relevant causal variables should not be taken as reason for rejecting the use of logical implication (deduction) in theory. After all, theory is inherently abstract. Propositions contain concepts that are abstractions. The relations between concepts are themselves abstractions. It is the purpose of logical implication to assist us in manipulating and understanding these abstractions. Indeed, logical implication is usually how theories produce different and sometimes novel conceptual propositions. It is also possible to examine theories for logical coherence. In other words, one important attribute of theory is whether or not the propositions are self-contradictory or consistent with one another.

Deduction or implication is at the core of theoretical explanation. As Homans (1967) observes, what we mean by explanation is indeed nothing other than the deduction of a particular event from more general and abstract propositions. For example, if I drop my textbook in class and then ask students to explain why it fell to the ground, students invariably say "the law of gravity." Of course, the "law of gravity" is actually a complex theory, but we feel an occurrence has been explained once we show that it is "covered" by a more abstract set of propositions. This deductive view of explanation is sometimes called the "covering law" model of explanation because it subsumes the particular event under a more general proposition.

The great strength of deductive implication is its *certifiability*. That is to say, if a theory is proposed as a logical theory, then there are rules of logic that allow us to judge if indeed the theory is logical. Having a logical theory allows for the deduction of novel hypotheses and the explanation of particular events. Thus most, if not all, scientific theories would prefer to be logically coherent.

Defining Scientific Theory

Defining a scientific theory is easier once one has explained the processes of induction and deduction. *A scientific theory is simply a set of logically related conceptual propositions, some of which are empirical lawlike propositions.* This definition is similar to those provided by many others writing in the philosophy of science (e.g., Rudner, 1966). It incorporates the basic elements of propositions, concepts, logical relations, and empirical lawlike propositions. The problem with such definitions is that they fail to consider the process. Scientific theories begin with ideas. The ideas are tied to observations and as theorists think about this, more propositions are developed and perhaps even linked to other theories. The process of theorizing is as important as the product.

Inductive observations supply the empirical lawlike statements used in scientific theory. It is this empirical ingredient that makes scientific theory different from other forms of logical theory. As I previously stated, the inductive processes are not logical in the same sense as deduction. There are no rules to tell us when to or how to see a cluster or set of empirical observations as a conceptual entity. This would be considered the "creative" and "generative" part of the theoretical process. In family studies, this is the part of theorizing occupied by such approaches as "grounded theory," "phenomenology," and other empirically "emersed" approaches (e.g., Berger & Kellner, 1964; Gubrium & Holstein, 1993; Strauss & Corbin, 1997). Kaplan (1964) would see this as taking place within the "context of discovery." Once induction has produced these empirical statements, however, they may be added to other conceptual propositions to compose a theory. This process of building theory is also not subject to well-defined rules and is properly in Kaplan's "context of discovery."

Once the theoretical propositions are formulated, we may move to what Kaplan calls the "context of justification." In this context, the logical structure and coherence of the theoretical propositions can be analyzed and improved. In addition, deduction may produce unseen conceptual propositions and supply "covering law" explanations of particular events. Furthermore, deductions supply empirically testable conceptual hypotheses that may be falsified. Thus in the context of justification we see if the theory "holds," logically and empirically. If there is no reason to reject the theory, it is tentatively held until it is eventually refined or supplanted.

One of the most critical differences between scientific theory and other forms of theory is this tentative nature and the expectation that empirical refutation is possible. When we reviewed the history of science, we found that early scientists believed that events could be explained by examining the physical world and its regularities without recourse to gods or other supernatural beings. The empirical nature of scientific theory goes even further and presents a basic premise that theories can be tested and overturned. Thus, unlike religion, "truth" and "belief" in science are always tentative, and the one certainty is that our theories will, in time, be supplanted by more adequate ones.

Two comments need to be made at this point. The first is to recall Black's statement regarding mathematical models cited previously in this chapter. Black's comment applies equally well to deduction. Indeed, once a theory is systematically stated, all of the resulting deductions are only bringing out what is already contained within the theory. Although the deduction of some propositions may seem novel, they would nonetheless be already contained in the premises.

The second point is that when I discussed explanation, it was paramount that some lawlike statements be included. Scientific theories rely on these empirical lawlike propositions for their falsifiability and for explanatory power. Indeed, a theory with no empirical or sensible referents would not be a *scientific* theory. It is this empirical character that allows a completely logically true theory to be empirically falsified. It is also the "covering laws" that do much of the explaining of particular events. In the following pages I will take a more detailed look at the production of these lawlike statements.

Data

It is sometimes surprising to me that the theoretical nature of "data" is often not well developed by theoreticians. Certainly many of us think of "data" as being "given," "immediately observable," or "clear and distinct." The truth of the matter is that data are as much a theoretical construction, if not more so, as any social or physical theory. Kuhn (1996) remarked on this in his observation that "the distinction between discovery and invention or between fact and theory will, however, immediately prove to be exceedingly artificial" (p. 52). Although Kuhn argues that facts are constructed as part of theory, and I do not disagree with this contention, it is also possible and very usual for facts to be generated by their own theory. The area that composes this theory is called "measurement theory." In this section, we delve into this area of theory so that we can better understand the overall relationships among data, models, and theory.

What is the simplest form of knowledge you can have and still call it knowledge? If we think very deeply about this question, we will come to the conclusion that the simplest form of knowledge we can have is a basic distinction between presence and absence. For example, a qualitative researcher collects the following statement from a respondent:

"I wanted to be a mother."

We can break this statement down into the information that the respondent either

(a) "wanted to be something"

or

(b) "didn't want to be something"

and the respondent wanted to be

(c) "a teacher"

or

(d) "other than a teacher."

In both the first and second statements, one may be true but the other cannot be true. The respondent is telling us that statement (a) and (d) are true, whereas (b) and (c) are false. Of course, meaning is broader and more illusive than captured in a truth function, yet I would contend that the smallest unit we can call knowledge is just such a function. Imagine a researcher going out to do a qualitative interview. The first important piece of information is whether or not the respondent is at home (1 or 0). Indeed, as we know from information technology, with a sufficient number of "1's and 0's" we can produce a continuous flow of music or movies. Even the most complex of photographs can be digitized. Although this fact is well accepted in neuropsychology, it is less well understood by qualitative researchers. The fact is, however, that most qualitative researchers are aware of the many text-analysis software packages available to assist their research analyses, which would testify to the presence of this elemental level of information.

The fact that presence or absence, "1" or "0," is the smallest component of information is most instructive for measurement theory. Indeed, it is the basis for measurement theory. The assumptions behind making any distinction such as "presence or absence" are foundational to measurement theory.

Definitions and Facts

The first assumption we must make is that the "thing," "entity," or "event" we will describe as "present or absent" is defined so that we know when an observation indicates its presence or absence. This is actually a relatively complex procedure involving (1) a universe of observation, (2) definition of object, and (3) the definition of presence or absence. For example, if I want to know if a particular student, Janet, attended my lecture on Wednesday I would have to state the universe of observation (10–11 A.M. on Wednesday, September 3, 2003). Next, I would have to define the object such that only one case will satisfy being Janet (Janet's physical appearance). Finally, I would have to decide what constitutes the attributes of "presence and absence." So if I take attendance at the beginning of class does that mean Janet did not attend class? I would have operationalized presence to mean only her physical presence at the beginning of class and she may leave thereafter yet still be counted as present.

The assumptions we make are relatively formal. First, the universe of observation may be treated as a set of possible observations where Janet is an element of the set of students enrolled in the course. The set of observations is then mapped onto the set of attributes of observations. In our example each member of the set can be mapped onto the attributes of presence or absence. This mapping can be seen in Table 4.1.

Table 4.1 shows I have six students enrolled in the course. I take attendance on each day, but the observations in the diagram are only for September 3. On that day there were two absences for the set. If we think about this, the students enrolled represent the finite set of possible cases. At any point of observation, each case may be either absent or present. This measure is exhaustive of the possibilities for the attribute; the student is either in

Table 4.1   Mapping Objects, Observations, and Attributes

Set of Students in the Course	Observation (Attendance on the 3rd)	Attribute (Measurement Variable)
Janet	O_1	A
Roscoe	O_2	P
Bill	O_3	P
Jim	O_4	P
Sue	O_5	A
Joanne	O_6	P

attendance or not. Furthermore, the attribute qualities, present or absent, are mutually exclusive; a student cannot be simultaneously both present and absent. Indeed, the basis of all qualitative distinctions is founded on the assumption that "1" and "0" are mutually exclusive and exhaustive of the attribute space.

An attribute space is said to be the possible degrees, levels, or types on which a set of objects might be graphed (the range of the function). In the preceding example, we mapped students onto the nominal attributes of presence and absence. It is, of course, possible to move to higher levels of measurement such as ordinal and interval scales. For example, if we could order (< or >) the observations, we could map onto ordinal categories such as high, medium, and low. And if we can order the objects by some attribute and also assume there are equal intervals between the orderings, then we would have an interval scale. Kaplan (1964, pp. 177–186) provides an excellent introductory discussion, and McGinnis (1965, pp. 274–290) follows a more complete account of these details in measurement theory. These sources should be consulted for the formal analysis of measurement.

What should be clear, however, is that the attribute space is, of course, a theoretical decision. Whether we believe the relevant attribute for class attendance is simply "presence or absence" or "degree of presence" is a matter for our theory. I know it seems odd to think of attendance as a theoretical area of discourse, but if we measure it then it must be. Facts are not created *ex nihilo* but are created from theory. Someone had to believe that attendance in class is an important component for learning and that learning is the goal for any class. The assumptions we make are theoretical assumptions that then construct our observations and measurement. Thus what we regard as a "fact" represents a series of complex theoretical decisions.

We have already seen that simple factual statements such as "Joanne wasn't in class today" consist of a series of theoretical decisions. But most of our common everyday "factual" world is also constructed in such a way. For example, "The red Volvo was hit by the blue Toyota." Certainly the color is an attribute of the automobile classification. But for the moment, focus on the word "hit." Does this mean "one car damaged another," or that "any minute force was transferred from one car to another"? Can the Volvo driver feel the "hit" while the Toyota driver does not? Clearly we need some common assumptions about the meaning of "hit," and if the drivers cannot establish a common understanding then the courts will assist them.

In science, we are in exactly the same relationship to facts. As I have said, facts are developed from theoretical assumptions. However, the "meaning of a fact" implies that the set of assumptions that produce the fact are so widely agreed on that the "fact" is taken for granted. In science, we have some such measures for extensions such as length and time. Kaplan (1964, p. 187) argues that there are two kinds of measures in science, fundamental measures and derived. A fundamental measure is one that is not decomposable into simpler measures. For example, Carnap (1966) has argued that length and time are fundamental measures in physics. However, a measure such as volume would be tied to more fundamental measures such as length ($v = h \times l \times w$). Many of the fundamental measures in the physical sciences originated from commonly agreed-on everyday assumptions. This gives the physical sciences a "commonsense" foundation even though many of these common assumptions are now being questioned (see Davies, 1995).

One important function for such "fundamental" measures in any scientific field is that they provide a set of measures that stand as "independent" from the theory. Derived measures, although not necessarily being constructed according to a particular set of theoretical assumptions, often are based on testing theory "A" or theory "B." The fundamental measures assure us there is a set of measures that have been developed as independent of any given theory but that every theory within a given field should be able to relate to those measures. So, for example, most economic theory can be related to "money" as either a measure of "value" or as a measure of "output." In physics, most theories relate to time and space. The fundamental measures ensure a coherence in the field and help define the field.

In the social sciences, we are less sure of commonly agreed-on assumptions. Certainly some social science fields such as economics contain some fundamental measures such as "money" that gives them this "commonsense" foundation in their measures of consumption and production. Indeed, this is recognized and appreciated in such ways as there being Nobel Prizes in physics and economics. Many of the other social sciences, however, including family studies, lack fundamental measures that have consensus in both the lay and scientific communities. Although this does not mean these endeavors need be any less scientific, the struggle for legitimacy in the eyes of the public and for consensus on measures within the community of scientists is continual. This consensus, or lack of consensus, in social science will be discussed later.

Theory-Model-Data Triangle

Models, theory, and data are all interconnected. This was emphasized in the previous discussion regarding the theoretical nature of "data" and "facts." Understanding the intimate connections between these three components, however, is critical to understanding theory because theory does not exist in isolation from these other components and the relations between them. Leik and Meeker (1975) developed a diagram of the relationships between theory, models, and data that I continue to find helpful (e.g., White, 1991). This diagram supplies a rich and intriguing picture of the many ways that models, theory, and data are related. I have now explicated the notions of models, data, and theory so that we can now focus on the relations between them.

Although where we start in Figure 4.3 is relatively arbitrary, it might be helpful to assume the ordering in the old induction-deduction model for the production and testing of scientific hypotheses simply because of familiarity. So let us begin with the relation moving from data to theory (I4). This is called "substantive interpretation of data" but may be simply examining data (qualitative or quantitative) for a "story." Because this interpretation comes after the fact (*ex post facto*), it will have no logical necessity nor be any more compelling than many other possible interpretations. Homans (1967) used an example from his boyhood swims in the bays of Massachusetts. He observed over several of his summer swims that sometimes the water on one side of the bay was much warmer than on the other side of the bay (data). His interpretation (I4) was that, like air, warmer water must rise to the surface. But that would not account for one side of the bay being warmer. He then reasoned that wind might displace the surface water to the windward side of the bay, causing colder water to surface on the lee side. As a result, it is possible to deduce that one side of the bay would have cold water and the windward side would have warm water. Now, if you formalized this "story" into propositions you would have a theory. Indeed, we could envision propositions about warm water rising and wind displacement of surface water. When stated as formal propositions, this would yield a theory that would deduce (D4) that the windward side of all bays would be the warmest. The problem is of course that tides, topography, and ocean

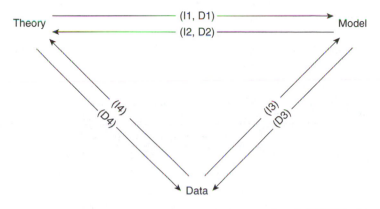

Inductive Modes:
  I1—Mathematical generalization of theory.
  I2—Substantive interpretation of mathematical patterns.
  I3—Mathematical generalization of empirical patterns.
  I4—Substantive interpretation of data.
Deductive Modes:
  D1—Formalization of theory.
  D2—Derivation of substantive hypothesis from mathematical patterns.
  D3—Mathematical prediction or extrapolation.
  D4—Substantive prediction.
The term "substantive" implies reference to a particular area of interest such as
social mobility, small-group interaction, and the like.

Figure 4.3   Theory-Model-Data Triangle

SOURCE: From *Mathematical Sociology* by R. K. Leik and B. F. Meeker. Copyright © 1975
by Prentice-Hall. Reprinted with permission.

currents would play havoc with this prediction. Indeed, this theory fails to
incorporate boundary conditions and control variables and fails to specify
the relevant model or models (misspecification).

Imagine that we pursue Homans's childhood theory and add a set of
boundary conditions such that the theory only operates when the effects of
topography, tides, air pressure, and currents are controlled. The next question would be to more accurately specify the relations in a formal model
(I1, D1). Most importantly, we would want to specify the wind velocity
needed to transport the water to the windward side of the bay. For example,
if this is a linear relationship, then as the wind got stronger the windward
side of the bay would get warmer. But clearly the windward side can only
reach the temperature of the warmest water, so there must be an asymptote
or point at which no further increase in wind can produce increases in
temperature. There also might be a lower threshold where the wind is not

sufficiently strong to move the water, in which case this might be a logistic function. Furthermore, what if the wind has been blowing hard but then dramatically abates? The windward side of the bay would have residually high temperatures even though the wind velocity is low. Somehow our model must accommodate occurrences such as "history." It is fairly obvious that formalizing our theory forces us to confront details that we might not have included in our interpretation. It also makes our language formulations take on increased precision. For example, instead of saying "is related to," we now specify the form of the relations (logistic function). This is achieved through the formalization of our theory.

Once the model is specified, we can predict (D3) the temperature (given certain initial conditions) for bays with any given wind velocity. For instance, if the model is a logistic function, then for very low velocities there might be no significant change in the temperature of the windward side of the bay. It is also a result of the model that the data must be in a certain form in order for the testing of the model to occur. For example, some models might be able to analyze continuous and discrete data while other models might not. Thus the model constrains the data. In our present example, we would like our data to be continuous temperatures and wind velocities over time.

Once the data are available, we can assess our model (D3) and use inductive parameter estimates (I3) for the model. There may also be a need to reassess the model's empirical utility against competing models. In this sense, the empirical data assist in refining and redefining the model (I3), which in turn may add to or modify the theoretical propositions in the theory (I2, D2).

The process of "doing" theory would traverse all of the relations identified in Figure 4.3. It is important to point out that, although I have discussed the relations in Figure 4.3 as fairly systematic and sequential, this systematization and sequential character may be more illusory than real. Several scholars, such as Knapp (1997), have noted that the distinction between induction and deduction is not as useful as once imagined, and some philosophers, such as Peirce (Buchler, 1955), have argued for a third process. Peirce, for example, sees a third process he labels "abduction," and further discusses "inductive abduction" as an important part of explanation in science. Regardless of Peirce's claims, his argument points out that there may well be complex mixtures of forms of logic when we reconstruct certain scientific discoveries. Almost any scientist reflecting on the process of logic used in formulating and testing theory would admit that often there is a mixture of logics and processes. This fact does not change the need to justify our claims logically and empirically, but it does give us a more realistic and human picture of the processes scientists experience and employ.

Formalism and Metaphor

Given the discussion of metaphors and models at the beginning of this chapter, it is only appropriate to address the degree to which theories and models are literal versus metaphorical. It is important to note, however, that a term may be metaphorical in one context but literal in another context. "Don't force me to tell on you" and "Force equals mass times velocity ($f = ma$)" are two sentences using the word "force." The context leads us to believe that force is metaphorical in the first context and literal in the second. Similarly, there are multiple contexts in science. One way of isolating these contexts is by identifying the way in which we want theory to function. For example, asking for a theory to "explain" an outcome and asking a theory to "accumulate" and "file" research findings are two distinctly different functions. In the next chapter I turn to an examination of theory as metaphor in relation to the major functions theory performs in social science.

The most essential point in this chapter is that much of what we do in science and theory is really metaphorical. There are, of course, many different types of metaphors. But the essential message is that the pretense of certitude and analytic formality of the "theory constructionists" can be seen as simply providing us with precise and detailed metaphors. It is, however, just as important to theory and understanding that these metaphors are creative and bring us new insights and connections for understanding families and their environments.

5

Functions and Types of Theory

In the introduction to this book I partially addressed the "so what?" question. One of the biggest problems I perceive in family theory is that researchers do not amply appreciate what theory does for them, for the field, and for knowledge in general. There is the mistaken perspective tied to empiricism that facts speak for themselves. But as we have seen, facts are theoretical constructs. Furthermore, I believe there is some misunderstanding of the functions of theory because the metaphorical foundations of explanation and interpretation have been deemphasized. White and Klein (2002) list seven distinct functions that theories serve in the social sciences. Although I will follow the list offered by White and Klein, I must stress that the emphasis here will be not just on the functions of theory but on the way theories use models and metaphors to achieve these ends.

Accumulation of findings is a major task for theory. This function is more important for today's social science, with its exponential increase in "data" and "findings," than it has ever been in previous eras. This function is achieved in two ways. First, theories organize data and findings by clustering research on particular concepts or categories. These concepts or categories are often used as "dependent variables" in studies. For example, research using various family, social, and economic variables to predict child well-being would be clustered under theories that deal with the concept of "child outcomes" or "child well-being." In general, only two family theories spring to mind in regard to such concepts, and they are rational choice theory (Coleman, 1990) and functional theory (Parsons & Bales, 1955). This leads us to the second way in which theories "accumulate" findings, and that is in regard to clustering "empirical relationships" found in the research.

Theories offer general propositions, but the specific empirical relationship findings can be viewed as particular incidences of those more general propositions. For example, Coleman's general proposition regarding the family as a form of social capital that influences child well-being can be tied to specific research findings on single-parent families and negative effects on child academic success. So findings are "stored" and "accumulated" within the more general concepts and more general propositions of theory.

It is very important to realize that this function and the way it takes place is using theory as a metaphor. Lakoff and Johnson (1980) define metaphor similarly to Black (1962). They state that "the essence of metaphor is understanding and experiencing one kind of thing in terms of another" (1980, p. 5). The example, using Coleman's theory, basically *maps* specific and particular findings onto a generalization. To do so, the theoretical concepts must be at least as inclusive, if not more inclusive, than the concepts in the specific finding. When the concepts and therefore the theoretical propositions are more inclusive, they necessarily contain many other analogs of the specific finding. These other "examples" serve as analogies to the specific finding. So the accumulation function for theory is in large part using theoretical concepts and propositions as metaphors for the specific relationships and findings.

Precision is achieved when vague hunches or hypotheses are made clearer and well defined by using precise theoretical language. Note that this previous sentence should sound like an utter contradiction to what I have said before, namely that theoretical concepts and relationships are more general. However, theories are supposed to say how and why relationships occur. That entails specifying the mechanisms that are causally operating to produce consequences. As a result, vague statements such as "single-parent families (as opposed to intact families) are related to children's lower academic performance" may appear to be theoretical but fail to satisfy the basics of identifying what it is about family structure that produces this correlation. The theory should specify *why* this is so and *how* it occurs. Returning to our example from Coleman's theory, Coleman specifies that closure of a social network allows for the reinforcement of socialization by multiple agents. Single-parent structures lack closure. Thus as a group structure, single-parent families have lower social capital than two-parent families. Although we could go on and add much more detail in this regard (see Coleman, 1990, pp. 300–321, and particularly pp. 595–597), it is clear that theory provides more precision, especially for a vague statement such as "is significantly related to," which often appears in empirical literature. Indeed, no matter how many control variables or how robust the parameter estimation, the empirical finding often fails to tell us why and how something happens. That is the job of theory.

Precision is gained by mapping relatively vague empirical relationships (x is positively related to y) and findings onto much more detailed theory. In this sense, theory is the literal part of the metaphor while the empirical relationship is the figurative aspect of the metaphor. The precision suggested for future research is to define and examine the nexus of factors and mechanisms suggested in the more detailed argument of the theory. So although theory may be more general, it is not contradictory to say that it allows more precision because it identifies the mechanisms through which causal efficacy is carried.

Guidance is a function that is closely tied to the preceding discussion about precision. As we use theory to specify the how and why of findings, the same specification suggests new and potentially fruitful avenues of research. Once again, returning to Coleman's notion of closure of networks, we could investigate hypotheses dealing with extended family forms compared to two-parent forms. Both would have closure, but the availability and density of network relationships would be different. Indeed, this might also suggest the development of a metric (measure) combining closure and density of social networks for the determination of child outcomes.

When a theory guides the empirical researcher to new hypotheses, this is clearly metaphorical. The theory "points to" new areas of research. The theoretical concepts and abstractions are the figurative components leading to the concrete and literal realization in hypotheses and measures.

Connectedness describes how theories relate to other sets of ideas, and how they connect us to other ways of seeing. Previously, we have seen that theories give us new ways of seeing data and findings. However, "connectedness" refers to connections between theories and clusters of ideas. For example, the notion that family transitions are dependent on the history the family has traversed led Magrabi and Marshall (1965) and later White (1991) to see this more vividly as a mathematical model known as a Markov process. Prigogine and Stengers (1984) envisioned their similar work in chemistry as having ramifications for any "system" conception. In general, connectedness may be within a discipline or school of thought and between various disciplines and schools of thought. Connectedness may suggest that parts of theories or concepts are possibly connected to knowledge acquisition in a seemingly unrelated field. A good example would be those scholars such as Bronfenbrenner (1979, 1989) that first envisioned ecological theory for biology as being relevant to child development (see White & Klein, 2002).

The notion that we can take one set of ideas and see them as relevant to another set of ideas certainly fits the definition of metaphor by Lakoff and Johnson (1980) cited earlier. The problem of which is the literal component and which is the figurative component is resolved by which theory or set of ideas is most familiar—the most familiar supplying the domain for the mapping and the more foreign supplying the range. Once again the function is metaphorical.

Interpretation is one of the three main functions of theory—explanation, prediction, and interpretation. All three of these are captured as relations in the theory-model-data triangle (Chapter 4, Figure 4.3). Interpretation in Figure 4.3 is represented by two relations (I2 and I4). In the first of these (I2), the model is interpreted by the theory. Another way of saying this is that the calculus or abstract mathematical entities in the model are given language meanings in the propositions and formulations of the theory. For example, if we used a linear model ($Y = a + bX$), we might interpret this model to mean "the greater the social capital in the child's family (X), the greater the child's academic achievement (Y)." Here, an interpretation clearly means the mapping of the concepts onto the symbols of the model. To interpret the model is to perform this mapping.

The second relation (I4) in Figure 4.3 interprets the data. The data are mapped onto the concepts of the theory, and the relations in the data are mapped onto relations between concepts in the propositions. A much more practical way to say this is that the theory provides us with an after-the-fact (*ex post facto*) story about what happened. So, for example, if our data were a case where a child named Billy is doing poorly in school and Billy's mom is a never-married single woman, we might invoke Coleman's theory about social capital to interpret this situation. Many of you might be tempted to say that this is an attempt to explain Billy's performance, but that would be less than accurate. Interpretation differs from explanation in that it is always *ex post facto*. In this sense, the mapping of data onto theory is always one "story" among many other possible "stories" that would also interpret the same data. For example, Billy's performance might be tied to the type of school Billy is attending. He may be attending that school because his mother has scant economic resources, and the housing she can afford lands Billy in schools that fail to assist his academic development. In this story, social capital is "spuriously" related to academic outcomes because the causal path is really through resources and housing. This is to say that it is the type of school and not the type of family that is causally related to outcomes. We could in no way determine which of these stories might be better, because the stories are generated after the fact (*ex post facto*). Philosophers of science, such as Popper (1959), have argued convincingly that there is no necessity to one story over another in *ex post facto* arguments. It is important to note that apparently many social sciences journal editors believe such *ex post facto* "stories" are important "speculations" in the discussion section of academic articles. Indeed, such *ex post facto* "stories" are similar to natural history arguments about evolution and descent. The big difference is that a theory of natural history would also predict other artifacts or archaeological information that would add deductive certifiability to the theory.

Prediction is sometimes thought to be the *sine qua non* of science. Theoretical propositions predict substantive outcomes (D4) in Figure 4.3. The relationship (D4) moves from propositions to data. The concepts and relations in the theoretical proposition are mapped onto the data. The assumption behind this metaphorical mapping is that the data bear some isomorphy to, or is at least a proxy for, the concept. Often the ability of data to serve as a proxy for the concept is tied to the "operationalization" of the concept as a measure. However, the operationalization is simultaneously tied to the metric or level of measurement used for variables and the way the relation is operationalized. The measurement aspects of the data are actually more tied to the mathematical model used to examine the data (D3), because the model will make assumptions that constrain the way data are measured. For example, a first-order linear equation constrains the data by requiring the data to be at the additive interval or ratio level of measurement. Prediction then entails both the adequacy of the proxy variable as operationalizing the mathematical constraints of the model and the adequacy of the variables to really stand as an adequate proxy or measure of the concepts and relations in the proposition (validity and reliability). As a result, prediction involves both the model and the theory simultaneously. Naturally, it is possible to have just the theory-data (D4) or just the model-data (D3) mapping relations, but without both either validity or analysis would be lost. For most predictions, we want to have valid measures that compose hypotheses that can be falsified. Without analysis (D3) we would have no disproof of theory and without validity (D4) we would not be sure of what we are falsifying. So most of science is concerned with both of these relations composing prediction.

Prediction is the ability of a theoretical proposition to make a claim about the world that is independent of that claim, at least in time. It is the independence of the data from the claim that makes these *a priori* arguments so compelling. So, for example, I could say an apple fell to the ground because of gravity and this *ex post facto* argument would have to compete with any number of other possible stories. However, if I hold an apple and say that when I let go of it the apple will fall to earth, it seems more compelling because I didn't have the outcome before I had the story—the prediction was *a priori* to the experience. In the case of prediction, I have a story—the theory—telling me what the outcome will be. Of course there are always boundary conditions, such as being in a gravitational field of a significantly larger mass, but that too would be part of the theory (boundary conditions). Another reason that prediction seems compelling is that it allows for the systematic exclusion of the other competing theories. Naturally, it is important to exclude the most probable alternative theories first.

Despite the compelling nature of prediction to convince us of a theory's credibility, it can never prove a theory because there will always be other stories or theories that have yet to be disproved. So although prediction is more compelling an argument than *ex post facto* arguments, it is nonetheless not an absolutely necessary argument and always leaves doubt and uncertainty.

Explanation is the last function of theory we list. In part it is listed last because to understand explanation, prediction and interpretation must also be understood. Many scholars, such as Homans (1967) or Hempel (1966), view explanation as a "covering law" or "hypothetico-deductive" system. This perspective argues that explanation is achieved when a particular phenomenon is shown to deductively follow from a set of more general and abstract propositions. Certainly this sounds impressive if it could be achieved. The problem is that there are a host of contingencies that make this process more arbitrary, relativistic, and less necessary than we would first believe. As I discussed earlier, the operationalization of a concept may not be valid. Furthermore, a model may not be correctly specified and some relevant variables could be omitted. Concepts may be poorly defined, leading to inaccurate specification of the model and in turn inaccurate analysis. Indeed, we could go on and on with potential sources of error that keep explanation from being much other than a plausible story. Even if phenomena could be deductively explained, at some critical juncture we would have to incorporate some "synthetic" or "empirical" propositions to make the theory an empirical theory rather than just a logical theory. Indeed, although some philosophers of science, such as Hempel (1952), have argued that prediction is explanation, others have argued a less necessary connection (see Kaplan, 1964, p. 346). When we think about it, it is quite possible that mathematical models might predict, in the sense of a "weather forecast," and yet have almost no explanatory value in that they cannot provide a story or interpretation as to why the weather is changing. Furthermore, there is also the possibility that some theories might be dependent on the emergence of new technologies (such as the microscope or telescope) before prediction is possible. But does that mean that prior to the development of measurement, the theory was any less explanatory? The less restrictive and more generous perspective on explanation seems to take these exceptions into account.

So what is explanation? Returning to Figure 4.3 we might say that an explanation occurs when all the relations in the triangle have been developed.

Another way of saying this is that we expect an explanation to provide both interpretation and prediction while fully recognizing there is no logical necessity validating any explanation as the correct explanation. Indeed, all explanations are fallible and tentative. All explanations should provide us with a story as to why and how things happen, and this story should be testable on independent occurrences, not the observations from which we generated the theory. And finally, explanations should be logical, not because we achieve necessity but because we want to understand. Indeed, the law of contradiction has no necessary foundation other than that I am not sure we could understand the world in any other way.

Function, Relativism, and Types of Explanations

The conclusion just given—that scientific explanation is always tentative and fallible—may seem to be heralding the dominance of some variety of post-modern relativism, but this is far from the case. It does see science as a "human endeavor" fraught with the normal frailties that go with that moniker. It does not see all knowledge, or specifically scientific knowledge, as being equally valid.

If knowledge is not absolutely "true" on the one hand, nor absolutely relative on the other hand, how is it to be judged? As is often the case, the most plausible positions lie in between the extremes of relativism and abso-lutism. For example, a pragmatic perspective would argue that it depends on the purposes. If the purpose is "explanation," then we would clearly expect a knowledge claim that would both predict and interpret. If the purpose of theory was to sort and accumulate, however, then theories would be judged on the basis of the adequacy of categorical schemes, clarity of definitions, richness of relations, and other characteristics necessary for sorting and storing findings. We judge the knowledge claims of theories relative to the functions we wish the theories to perform.

For a theory to explain, predict, and interpret as in Figure 4.3, it must have certain characteristics. Some of these characteristics I discussed earlier in the sections on theory and as we followed the paths in Figure 4.3. However, the basic elements of lawlike statements were only partially and incompletely discussed. As previously indicated, the ability for a theory to deductively generate specific outcomes from general propositions may be somewhat problematic. However, the problems I previously discussed are more tied to the assumption of necessary deductions than to the laws that make such operations possible.

Laws

Laws are statements of empirical uniformities. It is not unusual to say there are "laws" of planetary motion or to talk about the "laws" of gravity. Even in the social sciences there are lawlike statements, such as Michels's 1949 "iron law of oligarchy" (see Coleman, 1990, pp. 359–361 for a discussion), and in the area of the family we could point to lawlike statements such as "if families are 'out of sequence' with the normative ordering of family events, then the probability for later life disruptions is increased" (White & Klein, 2002, p. 101). Similar to the laws in the natural sciences, the laws in the social sciences refer to empirical uniformities such as the tendency for any organization to become an oligarchy (Michels) and the tendency for early life course deviance to affect later deviance in life course events. But we can already see from these examples that several different forms of generalizations may be covered by the term "laws."

Kaplan (1964, pp. 109–113) identifies the content of laws as being of several forms: statistical laws, taxonomic laws, and temporal laws (pattern laws, genetic laws, and interval laws). All of these types of laws follow a similar logical form in which some observation or finding presents a relationship (r) between empirical measures "x" and "y" (x r y). This relationship is then generalized to concepts A and B, so that "x r y" inductively implies "A r B." This argument is familiar to readers of White and Klein as Figure 1.1 (2002, p. 15). Now the conceptual generalization must be brought into relationship with at least some other propositions in order to form a logical explanation (see White & Klein, 2002, p. 13).

Statistical laws are those statements about the relations between categories or variables within defined populations. Kaplan (1964) views "causal laws" as a subset of statistical laws where there are no exceptions to the association, and one element "A" must always precede the consequent "B" in temporal order. Kaplan goes on to add,

> Causal laws, it must be said, are not at all so important in science as philosophers of science have often assumed. The ordered simultaneity which they affirm, if it can be made precise at all, is in any case a very special type of constancy. Atemporal and therefore noncausal laws are easily at least as important as the causal ones, for the purposes of science itself. (pp. 112–113)

This statement may further explain the failure of the theory constructionists in the 1960s and 1970s because much of their focus was on causal relationships.

Taxonomic laws are those that sort the empirical elements into categories where the categories have general statements attached to them. For example, one could put poinsettia flower in the category of "poisonous plants," which would say that eating plants in this category is hazardous to humans. Taxonomic laws, as I stated in Chapter 2, are perhaps some of the first types of laws to emerge because humans need to know what things in their world are dangerous and harmful.

The last three types of laws identified by Kaplan (1964) are all forms of temporal laws. Although the long-range goal of science is to find laws that cover phenomena regardless of time, Kaplan notes that temporal laws may indeed lead to more general laws. Pattern laws are one type of the temporal laws that take a "zero" starting point. The evolution of a species or the development of an individual both take the birth date as the starting date for the life course. As we shall see later, developmental-life course theories of the family might use this type of temporal law. A second form of temporal law is genetic laws. These are sequential laws that are especially well known in developmental theories where a series of stages are determined, such as Freud's oral, anal, and genital stages. Again, family development and life course theory is especially interested in general laws of this form. And finally, the last form of temporal laws cited by Kaplan is interval laws. An interval law is one that identifies "a relation between events separated by a distinct time interval" (p. 109). These would be laws about "stages" and about the effect of history. Kaplan cites the example of "metal fatigue" as a stage-type law. Once again, developmental theories about process, maturation, and stages of development fit into this form of law.

It is important to recognize the various forms of laws. Often the social sciences are all too convinced that we have little theory and no laws. However, Kaplan's examination of the types of laws leads us to conclude that such pessimism may be unwarranted. If indeed family social science has some lawlike statements, then we might also be optimistic about attaining "explanation" in the study of the family.

Types of Theory

Regardless of the form of the law, in order to have an explanation, the law must be logically and conceptually integrated with other propositions for a theory. For example, when we say that the "laws of gravity" explain why a book falls to the ground, we tacitly assume a host of propositions regarding measurement, boundary conditions, and so on. Indeed, "gravity" really amounts to a complex set of propositions in order to explain any given event. In family theory, Nye (1979) proposed a theory of sexual exchange.

If we were to observe a woman being picked up by a man for sexual purposes, Nye would argue that sexual activity is more valuable to the male than to the female and will, on average, have better outcomes for the male than the female. As a result, males must offer something greater in value to the female than sex alone because the activity is less rewarding and more costly for females than males. As a result, we would explain that the woman is probably getting paid. Not only does this theory have several propositions, but there are tacit background assumptions as well, such as in the observation that the woman is "picked up for sexual purposes" rather than getting a ride home.

Every theory has multiple propositions and assumptions. Kaplan (1964) divides theories into several types based on the way in which the propositions are related. The first type of theory is called "concatenated" and refers to theories in which most of the propositions are focused on one outcome. These propositions might come from different sources and are related by the fact that they are all concerned with explaining a particular outcome. For example, a theory about "divorce" or a theory about "fertility" might be of this form. A perfect example of family theories that are concatenated theories is in Volume I of *Contemporary Theories About the Family* (Burr, Hill, et al., 1979). For example, the Lewis and Spanier chapter on marital quality examined the empirical propositions related to predicting low or high levels of marital quality. To gain a systematic and coherent theory, Lewis and Spanier (1979) tied these propositions together using more general propositions from social exchange theory (e.g., Levinger, 1977). So the theory of marital quality these authors developed was a concatenation of theoretical and empirical propositions aimed at explaining marital quality. Most of the other theories developed in Volume I of *Contemporary Theories About the Family* were similarly of this form because the orientation of Volume I was to produce "inductive" theory.

Kaplan (1964) calls the second type of theory "hierarchical" theory. This form of theory deductively organizes propositions at various levels of generality, with the most general premises leading deductively to more specific conclusions. During the heyday of theory constructionism, these theories were known as "axiomatic theories" (Zetterburg, 1963). The second volume of *Contemporary Theories About the Family* (Burr, Hill, et al., 1979) provides several examples of attempts at forms of axiomatic theory. The previous example from Nye (1979) is one such example. However, all of these examples are not pure examples of axiomatic systems because the definition and empirical content always add a synthetic element.

Although Kaplan (1964) provides many other types of theories, the two mentioned earlier, hierarchical and concatenated, parallel similar distinctions used by others. For example, each volume of *Contemporary Theories About the Family* was focused on different types of theories, inductive and deductive, which correspond to Kaplan's concatenated and hierarchical. In traditional philosophy of science, theories might be clustered into synthetic versus analytic.

Regardless of the many authors focusing on the different types of theory, it is useful to pause and ask what difference such classifications make for the scientist rather than the philosopher. Indeed, Kaplan (1964) pointed out that how we arrive at a theory (context of discovery) should not be confused with the validation of the theory (context of justification). In that sense, whether we arrive at the theory inductively or deductively, analytically or synthetically, would make little difference to the validity of the theory. In turn, we might ask if the form of the theory makes a difference because it is individual propositions that are empirically tested, and the logical coherence of the theory would be examined regardless of the deductive or inductive origins. It would also make sense to make such distinctions if we had established rules or norms of inquiry used to produce "good" theories, but as I argued in Chapter 2, this is neither the case nor is it desirable. One lesson from the theory constructionists of the 1960s and 1970s is that when creativity and insight is sacrificed to rigid rules of conduct, all theoretical generation suffers.

Finally, it could be argued that the different types of theory actually are expressions of different epistemological assumptions and that these assumptions need be made explicit. For example, it could be argued that inductive theory is generated from scientists who are "realists" and believe that there is an independent knowable reality apart from our knowledge or perception. This position has been thoroughly criticized by family scholars such as Knapp (1997). In contrast, there is the epistemological position of "constructionism" or "instrumentalism" that assumes that our knowledge is created from our experience and mind but that there is no way of determining an independent reality. Many important and distinct positions within this broad constructionist perspective contradict one another on specifics, such as the difference between Dewey's (1929) "instrumentalism" and the radical position taken by Derrida's (1976) "deconstructionism." Most of these positions, however, argue that "truth" is to be found not in "reality" but in the current criteria of instrumental validity maintained within the community of scientists. Of course the criteria for validity change over time, as we have witnessed in our brief review of the history of science. However, "reality" in science is always defined by the current construction of what constitutes a valid proposition and evidence. As I argued previously, "facts" are not found but constructed and validated by the community of scientists.

Now we could embark on a long amble through this thicket of epistemology, but before doing so it is wise to ask what difference this might make in how we create and express our theories. Over the history of science, many different forms of construction have occurred, from Baconian induction to Newtonian deduction. However, to place the emphasis on form would be a grievous error and lead us once again to the rule approach to theorizing. This would do little but lead us away from the factors that make science and theory what it is: inquisitiveness and creativity. Even though Kaplan's "context of discovery" and "context of justification" is, I think, an important distinction for helping scientists keep track of the kind of work they are doing (exploring versus judging), it might be seen by some as a programmatic dictum. Kaplan (1964) reacts against such an interpretation when he states,

> I am not saying merely that the creative imagination plays a part in the *process* of theory formation, the context of discovery, but that it is also involved in the product, and so enters into the context of justification. (p. 308)

For example, some of the areas within the context of justification that involve creativity might be the areas of measurement, research design, and deduction. The important point here is that the types and forms of theory and epistemology should be taken as the reconstructions of philosophers and historians who are studying science and not some set of rules for the proper conduct of science.

Method and Explanation

The preceding discussion might seem to dismiss the work of philosophers and historians of science as being an *ex post facto* reconstruction of a creative scientific work for the purposes of producing a rule book for scientific enquiry. Perhaps this is in part true, but some of this "reconstructive" enterprise has been very useful in pointing out methodological problems that scientists, and especially social scientists, have been slow to visualize. Perhaps one of the most important of these problems for social scientists is known as the "intensional-extensional" problem. This problem shows up in family studies in our attempts to attribute motive and cause that often end up crossing and confusing various levels of analysis. To clarify this problem, we must first examine the larger philosophical problem of intensional and extensional forms of explanation and then turn to the problem of defining levels of analysis.

Intensional and Extensional

You may recall from our discussion of science in Chapter 2 that one of the hallmarks of science was that it does not look to gods or other worldly forces to explain what is observed. Indeed, citing causes for behavior such as "the devil made him do it" or "it is God's will" is systematically rejected as explanation in the sciences. Certainly early religions often envisioned all of the physical world as having some soul or *anima* that explained its behavior. Part of this rejection was based on the notion that science would find explanations based on the observations of physical matter alone. A basic metaphysical assumption of science has been that explanation of the behavior of plants or atoms, tables or stars, could be accomplished without recourse to the mentalistic perspective of religion and superstition (Lillegard, 2003).[1]

This perspective in science is expressed as its focus on extensional qualities of objects. An extensional quality is its dimensionality in physical space, such as provided by length, width, and time in the case of movement. Explanation in the physical sciences focuses on one set of extensional objects interacting with (or causing) some other set of extensional objects to either change their extensional properties or position in space.

It would seem silly for a scientist to discuss the "motivation" of an atom or to attempt to measure the current state of hydrogen atoms' "attitudes" about another group of atoms such as oxygen; do they really intend to bond? However, this is exactly what the social sciences attempt to do with humans. Indeed, a simple extensional perspective on humans would seem naïve. For example, it would seem ridiculous to describe the physical activity of driving an automobile without recourse to the rules of the road and the symbol systems that guide it, such as red lights and stop signs. In the social sciences, the extensional is often conceived as being controlled and guided by human intentionality, motivation, and interpretation.

These contrasting perspectives are responsible for some of the pessimism about the "scientific" status of the social sciences. Indeed, the social sciences use mentalistic constructs that were previously rejected by the physical sciences in their break from superstition and religion. However, social scientists such as Weber (1949) recognized that to treat humans as not mentalistic entities would provide the social sciences with no understanding whatsoever. This, however, is one of the major points Winch (1958) makes about the difference between what science does and the social sciences, and it is sometimes used as the very reason that the combination of "social" with "science" may be seen by some as an oxymoron.

Whereas some scholars might welcome the status of two different types of science, physical and social, others have not. Lillegard (2003) points out that social constructionists' antirealist positions allow for a convenient exit from the two-sciences perspective.

> If even the physical sciences are social constructions, then there should be no need to show that the social sciences measure up, in terms of predictive capacity etc. to the physical sciences. If the latter represent just one way of "constructing knowledge" with no special privileges or status attached to it, then social scientists should feel that their failure to find causal laws and sharp predictions somehow counts against the claim that their disciplines are "science." (Lillegard, 2003)

Lillegard is quick to point out that the "costs" of such a convenient perspective as just given is that we abandon the idea that competing claims about the world (such as, is Earth round or flat) become just a matter of "perspective" rather than disputes that can be settled by observations. As I have previously argued, such relativism is too high a price to pay for this convenience.

Besides rejecting relativism, most social scientists still hold on to the ideal of producing laws to explain human behavior. Although, as we have discussed previously in this chapter, there are several types of laws, the basic notion that a social science can produce lawlike statements is still preferred to idiographic statements, as is evidenced by the generalizations produced in most of the current journal articles (see, for example, *Journal of Marriage and Family*). Likewise, other so-called methodological solutions, such as Weber's advocacy of *verstehen* as a special way of understanding the perspective of the actor, have failed to address how a social science would ever produce nomothetic statements rather than be idiographic histories. However, a number of solutions have evolved in the social sciences so that individual mentalistic structures need not be contrary to producing laws. Most of these solutions rely to some extent on the notion of levels of analysis. So before turning to these solutions, an examination of levels of analysis is in order.

Levels of Analysis

Bulcroft and White (1997) defined level of analysis as referring "to the conceptual level at which theoretical explanations are formulated in a theory" (p. 137). It is impossible to understand the importance of this term and its consequences for theory and research without some appreciation of its history. Most of us realize that social theories may focus on individuals. Indeed, exchange theories and utilitarian theories have focused on the individual as the principal "actor" and offer propositions about the motives of actors to increase rewards and minimize costs. Indeed, many theories in the social sciences focus on the individual and attributes such as personality and motivation. When theories focus explanation and research on the individual as the causal agent, we say they are practicing "methodological individualism."

During the 1800s, several social theories developed using levels of analysis other than the individual. For example, both Durkheim (1949, 1951) and Tönnies (1887/1957) developed theories about larger "social facts" that they argued could not be reduced to the individual level. Theories such as these focused on "emergent" or "holistic" characteristics that derived from social interactions. Concepts such as social cohesion and group solidarity clearly could not be reduced to or derived from individual actors. Bulcroft and White (1997) give the following example:

> An example of research conducted from a holistic perspective is that of Trovato (1986) who demonstrated the effects of low community solidarity on the breakdown of the family institution by correlating provincial migration rates and provincial divorce rates in Canada. (p. 138)

Some theories about family may use multiple levels of analysis such as systems theories and ecological theories. Furthermore, there are theories that focus on population processes such as "genetic drift" or "natural selection," especially in biosociological theories of the family (see White & Klein, 2002), that view these processes as explaining the behaviors of individuals even though the individuals do not comprehend the processes that drive them. Finally, we see a great deal of theoretical and causal confusion about levels of analysis. For example, we can see theories about divorce (a dyadic or group phenomenon) that have attempted to explain this dyadic phenomenon by examining each individual's motive or reward/costs ratio while neglecting interactional processes that exist at the couple level of analysis.

Thinking about levels of analysis in the study of the family quickly results in the realization that there are more levels than just captured in the tradition distinction of microtheories and macrotheories. Indeed, Hill and Rodgers (1964) were among the first to point out that multiple levels of analysis were not only possible but important for understanding phenomena. Bronfenbrenner (1989) identified multiple levels in his ecological approach, as did White (1991) for family development theory. From the methodological side, several research scholars have also addressed the issue of measurement in relation to levels of analysis (e.g., Bulcroft & White, 1997; Thompson & Walker, 1982).

Confusions of levels of analysis lead to two type of mistakes. One is called the "individualistic fallacy," and the other is called the "ecological fallacy."

The individualistic fallacy occurs when we generalize from individual observations to a group or institutional level. One simple example of the individualistic fallacy has already been mentioned. Whenever we take a measure of marital satisfaction on individual spouses and then generalize this to the marriage (couple phenomena), we aggregate individual scores and the "couple" is not measured but only the individuals in it. To further clarify this, the couple may interact in ways that are not dependent on individual scores and may be more dependent on habit and other historical features of the interaction pattern. Even if it were possible to aggregate the husband and wife individual scores, we would need to know if these scores should be equally weighted or if the wife's satisfaction is more salient to the couple's interaction than is the husband's individual score. Besides the study of divorce, the very definition of the "family" supposes that we take the social group of the family as a level of analysis rather than individuals.

The "ecological fallacy" occurs when observations at the social group level are generalized to the individuals. For example, when we take measures on school districts such as aggregated academic performance scores, we cannot then generalize about students since only districts were observed. Likewise, research and theory dealing with the characteristics of the "marriage market" should not generalize these macrocharacteristics of the "market" to individuals in the market. At a theoretical level, ecological fallacy would occur when a process such as family cohesion is generalized as an attribute of an individual family member. Although such mistakes are most often tied to measurement confusion about the reporting unit and the sampling unit and how these are tied to the level of analysis (see Bulcroft & White, 1997, for a more detailed discussion), we are principally concerned with the theoretical ramifications.

The distinction between levels of analysis is critically important in understanding the substantive theory in the chapters to follow. Furthermore, much of the theory that is currently being developed in the area of the family deals with multiple levels of analysis. In part this is because statistical techniques such as hierarchical linear modeling (HLM) have gained quick and wide acceptance in the social sciences and especially in the area of family research (see Teachman & Crowder, 2002). I believe another reason is that the two substantive theories I examined in Chapters 4 and 5 demonstrated that multiple levels of analysis are useful for organizing and explaining family phenomena.

For the moment, the principal theoretical ramification for levels of analysis is to assist us in understanding the solutions that the social sciences have attempted as resolutions to the intensional-extensional debate. That debate focused on the fact that the physical sciences have rejected any mentalistic (intensional) character of phenomena they study. Indeed, one of the hallmarks of physical science is to disallow appeals to the internal intent of physical objects found previously in religion and superstition (see Chapter 2). However, most social science has, to various degrees, had to deal with the admission that their subjects (humans) are at least to some degree intentional and that understanding that intentionality is necessary for explanation. Yet it remains unclear whether such intentionality can be successfully integrated with the nomothetic goals of science.

Solutions Within the Nomothetic Goals of Science

One of the oldest questions in social science is whether a science of the social is at all possible. Although aspects of this argument hinge on arguments such as the reflexive nature of humans and their knowledge, understanding versus explanation, and so on, much of the central focus is on the seeming impossibility of using methods and approaches appropriate for extensional objects in order to investigate intensional objects such as humans. I find it interesting that in many of these discussions the relevant disciplinary examples are drawn from physics (extensional) and psychology (intensional). The reason this is of interest is that it somewhat skirts the issues that many of the natural or life sciences would have in regard to both extensional and intensional approaches. Indeed, sciences that deal with organisms cannot easily reject either of these two approaches. So the arguments I address here pertain to a larger number of disciplines than would just be covered under the aegis of social science. Below I outline several different approaches and how they attempt to resolve the conflict of extensional and intensional methods. Although I intend to survey these approaches rather than critically assess them, we will need in the next chapter to use this discussion in the analysis of the theories presented.

A Priori Mentalistic Structures

Lillegard (2003) points to theories of *a priori* mentalistic structures as one way in which social sciences have attempted to address the creation of intensional laws that are similar in form to extensional laws. The term *a priori* refers to the fact that these mental structures would precede experience and hence would not be learned from experience. However, if these structures are not learned, how are they acquired? Most of the theories falling in this category of *a priori* mentalistic structures believe these structures are species specific. Hence the mentalistic structures in such theories tend to be ontogenetic in that they are contained in the organism.

There are several examples of this form of social theory. Certainly Chomsky's (1965) theory of syntax, and most particularly his idea of a species-specific "deep structure" of language, would be an example of such theories. Levi-Strauss's structuralism, especially in *The Savage Mind*, points to a similar type of mental structuralism, although it is somewhat vague as to whether this is ontogenetic or "cultural." Certainly most ontogenetic theories in developmental psychology, such as Kohlberg and Piaget, would be of this form.

All theories in this category tend to produce laws that are tied to the species. These laws would be similar to saying that "all humans have ability X." Although there may be some general boundary conditions and constraints such as "with proper protein in their diet," these laws are very general. The theories are usually deductive theories formulated from inductively generalized observations, often about temporal patterns. Note that theories of universal psychological characteristics, as well as theories that Kaplan labeled temporal theories, are of this form.

Institutionalism

Institutional theories produce laws based on the rules that govern societies. Both Winch (1958) and Black (1962) discuss the philosophical foundation behind this approach. An example helps make the logic of this approach clear. Imagine that you could watch as many chess games as you could stand to watch but that you were not allowed to inquire about or receive the rules of the game. Most astute observers, given sufficient observations, would be able to piece together all but the most obscure rules. Indeed, the astute observer might even become proficient at playing the game. So this part of the analogy assumes that social systems such as language, games, and other forms of conduct must necessarily be rule governed and these rules shared by a large number of players in order for the game to operate. To extend the metaphor, imagine an anthropologist observing that a statue in the center of a village square is never touched by the villagers. When the anthropologist inquires about this, the villagers refuse to talk about the statue. The anthropologist infers a taboo about touching and naming the statue. The laws that result from this approach are the inductively generalized observations of patterned behavior that is so uniform as to inductively infer "rule-governed behavior." It should be noted that many familiar concepts in the social sciences would fit with this approach, such as social norm (rule) and expectation (anticipation of rule behavior) and social role (behavior tied to a position). The theories that result from such approaches can be powerful deductive theories under the assumption that the social system is organized to not be contradictory. Thus we can deduce norms from conjunctions of other sets of norms.

There are many examples of theories about the family that use such an approach. Certainly many social scientists would immediately think of symbolic interaction theory as being the most obvious example. Mead, as you will recall from White and Klein (2002), developed two stages of socialization with the more mature stage occurring when children learn to take diverse roles and to follow rules in a game such as baseball or hockey. White (1991) developed an elaboration of family development theory using this approach to norms and later developed this position more extensively (White, 1998).

The laws from this approach, however, must be probabilistic laws based on the salience and power of the norms. The strength and adherence to norms is quite variable. For example, most people follow the rule about not killing others, and we could state it as a law with high probability if we were to add boundary conditions for excluding war. However, we would have a far less viable law in regard to automobile drivers not entering an intersection on a yellow light. One of the principal liabilities of this type of theory is that in highly voluntaristic societies such as North America, many social norms would not aid greatly in explanation. So although the logic is appealing, the actual laws that would result would seem not to be like extensional laws in the physical sciences. We will have the opportunity to further discuss this type of law in the next chapter.

Reductionism

Reductionism attempts to reduce social action and intentionality to lower-level physical laws. Several recent examples attempt to explain behavior as a function of physical states determined by hormones or neural connections. For example, Booth, Carver, and Granger (2000) state,

> Behavioral endocrinology is in the forefront of the integration of biological measures into studies of children and families because recent research has shown that hormones may play an integral role in furthering our understanding of individual differences in developmental trajectories, family relationships, and factors that mediate these processes. (p. 1019)

Behind this perspective is an emphasis on the individual organism as the level of analysis and confidence that we can somehow move levels of analysis (individual to family relationships) based on individual variations in hormones. Certainly reductionist perspectives are not new, but they are relatively new as explanations of higher levels of analysis such as relationships and family.

Laws from this perspective would be complex because each human not only produces different quantities of hormones at different times, but in addition, the individual's receptors vary in their reactions so that the same concentrations have different effects on different individuals. The number of boundary conditions and constraints required to produce laws that would explain would be formidable.

Invisible Hand Holism

Perhaps the most popular way of resolving the tension between extensional and intensional approaches is what Lillegard (2003) terms "invisible hand holism." Several theories use such approaches, and two of the best known are economic or rational choice theories and Darwinian or selection theories. In both of these approaches, individuals have conscious motives such as profit (rational choice) or survival (selection). What is unique about these theories is that when the effects of the individual behavior are aggregated to a population level of analysis, the effect is quite different. Classical rational choice or economic theory argues that in a free and open choice system people will act as rational actors, but the aggregation of actions produces the laws of supply and demand that function as an "invisible hand" to produce the public good (Lillegard, 2003). Likewise, in natural selection theories, individuals adapt to their environments in order to live. However, some of those who are poorly suited to their environment will be selected out (die) and those who survive have a stronger gene pool that is more adapted to the environment. Although both of these theories have been recently been refined (see, for example, Coleman, 1990, for rational choice and Gould, 2002, for selection theory), the general form of the explanatory laws has changed little.

In both examples, laws are formulated regarding individual motivation or intention but within a context of constraints. The individuals acting within constraints, such as supply and demand and selection, then produce aggregate behaviors that can be formulated as population- or aggregate-level laws. Clearly, these types of theory are theories of aggregation rather than reductionist theories. I will need to more fully discuss this type of explanation in the next chapter.

Conclusion

This chapter has traversed some difficult intellectual terrain. It began by discussing the functions that theory serves, interpreted through the previous discussions of models and metaphors. Then these ideas were extended to the nature of theory and types of laws. Finally, intensional and extensional laws and types of social science theories that could produce nomothetic laws were discussed.

This terrain has only been visited, and it is incumbent on students and scholars to revisit this terrain throughout their careers. Furthermore, I have represented only one of many possible guides through this topography and others might know better shortcuts or more encompassing lookouts. The important issues in this chapter, however, cannot be and should not be ignored by researchers and theorists of the family. This will become clearer as I turn to substantive theories of the family in the next chapters.

Note

1. This discussion owes a great debt to the more detailed and profound discussion by Norman Lillegard (2003) in his lucid essay "Philosophy of Social Science."

PART II

Advancing Substantive Family Theories

This section examines in some depth two substantive theories about families: rational choice theory and transition theory. Although it might seem that these two theories bear little resemblance to one another, our previous discussion in Section I will assist us in seeing many common problems and issues.

You may wonder why these two theories were selected rather than some others. The answer is complex. First, I believe these two theories represent two of the best developed theories in the area of family studies. The only other one that comes close to these is role theory (e.g., Burr, Hill, et al., 1979); however, it is not a theory that necessarily deals with the family as a group. A second reason for selecting these two theories is that each deals with the family as a group. So many theories used to understand families have no place for the concept of the family group (e.g., close relationship theory). Both of the theories selected pay special attention to the study of families. A third reason for selecting these two theories is that each provides strong formal elements that reveal the structure of the theory. A fourth reason for choosing these two theories is that each is an example of "grand" theory that provides explanations at multiple levels of analyses. And, finally, the last reason is that both of these theories are often overlooked by family researchers and scholars.

Besides being viewed from the substantive perspective, these two theories can be viewed from a methodological perspective. Each of these theories stands in bold relief when compared to the other one. For example, rational choice assumes a stance of methodological individualism, whereas transition theory assumes a position of methodological holism. Rational choice focuses on motivation using the concept of marginal utility, whereas transition theory is clearly a normative theory. Comparing these two theories highlights many of the discussions in Chapter 3 as well as the usefulness of the distinctions that were introduced in Chapter 3.

The first theory to be discussed is the rational choice theory as presented by Coleman (1990). Rational choice theory bears a resemblance to some of the earlier versions of social exchange theory, especially that of Homans (1950) and Nye (1979). It should be noted that other forms of social exchange, such as Emerson (1976) and Thibaut and Kelley (1959), have moved closer to what is called interdependence theory. Yet Coleman's work systematically organizes exchanges up to the level of social organizations and institutions. Coleman also offers one of the clearest explanations of the production of social norms from the motivation of individual profit. In the study of the family, Coleman's concept of social capital is the one that is used most often (Bianchi & Robinson, 1997; Caspi, Wright, Moffit, & Silva, 1998; Haveman & Wolfe, 1994; Hetherington, 1999; Marjoribanks & Kwok, 1998; Teachman, Paasch, & Carver, 1997). Indeed, other important parts of Coleman's theory that are equally relevant to the study of families are neglected or ignored. This chapter attempts to address this oversight.

The second theory is a temporal theory and represents the only theoretical school that originated within family studies. This theory combines the approaches of role transition theory, family development theory, and life course theory into one multilevel theory framework called "transition theory." This theory is dynamic in that time and duration assist in predicting the transitions that families experience. In the first statement of this theory, the individual life course is viewed through the lens of role transitions, the dyad level (parent, child, and marital) is examined using "oscillation theory," and the family group is analyzed by means of timing and sequencing norms. Institutional and cross-institutional norms are discussed at the societal level. The theory as laid out here is incomplete, and readers are urged to apply the more formal elements of both life course theory (Bengtson & Allen, 1993) and family development theory (Rodgers & White, 1993; White, 1991) to expand the discussion in this chapter.

Both of these theories, rational choice and transition theory, are theories that are advancing in new and profound ways. Rational choice offers scholars an unusual and unexpected treatment of what Coleman terms "primordial" relationships. Interestingly, such relationships are mainly family relationships. Coleman awakens distinctions such as mechanical and organic solidarity (Durkheim, 1949) and *gesellschaft* and *gemeinschaft* (Tönnies, 1957) in his treatment of rational choice. I believe this takes us in a new and profound direction in social theory of the family. In contrast, transition theory continues to move the study of the family toward a more dynamic focus. This focus eventually leads to cross-institutional and cross-cultural norms. This theory of how and why change and transitions occur is destined to move us to a theory that can incorporate and explain aspects of the coming crisis in the study of the family. That crisis is provoked by scholars facing a nation of families that are both internally and externally diverse in normative culture. This is the globalization of family. The treatment here is just starting family theory down that road.

Finally, these two theories should be integrated into the broader set of frameworks available in White and Klein (2002). The frameworks that White and Klein survey provide a broad perspective on the many varieties of theory contained both within and between frameworks. The two theories presented here can be compared and contrasted with these various approaches. Part III assists with such comparisons by presenting a metatheoretical classification of theories.

6

Rational Choice Theory and the Family

The very idea that the family and family members' behavior can be understood as "rational" behavior may appear an oxymoron. Indeed, families are the site of extreme emotion, attachment, and even violence. Families are where many of the seemingly "irrational" decisions of life are made. For example, it is currently estimated that the costs of raising one child to the age of 18 is about a quarter of a million dollars. So we invest our time, energy, and money in our children so they can grow up and leave us. That is considered parental success. Yet, as an economic decision, how can this be considered a "rational" choice? Children are clearly an economic liability, and the days when we could count on them for care of elderly parents appears all but vanished. Likewise, anyone observing sibling fights or marital discord is usually appalled at the level of discourse and language used. The volatility of these interactions fails to suggest that these are "rational" actors.

So who in a rational state of mind would propose rational choice theory as a possible explanation of family affairs? In fact, White and Klein (2002) point out there is a long list of scholars who would argue that this theory pertains to family phenomena. Certainly, Malthus's (1798/1872) original work on the relationship between fertility and food supply would count as an application of economic ideas to one area of family behavior. There are, however, more recent applications that provide examples of much broader applications (Nye, 1979; Sabatelli & Shehan, 1993). Nye (1979) called his approach "Choice and Exchange," and although he paid some passing homage to social norms such as reciprocity, most of his theory focused on understanding family members' behavior as a function of the marginal utility or profit for the actor. For example, Nye provides theoretical propositions that attempt to explain gender differences in sexual behavior, such as marriage and prostitution, by focusing on the costs/rewards ratio for males and females. His theory is founded on the idea that any rational actor would desire to maximize rewards and minimize costs. So even in this intimate area of discourse Nye envisions actors behaving as though choices were arrived at rationally.

Probably the single clearest indication that rational choice theory does pertain to the family is the fact that Becker was awarded the Nobel Prize in economics in large part because of his extension of traditional economic thinking into the "emotional" and "irrational" area of the family. Becker's *A Treatise on the Family* (1981) extended rational economic theory into areas of the family such as fertility and consumption. Furthermore, his approach sparked other researchers to move into this area sometimes known as the "new home economics."

Becker's work has had a profound effect not just on economic theory but also on social theory. Coleman (1990) is one of those whose social theory has been most affected by Becker's ideas. Notably, Coleman spent six years as coleader with Becker of the Faculty Seminar in Rational Choice at the University of Chicago (p. xv). As a consequence of these seminars and his own theoretical training from his research supervisor Robert K. Merton, Coleman embarked on one of the most ambitious theoretical projects in recent social theory. Coleman's *Foundations of Social Theory* (1990) attempts to use a rational choice approach to explain the emergence of social organization and social institutions. His book provides extensive discursive treatment of social theory, and much of what is said is accompanied by the mathematical models that formalize the discursive theory. As social scientific theory goes, Coleman's work must stand as one of the outstanding efforts in the 20th century.

The topic of the family, so often relegated by other theorists as "any other social group," is especially singled out for theoretical treatment by Coleman (1990). Perhaps Coleman's previous work linking family contexts to child outcomes (Project Headstart) provided him with motive to focus some of his discussions on families and children. Even more importantly, Coleman identifies one of his central concepts and its properties, *social capital,* as a component in explaining aspects of family behavior. Finally, Coleman uses family as a backdrop for one of his most pertinent and interesting discussions regarding the emergence of the *corporate* actor and the contrast with the *natural* actor. Undoubtedly, the family is considered as part of the larger social theory, but few other social theorists have taken the family unit so seriously.[1]

The organization of this chapter is designed to first discuss Coleman's theory as it pertains to the family and then to turn to a discussion regarding the critiques of this theory. The chapter begins with a discussion of Coleman's perspective on social theory and his unrepentant adoption of *methodological individualism.* Then the discussion turns to the manner by which Coleman sees social groups and norms as emerging from individual rational choices. This is, of course, a critical problem for social theorists who focus on the individual as an ontological "reality" (e.g., methodological individualism). Then the discussion moves to the concept of social capital and its properties. This concept is then applied to family structure and child outcomes, and the propositions Coleman argues follow from his application of social capital to families. Finally, we focus on Coleman's discussion of the natural versus the corporate actor and Coleman's surprising argument about the possibility that rational choice may be as much prescriptive as descriptive.

The next section of this chapter turns to critiques of rational choice. The major critiques come from three distinct areas: mathematical game theory, prospect theory, and metaphor theory. Taken together, these three critiques argue strongly that the rational choice theory works in part because of the prescriptive nature of the theory and that Coleman's worries regarding the corporate and natural actors may indeed be founded in the prescriptive nature of rational choice theory.

Methodological Individualism

I have previously discussed methodological individualism in regard to levels of analysis (see Chapter 4). In that discussion, I pointed out that methodological individualism is a theoretical assumption that the individual is the principal causal agent. There is, however, usually more to this assumption than such a characterization captures. Most social science theories assume "reality" resides at some level of analysis. For example, for Karl Marx the individual was not the ultimate level of reality; instead the historical processes and the forces it unleashed composed "reality." Individuals were, in the Marxist view, just particles blown by the winds of history. Other macroscopic theorists have also viewed the social system as the ultimate reality and individuals as simply carrying on the normative culture to the degree that they are properly socialized.

There is, however, a long tradition in the social sciences, especially psychology and education studies, arguing that the individual human being is the ultimate reality. This perspective might be called "ontological individualism" as easily as "methodological individualism" because the individual is imbued with a degree of reality that other levels of analysis cannot claim.

In this perspective, any claims about effects of groups or organizations must ultimately be reduced to the effects on individuals. For example, if there is the claim that a "lynch mob" has a "mob mentality," the methodological individualist would argue that if this is indeed the case then we should be able to find such a mentality residing in the individual members of the mob. The idea of there being any "emergent group phenomena" is seen as reducible to the individual members of the group.

To digress further for a moment, the traditional difficulty for social theorists adopting a stance of methodological individualism is that macroscopic phenomena such as social organization, norms, and culture, must all be reduced to the individual for both its production and demands. For example, if each individual is a rational actor acting so as to maximize profit, how is it possible to produce social norms that limit each individual's choices and hence, ability to fully profit. Individualistic theories that invoke a norm of reciprocity or a norm of equity clearly announce that these norms condition the individual's choices, and hence the individual is affected by something that might be at a societal level. Where do such norms come from, and how can they be explained by individual behavior? This is the production question.

In contrast the demand question poses the following: If each individual is a rational actor acting to maximize profit, then how does any social organization convince the individual to abide by informal norms such as turn taking, lining up, and so on? In other words, how is "the public good" seen as an individual profit? Imagine a long line of two lanes of traffic merging into one lane. The public good would be served by an orderly process that reduces conflict, such as taking turns merging into the one lane. However, a rational actor concerned with his or her own profit would simply "butt" in line at the first opportunity. Even if you were to answer that individuals are "socialized," the question would remain as to who or what is socializing people into norms that would be antithetical to individual profit. The Hobbesian solution of the social contract only works if behaving against the contract is sanctioned, yet there are few consequences for butting in line or transgressing the many informal norms of civil society.

The challenge to methodological individualism is to answer such questions as these while maintaining that all explanations must be reducible to, and in some sense, measurable on individuals. Because we are all individuals, the notion that the individual is more real than other aggregations such as social groups and institutions seems to fit our world view, especially in the individualistic cultures of the West. Usually theorists have no problem attracting adherents to this perspective. The problems reside rather in the ability to explain social and cultural realities such as normative behaviors, rituals, and traditions.

Coleman (1990) explains that his position is a variant of the traditional perspective on methodological individualism. Coleman states that his variant is mainly concerned with societal-level explanations rather than individual-level explanations. He notes that the major problem for social theorists proposing methodological individualism is the inability to move to the macroscopic levels of analysis. I think he quite insightfully uses the example of the widening gap and poor linkage between microeconomics and macroeconomics as "a weakness papered over with the idea of 'aggregation'" (p. 6).

The variant of methodological individualism assumed by Coleman (1990) is surprisingly familiar. He states,

> The individual–level of action I will use in this book is the same purposive theory of action used in Weber's study of Protestantism and capitalism. It is the theory of action used implicitly by most social theorists and by most people in the commonsense psychology that underlies their interpretation of their own and other's actions. (p. 13)

Coleman goes on to add the specific and more precise notion of "rationality." He states he "will use the conception of rationality employed in economics, the conception that forms the basis of the rational actor in economic theory" (p. 14). In other words, he adopts the stance shared by Becker and others that human action is purposeful in that it seeks to maximize utility.

Coleman then turns to some of the major criticisms of this perspective. A couple are especially worth noting. First, it can be argued that much, if not all, action is irrational, expressive, or impulsive. Coleman cites the work of Tversky (1972) and Kahneman, Slovic, and Tversky (1982) as demonstrating that irrational choices seem to be more the case than rational choices. Coleman's response to this criticism is that if we assume humans are rational actors and develop theory according to that assumption, then the degree to which the theory fails to explain and predict is the degree to which the assumption was wrong. The problem with this logic is, of course, that some other set of assumptions might be an even better explanation. Coleman also says that the assumption of rational action also accompanies much of Western moral and political thought, such as John Locke and Jeremy Bentham. He cites the view of man as "purposive and a responsible actor" as further justifying this assumption. Naturally, Coleman does not cite Nietzsche, Kierkegaard, or Heidegger as support.

A second critical objection is that an explanation assuming rational purpose is largely teleological. That is, "man does X so as to gain a rational outcome" assumes that behavior is not determined by antecedent states but in terms of future states. Indeed, causal direction is backward. Coleman's (1990) response to the teleological criticism is instructive. First he acknowledges that teleological arguments at the societal level led directly to the problems with and eventual abandonment of "functional" explanations; however, he does not see his assumption as leading him to the same fate, for a very intriguing reason.

> When the actions treated as purposive are actions of individuals, however, and the action to be explained is the behavior of a social system, behavior which derives only very indirectly from the actions of the individuals, then the explanation of system behavior is not in terms of final causes but in terms of efficient causes. (p. 16)

This is an interesting twist on the problem of teleology. Coleman is saying that because he is concerned with an aggregated effect that is at a different level of analysis, the assumption of rational action does not make for teleological explanations at the societal level where concepts as "norm" and "capital" are used rather than individual rational purpose. The only way to properly analyze this claim by Coleman is to understand how he moves from the individual actor to the societal level. Although Coleman uses the concept of maximization of utility for generating the mathematical models for the theory, he does note that it is not a necessary component of the theory in the way the rational actor assumption is necessary. He is quick to note, however, that when moving to the societal level of behavior, maximization of utility clearly assists in understanding how aggregates of individual behavior form macroscopic effects. For example, the overgrazing of sheep by one farmer clearly minimizes the range available to others and constrains their maximization of utility. This is called an "externality." So although Coleman clearly acknowledges the challenges to the assumption of methodological individualism, the rational actor, and maximization of utility, he is undeterred by these critiques and foresees great theoretical gains as a result of these assumptions.

Emergence of Organization and Norms

The explanation of social organization is critical to the success of any social theory, especially those dealing with the family group. Coleman approaches this problem in several ways. Among the more important ways in which Coleman addresses the construction of social organization are his discussions of exchange relationships and interdependency of actors, contracts, rights, and authority. However, none of these is as central to understanding the pervasiveness and enduring quality of social organization as the discussion of social norms.

Coleman recognizes that the discussion of social norms can be divided into the emergence of norms and the maintenance of norms. Although significant social theories may take social norms as given and proceed from that point (see Chapter 7), Coleman needs to demonstrate that social norms (macro) may be generated from the individual's maximization of utility (micro). As Coleman notes, "as much as any other concept in the social sciences, a norm is a property of a social system, not of an actor within it" (1990, p. 241). Coleman is adamant about the task of identifying the emergence of norms. He says, "I refuse to take norms as given: in this chapter I ask how norms can emerge and be maintained among a set of rational individuals" (p. 242).

Coleman defines norms as follows:

> I will say that a norm concerning a specific action exists when the socially defined right to control the action is held not by the actor but by others. (p. 243)

This definition implies there is a consensus about the right to control the same action among a large number of actors. No norm can exist if an actor has the right to control the action. However, Coleman is quick to point out that when the actor internalizes a broadly held social norm, that internalization does not change the fact that the right to control that behavior is held by other actors. For example, I may believe that monogamy is the correct, normal, and moral type of marriage because I have internalized the teachings of church and Western society. That fact, however, does not remove the legal sanctions for bigamy nor make this totally an individual choice. Coleman points out that individual choice (microactions) are affected by the system-level norms in order to produce the individual-level action of conformity to the norm. Thus the interaction between the microlevels and macrolevels is most evident in regard to the normative system.

As previously mentioned, some of an individual's behavior only affects the individual, but much of individual behavior affects others. When behavior affects others either positively or negatively, it is said to have "externalities." For example, if one shovels the snow off the sidewalk in front of a house, that is a positive externality, and if one smokes cigarettes in a closed social space, that has negative externalities for the nonsmokers (Coleman, 1990, p. 249). Norms arise when a significant number of people experience an externality in the same way (good or bad) and no individual actor (e.g., monarchs) has the authority or control to change the behavior.

The emergence of norms is based not just on the externalities of the action but also based on the fact that no one actor can control the behavior. As a result, Coleman (1990) argues that

> In the absence of an externally imposed solution to the public-good problem, some kind of combined action is necessary if a social optimum is to be attained. The combined action can be the mutual transfer of rights that constitutes establishment of a norm; but for the norm to be effective there must also be an effective sanction to enforce it, if any of the actors should give indications that he will not contribute. (p. 269)

It should be obvious that sanctions may be positive, such as rewarding certain behaviors, as well as negative punishments and costs.

Coleman's solution, then, is to see norms as emerging from common causes among a majority of social actors affected by the externalities or consequences of an act. Although this fits with somewhat similar proposals by political philosophers such as Hobbes and Locke, this solution also raises some critical questions. The major question is what has become known as the "second-order public good problem." Imagine that the emergence of norms really involves two steps. The first step is the identification of a rule or norm to constrain or promote the externalities of the behavior. So, for example, we might decide we would like everyone in the municipality to clear the walks in front of their property within 24 hours of a snowstorm. The second step is attaching sanctions that would reward those who do so and punish those who do not. The first step only involves consensus, whereas the second step involves enforcement.

It is this second step that provides the basis for the second-order problem. Coleman provides a splendid example from one of Aesop's fables. A mouse society is being plagued by the externalities of a vagrant cat who insists on eating the mice citizens. The mouse council reaches a consensus that a bell should be affixed around the neck of the cat so all can be warned of the approach and presence of danger. In other words, the council has in effect decided to sanction the cat for his deviant behavior. Now the second-order problem is, who will step up and volunteer to put the bell on the cat?

Now, the fable may seem disconnected to most human social norms, but the parallel is instructive. Imagine we are standing in line for concert tickets. A couple of people come "butt" in line ahead of us. Clearly the norms regarding "queuing" or "lining up" have been violated, but who will say anything or sanction the behavior? Those people not saying anything are termed "free riders" of the normative system because they receive the benefits but not the costs. In contrast, "zealots" are anxious to enforce any infraction of any norm regardless of how inconsequential the externalities. Coleman uses payoff matrices to predict when the costs of sanctioning outstrip the rewards the individual receives from the norm. Even without mathematical modeling, it is obvious that the costs of sanctioning an act should not exceed the consequences or externalities of the original act, otherwise the costs would not warrant the norm. In the end, in Coleman's view, unenforceable norms are destined to have a short life as norms.

Coleman's view of norms, when coupled with his discussion of authority, rewards, and exchange, allows us a fairly comprehensive picture of the emergence and maintenance of social structures and organizations. However, Coleman's project is far from complete at this stage because the social structures that emerge then interact with the norms, forming networks of norms and sanctions as well as structures that impede or propel. Indeed, he points out that the second-order problem is more effectively resolved by group structures that have "closure" (explained in the next section). Furthermore, Coleman (1990) argues,

> The social system has within it a potential, analogous to the potential in an electrical system. That is, when one actor carries out an action, thus experiencing costs, and others receive the benefits, the return that the actor experiences is not merely those benefits transmitted back to him through the social structure but those benefits amplified by this potential that exists in the structure. (p. 277)

Indeed, as we will find out in the next sections, these properties of social structures are especially relevant for understanding families.

Social Capital

Although Coleman's (1990) 950-page treatise on social theory contains considerable richness and conceptual sophistication, much of the literature citing Coleman mainly uses the notion of social capital found in his earlier work (Coleman, 1988). In many regards, Coleman's theoretical work is best known for the concept of social capital (although several other theoreticians, such as Bourdieu, 1986, may also lay claim to the idea). For Coleman, the idea of social capital helps further forge together his notions of social structure and norms. The idea of social capital is also one of the concepts most relevant to families.

Coleman begins by distinguishing among three types of capital: physical capital, human capital, and social capital. Physical capital is entirely physical and constituted as tools that are aimed at production, such as a computer. Human capital changes people by giving them skills, knowledge, and abilities so their actions are enhanced. Finally, social capital concerns the relations between people that change their activities.

Understanding the difference between physical capital and the other two forms is not difficult because physical capital is entirely physical. However, the difference between human and social capital is more difficult to understand. Both human and social capital change the individual's abilities. They do so in different ways. Coleman uses a triangular diagram to explain this. He points out that the points composing the vertices of the three angles represent human capital whereas the lines between the vertices represent social capital. Human capital is contained in the individuals (vertices); and social capital is the relationships between individuals. Coleman (1990) states,

> if B is a child and A is an adult which is a parent of B, then for A to further the cognitive development of B, there must be capital in both the node and the link. There must be human capital held by A and social capital in the relation between A and B. (p. 304)

Coleman is quick to point out that the relationships of social capital are where person A controls some outcomes of interest to B and likewise B controls some outcomes of interest to A. So the relationship is an exchange relationship. He characterizes the relationships, and hence social capital, as having three properties: closure, stability, and ideology. These three components create variation in the degree of social capital available to an actor.

Closure is a social system of relationships where all those affected by an actor's externalities are also in social relations with that person. This entails that every member of the social group must be related directly or indirectly (through another person) to every other actor. Closure is important in the development of trust because it involves intermediaries in the structure. Closure is important in generating and enforcing norms because the actors all bear the same externalities or consequences. For families, closure represents both trust and normative culture.

Social structures that can be maintained as stable organizations in the face of instability are said to be "stable." This is a second component of social capital. One way to achieve such stability is, of course, commitment of actors, such as in the family where marriage is for life. Another way to maintain stable relationships is to have positions that are related to other positions, and these relations are not dependent on the individual incumbents. Most modern social organizations function in this second way to maintain social capital.

The third component of social capital is the ideological demand that the actor relates for some purpose other than for the self. This could be a religious ideology or a collectivist ideology or a family estate. The negative side of ideology would be egoism or individualism to the extent that the actor is only acting for his or her own welfare. It is interesting to see how the normative culture returns to affect this structural element of Coleman's theory. All three of these properties of social capital have ramifications for families.

Family Structure and Social Capital

For most children, the family is the single most important source of social capital. Indeed, the social capital of the family provides the child with choices in acquiring human capital. However, the inverse of this proposition is even more important; that is, the social capital inherent in the strong relation between an adult and a child is important or necessary for the development of the child (Coleman, 1990, p. 593).

The three properties of networks predict the amount or degree of social capital. A collectivist ideology would predict the concern and investment of other members in the child's well-being as part of the collective. The stability of the group clearly is important for the child's development of trust and feeling of security. The property of closure requires a more detailed analysis because it occupies a central role in regard to Coleman's propositions about the family.

Coleman (1990) describes the effects of network closure on children in the following passage:

> Closure is present only when there is a relation between adults who themselves have a relation to the child. The adults are able to observe the child's actions in different circumstances, talk to each other about the child, compare notes, and establish norms. The closure of the network can provide the child with support and rewards from additional adults that reinforce those received from the first and can bring about norms and sanctions that could not be instituted by a single adult alone. (p. 593)

Coleman also points out that adults can and need to reinforce each other with patterns of discipline and rewards to strengthen approval and disapproval of the child's behavior. Closure becomes essential for the consistency and reinforcement of the child but also for the transmission of potential human capital to the child in the form of knowledge and skills.

Coleman (1990) argues that the degree of social capital can be measured in several ways. For example, Coleman offers the following proposition:

> When both parents are present, there will be, if all else is equal, a stronger parent child relation than when only one parent is present. (p. 595)

He continues with four other propositions. He proposes that the greater the number of siblings the less the social capital, because social capital between the parent and child is diluted by more children. The more parents talk about personal matters with the child, the greater the parental interests in the child. The more a mother works outside the home before the child is in school, the less she is focused on the child as opposed to career. And finally, the greater the parental interest in the child attending university the greater the parental concern with the child's future.

It is extremely difficult to justify these five propositions as derived from the theory rather than expressing Coleman's previous empirical findings or simply cohort biases. However, Coleman argues that single-parent family structures lack the closure that is possible for dual-parent families. From the component of structural closure, Coleman "deduces" that the children of single-parent families are exposed to greater risks than children of dual-parent families. At times Coleman refers to these propositions as "measures" of social capital that have been derived from the concept, even though these would not necessarily be supported by his conceptual argument if taken in its entirety. Rather, most of this argument is founded on the closure aspect of social capital. Take, for example, the proposition regarding siblings. Certainly when siblings are spread out in ages, the oldest offer social capital to the youngest and the youngest provide social capital in terms of baby-sitting jobs and experience with young children, an asset for camp counselor jobs, coaching, and later parenting. Indeed, Coleman's view about only the parent–child relationship predicting social capital seems far-fetched in relation to closure, stability, and ideology in some large families.

Natural and Corporate Actors

Coleman (1990) summarizes the relation of the three major forms of capital as follows:

> Throughout most of history persons have been born with some mix of three kinds of endowment: genetic endowments that, when developed, constitute their human capital; material endowments in the form of land, money or other goods, which constitute their physical capital; and the social context surrounding and supporting them, which constitutes their social capital. (p. 652)

He goes on to say that the change in social capital is perturbing.

> Of particular note are an increase in physical capital resulting from economic abundance and a decrease in social capital provided by the primordial social organization of family and community. (p. 653)

Coleman (1990) views the holistic frame of reference used in the "primordial" relationships of the family as important in the successful maturation and development of children. Earlier he made this point by asserting "a child has a clear need for such a person or corporate actor" (p. 598). He argues that

> one question for the social structure of the future, then, is this simple one: Who will take responsibility for the whole child: who will be in a position to "claim the body"? If the family disintegrates, with natural parents performing only the function of procreation and then disappearing into their own networks based on self-interest, there is no natural replacement. (p. 598)

To demonstrate the notion that these natural relations are qualitatively different than role-segmented relations of corporate actors, Coleman (1990) uses the metaphor of "claiming the body" when someone dies. Coleman's argument, that there are corporate and natural relationships and that family is a more primordial natural relationship, is similar to the "defunctionalization" argument of Parsons. In fact, Coleman states, "the primordial structure is unraveling as its functions are taken away by new corporate actors" (p. 585). Coleman's perspective on family structure is clearly that two-parent families will have better child outcomes. Yet the notion of closure would indeed allow for single parents to be involved in social networks with closure. However, this line of thinking remains unexamined by Coleman, and he pursues exclusively his proposition regarding family structure (dual versus single parent). Indeed, rational choice seems to make many of the same background assumptions as functionalists of the 1950s, even though the conceptual clothing of types of capital appears new.

Coleman (1990) sees the family as tied to an important dimension of social capital for children. He argues that social relations consist of role-segmented relations, such as doctor–patient and lawyer–client, on the one hand, and natural relations where one person relates to another as a whole person, on the other. He argues that this whole-person relation is found in primordial families and kinship and constitutes a valuable and increasingly endangered form of social capital in modern social systems dedicated to role-segmented corporate actors. For example, the mother relates as a natural person to the whole child whereas the day-care worker, babysitter, and teacher relate to the child as role segments. He argues that the role-segmented or corporate role structure in general fails to deal with the child as a whole person. However, in discussing future social change, Coleman speculates,

There appear to be two general strategies that can be employed to ensure that in the society of the future the child will be attended to as a whole person. One is the nurturing or strengthening of the primordial relations of kinship, which have constituted the principal source of such attention and responsibility. The second is explicit creation of purposive organizations—that is, modern corporate actors—structured so that persons do give attention to and take responsibility for the whole child. (p. 598)

Thus family and kinship represent natural or primordial relations where the child is treated as a whole person rather than a role segment. As closure, ideology, and stability of the child's family increase, so does the degree that the family network affords the child social capital. This social capital then is tied to the child's further acquisition of human and physical capital, all of which are associated with "success" in modern societies. The question clearly remains for Coleman as to whether a child can be successfully raised without this holistic primordial relationship being present.

Critiques of Rational Choice

White and Klein (2002) discuss several major critiques of microexchange and rational choice theories (pp. 53–57). Among these are two that apply particularly well to Coleman's formulation of rational choice theory. These two critiques focus on the assumption of "rational actors" and "methodological individualism." Both are germane to Coleman, although they must be modified somewhat to fit the particular formulation Coleman offers. Coleman is very aware of the many criticisms regarding the assumption of the "rational actor." He is especially aware of the criticisms launched by game theory and Kahneman and Tversky's (1979, 1983, 1984; Tversky & Kahneman, 1988) research, and he cites both areas of discourse. So discussing the assumption of the rational actor *a la* Coleman is going to require a more sophisticated treatment than the generic treatment offered by White and Klein (2002).

Rational Actor Assumption

As I indicated at the beginning of this chapter, there are three major critiques of rational choice theory originating from somewhat different perspectives (see Lakoff & Johnson, 1999).[2] The first critique is almost accidental because it originates from a school of thinking that is largely supportive of rational choice theory. This first source is *game theory*, and in particular one family of games called the Prisoner's Dilemma. A second source is from what is known as *prospect theory* in psychology and economics and owes it foundation to the work by Kahneman and Tversky (1983, 1984; Tversky & Kahneman, 1974, 1988). This perspective questions the ability of humans to be rational and to make rational choices. The third and final source of criticism is from the theory of metaphor proposed by Lakoff and Johnson (1980, 1999). Lakoff and Johnson (1999) argue that although humans are not rational in some absolute sense, they may nonetheless demonstrate a form of contextual rationality. All three of these criticisms are interrelated and all the more compelling taken together.

Prisoner's Dilemma

The Prisoner's Dilemma is a classic game-theory model with two players. It originally was part of a story about two prisoners in a Russian court. The prisoners were both accused of the same crime, and each claimed the other had committed the crime. The judge decided he would offer an incentive for the truth and punishment for lying. He told the two prisoners (A and B) that if one of them confessed, thereby showing that the other one was telling the truth, the confessor would receive a sentence of 5 years and the truthful person would go free. If, however, both continued to say the other one did it and no one confessed, then each would get a 7-year sentence. Finally, if both confessed, they would both receive 10-year sentences. Now the actual story is designed to make the rational actors tell the truth. Both prisoners were sent back to their cells to decide whether to confess or not and had no communication with the other prisoner.

The "payoff" offered by the judge presents a complex set of contingencies. The person (A) that committed the crime would receive the lightest sentence by telling the truth and a heavier sentence by maintaining the lie of innocence. The truthful person (B), however, has a dilemma because if the guilty person (A) behaved irrationally and continued to lie, the truthful person could receive a 7-year sentence. The truthful person (B) could reduce this by confessing to the crime he did not commit, but only if the guilty person (A) continued to claim that he did not do it. However, if the guilty person (A) decided to confess and the nonguilty person (B) decided to confess, they would both receive a maximum sentence of 10 years.

Even the early experiments using the Prisoner's Dilemma yielded a diversity of responses. Certainly some actors behaved as though they might be rational, but others clearly defined the context of the game as so competitive that they would rather everyone lose than let anybody have a superior outcome to themselves. Thus there were guilty parties who would continue to lie even though they would spend two more years in prison than if they told the truth. This was true even when outcomes were positive. (See Sprey, 1979, pp. 148–150, for an application to marriages.)

The nature of the Prisoner's Dilemma depends in part on the players' interpretation of the context. For example, is the context basically one of trust and cooperation or, in contrast, is the context interpreted as a "dog-eat-dog world" where the ultimate "win" is "sticking it to the other player before he can stick it to you." Sprey (1979) reports several studies conducted by Epstein and Santa Barbara (1975; Santa Barbara & Epstein, 1974) using married couples in games of Prisoner's Dilemma and Chicken. Four personality types emerged in this study, and the most aggressive were what they termed "Hawks." Sprey (1979) notes that "Epstein and Santa Barbara report that Hawks tended to be more suspicious and defensive than all others, and also exhibited a high degree of rigidity" (Sprey, 1979, p. 150). Clearly the fact that different personalities react differently in assessing pay-offs can only be accommodated in game theory if, on average, people behave rationally. Certainly in the context of marriage there exists some doubt.

So in the end, although Coleman and other rational choice theorist present the mathematical representation of "payoff" matrices and predict the ways in which rational actors would behave, this seems more of an assumption, an abstract model, than an actual way in which actors would compute their behavior. I will return shortly to further discussion of the context of "rationality."

Kahneman and Tversky

It is interesting that Coleman's work was guided and influenced by the work of 1992 Nobel Prize laureate and economist Gary S. Becker. It is even more interesting that one of the major criticisms of the assumptions shared by Becker and Coleman derives from the work of the psychologist Daniel Kahneman, a Nobel Prize winner in economics (2002) for the work that he and his colleague Amos Tversky produced over a period of 20 years. Even when Coleman wrote his major theoretical work (1990), he cited Kahneman and Tversky's work in several places.

Coleman recognized that Kahneman and Tversky's work represented a threat to the assumption of rationality. Indeed, he used very strong language—such as "have conclusively shown"—to refer to the antirationalist findings and conclusions of Kahneman and Tversky. He states that "Kahneman, Tversky and others (see for example, Kahneman, Slovic, and Tversky, 1982) have shown conclusively that persons, when intending to act rationally, have systematic biases that lead their actions to be less than rational, according to some objective standard" (p. 14). In addition, Coleman notes that using maximization of utility (profit) as a basic theoretical component is even more difficult to defend than the more general assumption of "rational actors."

Coleman (1990) defends his adherence to these suspect assumptions in several ways. One way he defends his assumptions is to argue that when we make such suspect assumptions "it then becomes an empirical question whether a theory so constructed can mirror the functioning of actual social systems which involve real persons" (p. 18). This is to say that if we make these assumptions and they produce empirically accurate predictions, then we can accept them even though we know them to be incorrect. The problem with Coleman's logic here is that it commits the "fallacy of affirming the consequent." He is saying that if we cannot empirically reject rational choice theory then the assumptions are warranted. Yet failing to reject empirical predictions would not mean that the theory is true but only that the theory is among the set of theories that would produce such predictions. In most cases this could be a very large number of existing theories.

A second argument that Coleman (1990) uses in defense of the assumption of rationality is that the assumption is consistent with political and philosophical thought regarding the human nature: "In a certain range of scholarly endeavor, including ethics, moral philosophy, political philosophy, economics, and law, theory is based on an image of man as a purposive and responsible actor" (p. 17). He argues further that "social theory which uses that base stands to profit from the intellectual discourse this common ground makes possible" (p. 17). There are two problems with this argument. One is that consistency with foolishness is no asset. The fact is that although some theorists have used the rational actor approach, especially from Locke to Bentham, others such as Nietzsche and Heidegger have not done so. Certainly Western law is largely founded on the thought of John Locke, but there is extensive philosophical writing both in the East and West that would not adopt the rational assumption so easily (e.g., American pragmatism in the hands of Peirce, James, Dewey, Rorty, and Haack). So to argue that the assumption is justified by being consistent with the political philosophers and economic theorists that one likes versus those one does not like is hardly compelling.

One final argument that Coleman (1990) raises in defense of the rationality assumption is that "much of what is ordinarily described as nonrational or irrational is merely so because the observers have not discovered the point of view of the actor, from which the action *is* rational" (p. 18). The argument seems to be that if we simply change perspective we will encounter how an act is rational and hence the assumption is indeed warranted. The problem with this argument is that if rationality is indeed "in the eye of the beholder," it would then lack any of the intersubjective (objective) nature that is usually tied to scientific theory and is the reason behind science (nomothetic laws). Naturally if rationality is so relativistic, then no one has a privileged position as to the correct interpretation of an act as rational or irrational. It is my guess this is not the theoretical outcome Coleman envisaged or desired.

Rational Actor as Prescriptive Rather Than Descriptive

It is this perspective that "rationality is in the eye of the beholder" that Lakoff and Johnson (1999) so ably address in their critique of rational choice theories. Most importantly, Lakoff and Johnson point out that the great success of the rational actor model may not be in the theoretical prediction of behavior so much as in supplying a *moral framework* of how corporations and the actors within them *should* operate.

> [S]o institutions have been constructed according to the rational-actor model. Contemporary economic markets are such institutions. . . . "Rational action" for a firm in a market is sometimes defined as nothing more than acting so as to maximize wealth, that is, to maximize profits and minimize costs and losses. (p. 530)

Lakoff and Johnson (1999) illustrate their point using the perspective of rational actors toward the environment. They first point out that the environment is, from the standpoint of the rational actor, perceived as a "resource" because it is not a rational actor but something in the state of nature. As a result, pollution is not seen as a cost to the environment because it is not a rational actor. Totally consistent with this view is the perspective that when corporations are forced to clean up pollution it becomes a reward. Even worse, money spent to clean up pollution is added to the gross national product and to the profits of the corporations doing the cleanup. Pollution then becomes a source of benefit—a good (p. 531).

Lakoff and Johnson argue that the use of rational choice theory to guide and justify any course of action is not science but morality. It is the invocation of one set of moral values over other moral perspectives.

> The choices of what such values should be are moral choices, not "rational" (i.e., interest–maximizing) choices. In short, any use of a rational-choice model to change the world, to make it more "rational," is a moral choice. (p. 533)

It may have been this value-laden quality that Coleman sensed in the latter parts of his *Foundations of Social Theory* (1990). Certainly there is some unease expressed by Coleman with the replacement of the natural actor with the rational, corporate actor.

Methodological Individualism and the Natural Actor

It is somewhat confusing for any reader of Coleman to spend approximately 300 pages establishing that from individual "rational actors" we can move to social norms and social organization. Indeed, Coleman pays serious attention to the theoretical move from microlevel analysis to macrolevel. It is, then, a great surprise to find the concept of the natural actor emerge late in the book and furthermore to find that this concept is not derived from the individualistic assumptions of rational choice theory. As Coleman (1990) points out, the natural actor is derived from "primordial" relationships.

> Of particular note are an increase in physical capital resulting from economic abundance and a decrease in social capital provided by the primordial social organization of family and community. The latter change (discussed in Chapter 22) reflects the growth of purposive corporate actors, which have replaced the household and community for an ever increasing range of functions and have thereby weakened those primordial corporate actors. (p. 653)

It is amazing that Coleman has already established that child development is well served by these primordial relationships and that family is best understood as an example of these primordial relationships. Indeed, I previously cited Coleman's question regarding how the role-segmented rational actors might be able to replace these holistic primordial relationships and the threat this poses to child welfare.

It is extremely tempting to become engaged in Coleman's angst over replacing the natural actor with the rational actor, or the angst of his predecessors over replacing *gemeinschaft* with *gesellschaft* (Tönnies), or organic solidarity with mechanical solidarity (Durkheim). However, that would miss the theoretical point. The theoretical point is that Coleman clearly moves outside of his own methodological individualism to a type of relationship not founded on nor derived from the rational actor's maximization of utility. To the degree that Coleman believes primordial relations are important explanations of norms, civility and social order, and child development, he also must believe his own theory of rational choice is inadequate. One thing is very clear in this regard: Family is a reservoir for these primordial relations and natural actors and as such is not explainable or derivable from Coleman's brand of methodological individualism.

Conclusion

Coleman's *Foundations of Social Theory* must be considered as one of the most ambitious and thorough theoretical treatises in recent time. Coleman accomplishes several important theoretical goals. First, he demonstrates how social norms and organization can be consistently derived from a position of methodological individualism. Second, he answers many of the questions regarding utilitarian explanations of altruism by reconceptualizing this as a problem of "zealotry." Finally, Coleman's discussion of social capital remains one of the more detailed explanations of what is sometimes a vague and ambiguous concept.

But, I think, the major gift that Coleman has given to family theory is that in his ultimate desire for empirical truthfulness, he has argued that there are distinct limits to the rational actor explanation. Family, child, and community all provide examples for Coleman of primordial relationships. Although Coleman may have left the job of explaining and explicating these primordial relationships to other theorists, he nonetheless showed great courage and honesty in not trying to stretch the rational metaphor to phenomena that he regarded as clearly falling outside the scope of his theory.

Notes

1. The exception to this would be Talcott Parsons (see Parsons & Bales, 1955).

2. The discussion in this section owes much to the form and content of that offered by Lakoff and Johnson (1999). Although the critiques were outlined before I encountered Lakoff and Johnson, their general format and understanding is consistent with mine and that of Klein and White (1996).

7

Transition Theory

I imagine that the first reaction by students and scholars to the title of this chapter would be to ask, "What is 'transition theory'?" They might well add that they have never heard of such a theory in their readings of sociological, psychological, or family theories. This would be true, and indeed, both of these reactions would be totally justified.

The reason they would be justified is that the name "transition theory" has not been used before, and so that name would not cause any especially significant associations to spring to mind. What I am doing in this chapter is creating an extension of family development (Aldous, 1996; Hill & Rodgers, 1964; Rodgers, 1973; Rodgers & White, 1993; White, 1991) and family life course theories (Bengtson & Allen, 1993). That alone, however, would not explain the need for a new name because White and Klein (2002) have already argued that these two are so similar as to justify merging them into one theoretical perspective. They call the new perspective by the somewhat unwieldy name "the family life course development framework" (p. 88).

Although these two theories have been previously united, there remains a significant body of relevant theoretical work that has not yet been incorporated into either family development or life course. Two significant components dealing with transitions are oscillation theory (Breunlin, 1988) and role transition theory (Burr, Hill, et al., 1979). Furthermore, a host of practitioner insights about the effects of transitions, in such books as Falicov's *Family Transitions* (1988) and several editions of Carter and McGoldrick's book on family therapy and the family life cycle (1980, 1988, 1999), add to the richness and applicability of a more general theory regarding transitions.

Certainly no one would argue that either life course or family development theory ignores transitions. However, life course theory is heavily focused on the basic concepts of cohort, period, and age rather than being focused on either the family or family transitions (e.g., Bengtson & Allen, 1993). Family development theory, in contrast, has traditionally been focused on family stages and describing what goes on within each family stage (e.g., Aldous, 1996). Even the more dynamic variations of family development (Rodgers & White, 1993; White, 1991) still carry the focus on stages and structure, although process is also considered.

I argue that a new name is justified by the blending of novel components at different levels of analysis. The theory discussed in the following pages is a blend of many influences. It would be a misnomer to label it with any of the previous labels. Furthermore, the previous labels lead people to look for similarities with the other theories. I believe this emphasis is a mistake. Some versions of these previous theories are outdated and mired in theoretical problems (Rodgers & White, 1993). For example, early statements from the family development perspective focused on a normative description of the "family life cycle" of U.S. families and fail to have much cross-cultural validity. To break free of the mistakes and useless baggage from earlier statements, it is necessary to adopt a new name. Of course, the new theory is also a blend of several theories dealing with "transitions" and as such is not fairly represented by any of the previous names. We must direct our focus on the unique and powerful theoretical vision such a blending and reconstruction allows.

The organization of this chapter is aimed at presenting this new approach. As such, I will assume the reader is somewhat familiar with family development theory and life course theory by way of such sources as Boss, Doherty, LaRossa, Schumm, and Steinmetz (1993) and White and Klein (2002). For example, rather than begin from the familiar moorings of the main progenitors of transition theory, I begin instead with a discussion of the concept of "transitions." I then proceed from the topic of "transitions" to the topic of "process." Both of these concepts are explicated using the insights of such scholars as Allison (1984); Elder (1974); Elder, Modell, and Parke (1993); and Tuma and Hannan (1984) to mention only a few.

After these two concepts have been introduced, I then turn my discussion to exogenous "contextual concepts and variables" that are largely identified by life course analysis and then to endogenous "family and relationship concepts and variables" that are largely drawn from family development theory. It should also be acknowledged that although the discussion of transition theory here focuses on the family, the theory is not restricted to one particular social group or level of analysis. The final part of this chapter is especially relevant in this regard because it discusses the transitions between macrolevels and microlevels of analysis.

Transitions

Ancient philosophers such as Heraclitus (536–470 B.C.) believed that only change is real. Indeed, he argued that stability is an illusion. Although this is not the position of transition theory, it is helpful to reorient our thoughts to process rather than structure. The problem, of course, is that we cannot get to process or even discuss transitions without some understanding of both change and structure.

Change and Structure

The idea of change Heraclitus put forth is that everything is in flux. However, this instantly brings up the problem of how we know or observe this "flux." Most elementary approaches in this regard assume "change" is determined by the nonidentity of some entity or thing observed at two different time points. If the observation at time 1 is identical to the observation at time 2, then we say no change has occurred. If the time 1 and time 2 observations of the entity are nonidentical, then we say change has occurred.

The implicit assumptions of the Heraclitian perspective on change are worth explicitly noting. First, there is the assumption that any two observations can never be the same or identical. After all, they differ in time and so cannot logically be identical. So what we mean by identical can, in reality, only be in regard to a close approximation or similarity rather than identity. Second, we usually focus on only some but not all of the dimensions or components of the entity or thing as being similar or different. Third, the amount of difference that is counted as change is probably on a continuum so that after some threshold we say the object has changed. Finally, there are several assumptions about the flow of time as monotonic and irreversible. Carnap (1966, 1974) and others (see Davies, 1995) have discussed the problem of the interdependency between things changing and our very notion of time. All of this said, we at least have an elementary understanding of change.

In what might seem an oxymoron, the measurement and conceptualization of "change" is dependent on structure and things changing. We can return to the mapping function of metaphors (see Black, 1962; Lakoff & Johnson, 1980) to better understand the nature of change and structure.

If we say entity X changes over time, we must have some instrument that operates independently so that it changes. Usually that instrument changes in what we perceive as a periodic manner. For example, a pendulum on a clock swings from one position to another with periodicity, as does the emission of Cesium radiation from an atomic clock. A mapping from the counting of the swings of the clock to observation 1 and observation 2 yields our version of time in relation to change.

The entity we are observing must be perceived as changing. That perception is *at minimum* based on what could be called a "state-space." Any object is said to occupy a state when the attribute of interest or its structure resembles all other elements of that set or state. A state-space is generated by identifying all possible finite states that an entity may occupy on successive observations. For example, if we were concerned with all marriages and only the attribute of living together or living apart, we would have a two-state space identified. If we were interested in the weather and said that the states that could be occupied are "nice, rain, and snow",[1] those states would compose a three-state space. If we wanted to construct a state-space for all single transitions, the possibilities would be the Cartesian cross-product of the states. Using the example of the three states for weather, the transitions would be as shown in Table 7.1.

Table 7.1   Cartesian Coordinates of Weather States

		Day 2		
		Rain	*Nice*	*Snow*
	Rain	RR	RN	RS
Day 1	Nice	NR	NN	NS
	Snow	SR	SN	SS

This matrix of course is too simplistic for any purpose other than illustration of a transition state-space. Indeed, we could envision a complex state-space constructed of Cartesian coordinates of continuous variables rather than discrete categories of weather. However, the basic idea would be exactly the same.

The basic notion in such a matrix is that it helps us identify systematic or patterned change. Now the matrix specified in Table 7.1 just shows first-order change where a change in the weather at time 2 is contingent on the previous day's weather (time 1). If there is no pattern or relationship between the weather states from day to day, then we would say that weather is random or not conditional. Of course, we could imagine a case in which the adjacent days do not show much of a pattern, but some aggregation of days (such as seasons) might be more useful. The first-order change is just the start for identifying patterns of change because we could move to a lagged analysis with many more days or an aggregate analysis where we change levels of analysis from days to months or seasons. This would constitute multilevel analysis.

Once a contingent pattern is discovered, then that becomes the "structure of change." There still are many questions to be asked regarding the structure of change. The single most important question is in regard to the stability of the pattern. Returning to the simple example, imagine we find that if it rains one day there is an 80% chance it will be nice on the succeeding day. Now we must ask if this probability fluctuates over longer periods of time than covered by our observation. For example, fluctuations could occur by some geologic period (ice age) or by the duration of a particular pattern causing a shift to another pattern. We would want to know if it does fluctuate, whether the fluctuation is predictable. In general, when the effect of a variable changes across time we say it is a time-varying covariate.[2] A parameter that changes over time may be part of a process at a higher level—for example, when the course of individual change is affected by nonindividual variables from eco-logical contexts such as the community and state (see the discussion of multilevel analysis by Teachman & Crowder, 2002).

Identifying the structure of change is, of course, the primary goal of science. It has been less of a primary goal of family studies. Many studies are cross-sectional and correlational in design. Even more important is that the theoretical thinking in regard to family change has been focused mainly on a few problematic elements of family life such as divorce. In many regards, only in the last 40 years of scholarship have we witnessed increasing interest in the life course of individuals and families. And only in the last 20 years have theories such as life course and family development begun to show interest in the patterns of change. From a theoretical perspective, one of the major elements in examining patterns of change is the study of change from various levels of analysis. As stated previously, moving to different levels of analysis is key to identifying and understanding patterns of change.

Levels of Analysis and Methodological Holism

As we have seen, Coleman (1990) argued that methodological individualism was an appropriate theoretical assumption. Part of Coleman's argument is that individuals are "real." This is in fact as much an ontological position as a methodological one. Indeed, I would argue there is no academic justification whatsoever for a scholar to defend such an ontological position.

The notion that one level of analysis is real and others are reducible to that one level is often called *reductionism*. Such arguments only serve to move us away from what science can know and into the realm of metaphysics. Although metaphysics is a proper concern of philosophy, it need not be a concern of science. The reason that science does itself a disservice by focusing on metaphysical and ontological reality is simply that it is unnecessary for the generation of scientific knowledge.

Sciences may analyze phenomena at various levels. For example, cancer may be examined at the gene level, cellular level, organ level, individual organism level, and epidemiologically at the level of region or society. Although one could say that the basic reason we investigate cancer is to help humans overcome that disease, it is also quite possible many scientists are simply curious and inquisitive. Furthermore, the ontological assumption of one level representing "reality," such as individuals, might curtail work at levels that are not credited with ontological reality, such as genes and cells. Indeed, the assumption of the ontological reality of one level may provide significant blockades to the acquisition of useful knowledge by deemphasizing other levels of analysis. Finally, the assumption of ontological reality is best left to religion and philosophy to discuss and contemplate, rather than empirical scientists.

The position of methodological holism adopted in transition theory approaches this topic in a very different manner. Rather than assume that only one level has ontological reality, transition theory assumes that the level of analysis is simply the choice of the researcher relative to any given research question. The usual levels of analysis used in social science research are the individual, relationship dyad, social group (family), organization, institution, society, and culture. This is not to say that other levels might not prove useful for research, such as cellular and hormonal (e.g., Booth et al., 2000). This version of methodological holism is indeed ecumenical because the property of an "entity" may exist at any level. Although this version is flexible, it is not without constraints, but as we shall see, the constraints derive from the theoretical propositions rather than ontological assumptions.

Norms and Normative Patterns

The remainder of this chapter is organized by levels of analysis. Before we proceed to the detail of that organization, however, it is useful to point out the theoretical themes that unite and give coherence across these diverse levels of analysis. Indeed, to understand transition theory as composing a coherent explanation across these levels of analysis, some of the basic principles need to be introduced.

The most basic concepts of transitions, states, and change have previously been introduced. The concept, however, that unites and gives coherence to transition theory is that of social norm. Patterned and systematic social behavior is viewed as being produced and governed by social norms. This perspective is not vastly different from Coleman's perspective once he generates social norms from individual externalities. The difference is that transition theory takes these norms as preexisting any individual and as not requiring an explanation.

Coleman (1990) critically remarked that "norms may be taken as axiomatic by many sociologists, but for others they constitute an unacceptable *deus ex machina*—a concept brought in at the macrosocial level to explain social behavior, yet itself left unexplained" (p. 242). He further draws the distinction between these two approaches:

> Whereas rational choice theory takes individual interests as given and attempts to account for the functioning of social systems, normative theory takes social norms as given and attempts to account for individual behavior. (pp. 241–242)

Clearly, transition theory accepts that norms are given and then uses them to account for behavior.

Coleman (1990) raises the issue of origins, and yet much of normative theory seemingly avoids this question of origins. Basically, Coleman and many others have resolved the origin question by means of invoking the idea of a social contract in which people give up some of their rights so as to consensually constrain the externalities of others.

I believe that normative theory does not adopt this perspective on the origins of norms not because of a lack of concern with origins but because the social contract approach is too simplistic. Transition theory would argue that the evolution of social norms was probably founded in biologically determined social organizations, similar to what we find in many primate groups or other social animals. The conscious control of social norms only comes when individuals or social groups can reflect on the nature of social organization and how it might be changed.

Using the example of Mead's (1934, also see White & Klein, 2002) "game stage" might help in understanding this perspective. Mead argued that children were only able to assume both the position of the other and the generalized other when they could envision the rules of game and see that although actors may act differently, their actions are following the rules or norms accorded the positions they occupy. A simple example is that the pitcher in a baseball game acts differently from the batter, but each may be following the rules for his or her position in the game. Once the entire game and its rules are grasped, then modifications can be made. For instance, if we were playing hide-and-seek in a situation where hiding places are more geographically spread out, we might consensually agree that those who are "It" or "Seeker" must count to 100 rather than to 10. We have agreed on a modification of the norm or rule to organize the game within a particular context.

The perspective Mead brought to the study of norms is also shared by others such as Black (1962). Black argues that social organization is similar to a game. For people to play the game or to take roles in society, certain rules are necessary. These norms or rules, however, can be changed but the change must be consensual. White (1991) makes a similar argument about consensus but adds that unlike small-group norms for games, social norms change by increasing variation and deviation from the norms. The more systematic the deviation and the larger the number of people deviating, the more quickly an old norm is replaced by a new norm. The particular example White uses is the relatively rapid change in norms about premarital cohabitation. Just 40 years ago, premarital cohabitation was largely isolated to a small percentage of the population and considered deviant. Today, premarital cohabitation is the modal path to first marriage and considered by many social organizations to be acceptable behavior. The change from a deviant path to a normative path supplies an excellent example of how norms change. We will revisit this example later in the chapter.

Transition theory takes the perspective that many transitions are organized and expected in the life course of an individual, relationship dyad, or family. Deaths, home leaving, births, and marriages may all be expected and normative events. However, these very same events may be out of synchrony with the normative expectations and hence unexpected and non-normative. A non-normative event might be random or part of a systematic variation that will eventually change the norm. Transition theory is first a description of the norms and normative patterns and distributions and second a way to predict macrochanges in the norms of the social structure as well as changes in the life course probabilities for experiencing various events.

Organization of Chapter and Levels of Analysis

The organization of the remainder of this chapter is based on demonstrating the theoretical applications at various levels of analysis. The individual level is first considered. Although a host of individual life course approaches rely on event histories and would make suitable examples of applications, many of these examples lack extensive theoretical development. Instead they rely on the basic and non-controversial premise that the past events in one's life affect the future events. Such approaches rely on conditional probabilities and lagged conditional probabilities (see Allison, 1984). A much more theoretical work that relies on norms as an explanation is the work by Burr, Leigh, Day, and Constantine (1979). Although this work is relatively dated, it has survived as one of the most complete accounts predicting the ease of role transitions.

The second level of analysis is the dyadic level, which provides fewer examples of research on transitions though two principle areas come to mind. Two areas that are dyadic and have received much research attention are the "transition to marriage" and the "transition to parenthood." There is a problem, however, in that the major format for research in these two areas remains at the individual level of analysis. For example, even though Cowan and Cowan (2000) examine the transition to parenthood, it is in regard to individual adjustments with only divorce being a measure of the dyad. More recent research in this area, such as the Feeney, Hohaus, Noller, and Alexander (2001) study that focuses on attachment, has nonetheless maintained measurement at the individual level. Part of this problem is undoubtedly due to the paucity of dyadic theory. Only a small number of theorists have focused on the dyad (e.g., Sabatelli & Shehan, 1993). It is even a greater challenge to find dyadic-level theory that integrates norms into the explanation of the dynamics of dyadic transitions. Here I examine part of the theory proposed by Breunlin (1988) in his application of oscillation theory to family development. This theoretical formulation has undiscovered potential in regard to the study of dyadic relationships, and in this discussion it is founded on an understanding of the dynamic between norms, expectations, and behavior.

The third level of analysis is the family group. The family level refers to the presence and interaction of at least three persons, so it is not similar to the dyad. The family group is capable of producing qualitatively different phenomena from the marital dyad. For instance, the group may form coalitions and consensus may not include all members of the group. Families are groups that can be characterized by measures such as cohesion and solidarity. I examine family dynamics at this level by using the concept of "stage" and "stage transitions" similar to that used by White (1991). It is at this level that I begin to discuss an overall model for developmental change in the context of cohort and period change.

The last level I discuss is the institutional level. This discussion, however, must necessarily move beyond the institutional level to include cross-institutional and extrasocietal influences of norms. The institution of the family, like those of polity, religion, or education, consists of norms that apply to individual behavior in family roles in addition to the family group. However, the group and the individual participate in other institutions and must integrate the complex sets of norms from religious, political, social, and educational institutions into behaviors that attempt to be consistent within and between these many roles and transitions. When the norms across various institutions are integrated and consistent we have cross-institutional normative articulation, but when these norms are contradictory we have confusion and possible *anomie*. Added to this complex picture of normative articulation among various social institutions is the component of societies blending normative cultures through immigration and cultural transfers such as television and travel. This final level of analysis discusses some of these major issues in relation to transitions for families.

Individuals and Role Transitions

Individuals occupy many roles during a lifetime. Some of these roles are delegated within the family. Such roles as brother, sister, uncle, grandmother, and so on are family roles. Although this section concentrates on family role transitions, it is absolutely necessary to have some clarity concerning the concept of "role." A social role comprises norms. Norms are prescriptive and proscriptive rules for the social action attached to a social position. A social position is the same thing as a "status" and is always part of a social structure that is acknowledged and understood by social members. So there are three components of social role: norms, position, and social structure.

The most difficult to understand of these three components is social structure. In terms of the family, every society inculcates a basic nomenclature and understanding of family structure. This elementary structure is kinship (see Levi-Strauss, 1969). The kinship structure focuses attention on what is regarded within any society as significant family dimensions. These dimensions, which are universal for all kinship systems, are gender and generation. Most kinship systems are more complex (with the exception of the Polynesian or Hawaiian-type kinship system). For example, traditional Trobriand kinship, according to Malinowski (1932), delineates kinship positions by descent or lineage on ego's mother's side (matrilineal). The positions in the kinship structure are given by the universal kin terms used by ethnographers, such as *mobr*, meaning *mother's brother*. The social roles, however, consist of all the norms prescribed for that social position *mobr*. Now as it happens, *mobr* in this type of kinship is prescribed actions—such as the socialization of the mother's children and passing on of inheritance, property, and family name to the mother's children—that in North American culture is usually assigned to the biological father. In matrilineal kinship, however, it is often the case that the social role of father is prescribed to *mobr,* whereas the social role of uncle (in North American terms) is assigned to the Trobriand biological father. This example serves to point out the important distinction of social position and social role. Indeed, if we did not have the concept of *social position* it would be impossible to do cross-cultural research on *roles.* We can, however, ask about the norms in any culture that are attached to the social position of wife, a married female. In some cultures that role may include gathering roots and tubers as a prescribed activity (norm) and in other cultures, shopping. It is important to note that for social roles to be defined there must be a commonly shared understanding of kinship structure. When kinship structures are not clearly defined in terms of positions, it becomes more difficult to define social roles.

Social roles consist of some norms that are duration specific or age graded. For example, the role of mother contains prescribed behavior regarding children, but that behavior is graded or distinguished by the stage of the child, such as infancy or adolescence. Understanding that the normative prescriptions or expectations change as the child changes leads to the insight that the normative content of a social role is not static but is dynamic. The change in the role content is not in any way tied to the social structure because the position of mother is static and structural. The social role as a set of norms does, however, change. In most cases, the normative prescriptions of a role change as a function of an age-graded relationship (mother–child) or as a function of the duration of time spent in a role. As an example of changes determined by duration in a role, think about how long one should be "engaged" before giving up hope of marriage. Is 20 years too long?

There is a difference between the continuous developmental changes within a social role based on changes in a relationship and changes from one role to another role. The continuous change, for instance, in the mother role blends and adapts older norms with newer norms. Feeding expectations may change from breastfeeding with infants to TV dinners with adolescents. This type of normative change is tied to the dynamics of the relationship and will be further discussed in the section on dyadic relationships.

In contrast, changes from one social role to another are more abrupt and discontinuous. For example, in the transition to marriage we add the new role of spouse and in the transition to parenthood we add the new role of parent. These role changes are more abrupt mainly because a new relationship has been added or subtracted. Such cases are explained by role transition theory (Burr, Hill, et al., 1979).

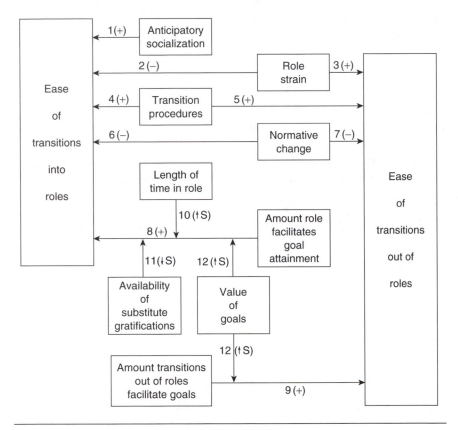

Figure 7.1   Causal Model of Role Transition Theory

SOURCE: From Burr, W. R., Hill, R., Nye. F. I., & Reiss, I. (Eds.). *Contemporary theories about the family* (2 vols.). Copyright © 1979. Reprinted with the permission of The Free Press, a Division of Simon & Schuster Adult Publishing Group.

Burr, Leigh, et al. (1979, pp. 84–89) discussed role transitions as but a part of their more comprehensive statement regarding role theory (symbolic interaction). Their statement regarding role transitions remains the most complete model identifying the propositions and variables for understanding the ease or difficulty of role transitions for individuals. Figure 7.1 graphically summarizes these propositions.

In Figure 7.1, each box contains a conceptual variable that is hypothesized to be causally related to the ease of transition into a new role or exit from an old role. The sign of the relationship is given within the parentheses. So, for example, the "amount of normative change" required either for entering or exiting a role is negatively related to the ease of a transition.

One way to understand this model is to walk through a major life event transition, such as the transition to motherhood (parenthood) for a female.

This would be a transition into a new role of "mother." Clearly, such prior experiences as parental education courses, prenatal courses, babysitting experiences, or simply and older sibling taking care of younger sibs would all contribute to the amount of anticipatory socialization (1). The amount of anticipatory socialization is positively related to the ease of the role transition. Although this proposition may seem obvious, some major contributions to the parenthood transition literature (Cowan & Cowan, 2000) have overlooked this variable.

If the new role will conflict or add impossible multirole demands resulting in role strain (2), then the transition will be difficult. For example, the young women who anticipate an early return to work and have no assistance with the infant from spouse would be likely to experience difficulty with this role transition. Likewise, if transition procedures are clear and well defined (4 and 5), this would facilitate ease of transitions both into and out of a role. For primiparous mothers these transition procedures consist of the event of childbirth and the care of the newborn. The transition procedures, such as bathing the infant and breast attachment, used to be attended to by the hospital staff when maternal stays were longer. Certainly we might expect some cohort and period variation with this relationship.

The amount of normative change (6 and 7) in the transition to parenthood is tremendous. The new mother undertakes a role that is similar to few others in our society and a role that is highly regulated. For example, some states will not let new parents leave the hospital with the infant until the baby is secured in an approved car seat. The norms governing "good mothering" are complex and come from kin, health care workers, and eventually school. There may be greater normative change in this role transition than almost any other we can imagine.

The degree to which the role facilitates goal attainment (8) is positively related to the ease of transition into the role of mother. For example, if the woman has dreamed of having a child and being a mother and having a family all her life, then the role transition would facilitate this goal. The relation between goals and ease of role transition is suppressed by the interaction of length of time she must remain in the role (10), availability of substitute gratifications from work or marriage or even a puppy (11), and the overall salience of the goal (12). As well, the importance of the goal of having a family or child (12) might facilitate the mother leaving roles such as work roles (9).

Clearly, as research proceeds we might envisage other interactions, such as a possible interaction between anticipatory socialization and the clarity of transition procedures, being added to this theory. What is important is that this theory represents an individual-level theory of transitions. Clearly, difficult transitions are more likely to not occur.

This is not to say that improvements to this model should not be addressed now. For example, in the case of motherhood, we would want to be able to identify mothers who are most likely to move through the transition based on this model. Age of the mother is an obvious candidate for an addition. We could further improve our predictions by adding components such as the "duration of the transition" itself as a component of "length of time in the role." Furthermore, the changing parameters of the model across cohorts and time periods would add a more comparative life course perspective. Despite these additions and modifications, this role theory approach provides great potential for analyzing transition to parenthood, transition to adulthood, transition to retirement, and many other individual-level role transitions.

Dyads and Behavior-Expectation Oscillations

Research has often confused individual and dyadic levels of analysis. For example, much of the research on marital quality (happiness, adjustment, satisfaction) has used measures that are typically administered to an individual, such as the Dyadic Adjustment Scale (DAS) or the Locke-Wallace scale. For years some researchers thought that one person's evaluation was a report on the relationship. Others argued that such measures were only an individual's subjective assessment of the marriage. Others thought that although both persons in a dyad need to be measured in terms of marital quality, the couple could be said to be "distressed" if only one of the two spouses scored below a threshold score (e.g., Gottman, 1979). Indeed, to say researchers have achieved consensus in this area of measurement would be unrealistic optimism. The confusion of researchers in this regard is equaled by theorists. Even Coleman (1990) found it difficult to deal with the dyadic level except as part of a group structure (note his treatment of two-person groups and social capital).

I think much of the problem in dealing with dyads can be resolved in a way similar to that used by Burr, Leigh, et al. (1979) in dealing with individual role behaviors. The roles consist of norms, and the normative culture both shapes and is shaped by actors in any role. In other words, the norms explain what is social and predictable about such behavior. In a very real sense this is also true of relationships. Relationships are structured by social understandings that guide behavior. However, in a dyad there is very much a "call and response" as we might find in musical duets. It is this dynamic property that has been very difficult for theorists and researchers to actually model.

This "call and response" character of dyadic interaction has certainly been a target of researchers. For example, Gottman (1979) investigated the *quid pro quo* hypothesis that one spouse in a dyad immediately reciprocates the affect of the other spouse. This simple hypothesis was largely rejected. Indeed, Gottman's (1979) analysis used a time-lagged Markov analysis to model the complex sets of conditional probabilities. The sophisticated methodological analysis did not get around the problem. The problem remained that the conceptual and theoretical understanding lagged behind the methodological tools at hand.

There is a basic theoretical insight about the nature of different types of relationships that is fundamental to analysis of dyadic relationships. As I stated in the previous section, some relationship transitions are mostly predicted by the normative content of the roles. Even the role-to-role transition is normatively prescribed. This is because the roles are well defined and, most importantly, the relationships between the actors playing the incumbents in these roles are normatively prescribed. For example, I was the president of a sizable academic organization concerned with families. When I stepped down and handed the position over to the next actor, we both understood what information and files needed to be transferred because this was largely defined by the norms of the positions we occupied.

The second type of relationship is less governed by prescriptive norms and is more developmental. This second type of role relationship places more emphasis on the relationship aspect. Certainly marriage and intimate adult relationships are of this sort, but so are parent–child relationships. These are relationships that are circumscribed by norms but are of such a relatively long duration (many are lifelong) that age-graded norms, cohorts, and historical periods may be traversed, as pointed out by both family developmental theorists and life course theorists. It is a far cry from one president leaving office and another taking over. Indeed, most family relationships are of this second form.

To digress for a moment, I might point out that what Coleman called rational role-segmented actors is akin to what I mean by role relationships of the first type that are largely normatively prescribed and of shorter duration. The second type of relationship is similar to what Coleman called *primordial relationships*. I do not agree with Coleman that these are "primordial" or in any way more biologically given or primitive than the first type of role relationship. Rather, these relationships are simply more complex than the others and more elusive for researchers and theorists.

The notion that the family is characterized by these relatively long-duration relationships was pointed out by White and Klein (2002) as being among the factors that made family relationships different from other social groups. It is not surprising, then, that family development theorists tackled this thorny problem. I believe the most successful theoretical treatment to date comes not from a purely academic theorist but from a theorist also rooted in therapeutic practice. Breunlin (1988) argued from a different orientation from predecessors in family development or life course theory. Breunlin argued that families *and relationships* make transitions,

> because, if nothing else, time never stands still and children in a family grow up. The only relevant questions are, how is a transition made, and how can the process become problematic? (p. 136)

Breunlin added the theory of oscillations to the study of transitions and by so doing added one of the best theoretical accounts of how these long-term relationships develop.

Breunlin (1988) describes oscillation theory in the following way:

> Oscillation theory hypothesizes that transitions occur not as step functions, where discontinuous leaps are made from one level of functioning to another, but rather through an oscillation between levels of functioning. (p. 140)

Although Breunlin acknowledges that events and discrete jumps in family structure and form do occur, he uses oscillation theory to approach the more continuous processes that occur within families and especially within dyads.

He argues that oscillations within the family and relationships always occur after a discrete jump where the structure of the family has changed or relationships have qualitatively changed. For example, relationships change with status changes from cohabitation to marriage, even though the dyad going through the transitions consists of the same actors.

The basis of oscillation theory is that it focuses on a more continuous variable than changes of status or relationship structure.

> Oscillation theory proposes that it is the competence of each family member that changes over the course of the life cycle, thus enabling a family to develop. When oscillations occur, they are expressed in terms of this competence and can be observed as a swing between overly competent and overly incompetent behavior. (Breunlin, 1988, p. 141)

The notion that competence is a variable is unique. It is in part unique because competence is an individual-level concept and not a dyadic level. Indeed, on the surface the notion that dyadic relationships and families could be examined by using competency appears somewhat strange.

Breunlin argues that within the broader pattern of discrete stage or state transitions often tied to changes in structure are what he terms "microtransitions." The microtransitions are changes that are continuous and move the relationship or family toward the next discrete stage transition. For example, a newly wed couple would traverse many microtransitions as they establish ways of managing conflict and developing clear communication before having a first child. The competency they achieve in this regard predicts the competency they have acquired to take on the task of parents.

The oscillation pattern is more obvious in the following example from child development:

> when a child first walks, walking does not abruptly replace crawling in a discontinuous fashion. Rather, sometimes the child walks (and frequently falls), and sometimes the child crawls. Likewise, during the microtransition, family sequences that regulate crawling and walking exist simultaneously. (Breunlin, 1988, p. 145)

Although this passage identifies the oscillation pattern, Breunlin appears hard pressed to define the exact mechanisms by which this occurs. I believe an extension of Breunlin's ideas offers a compelling theory of dyadic processes and sketch what such an extension would entail as follows.

Competency is acquired by the individual child. The process, however, by which the child develops competency is dyadic and not individual. Certainly Bronfenbrenner (1979, see also White & Klein, 2002, Chapter 8) and others have pointed this out. Even more importantly, the dyadic process by which this occurs accounts for both the old behavioral competency (crawling) and the new behavioral competency (walking). The key to understanding this dyadic process lies again in the concept of norms.

Most parents would share the understanding of the parental role as facilitating the competency of their children. This general norm is, however, translated into microtransitions as a very concrete age-specific norm. Parents may want their child to achieve academic success in high school, but how do they facilitate this when the child is one year old? They do so by continually setting and changing age and stage expectations (micronorms) for the child. When the child does not crawl, the behavioral expectation is that the child *should* crawl. The child responds by oscillating to the behavioral expectation until it is achieved. However, once it is achieved the parent shifts the behavioral expectation up a notch to walking, and a new oscillation begins again until competency is achieved. The norms that guide the parents are socially and culturally acquired, so in some cultures the trajectory of child competency may be somewhat different.

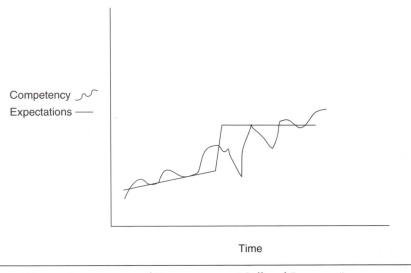

Figure 7.2   Competency and Expectations—"Call and Response"

Figure 7.2 graphically represents this dyadic process between child behavioral competency and parent expectations. Note that in this figure the child has achieved competency in crawling and the parent maintains the expectation until the behavioral output is stable and predictable. After stability is achieved, the parent changes the expectation level to the next developmental norm or expectation, requiring yet another series of oscillations from the child. Eventually the child will achieve the stability in regard to this competency and the expectation will once again be changed. This "call and response" series of behaviors are what compose much of child development and parent–child interaction.

If we move this analysis to marital dyads (or even bidirectional child development), we get a somewhat different perspective. The "call and response" interaction is still a factor. One spouse may have expectations for the other that are important in terms of the development of the relationship, but only when the norms are mutually viewed as legitimate or consensual do we see behavioral competency develop on the part of both spouses. In other words, adult voluntaristic dyads achieve competency as a relationship when each individual shares the norms for behavioral output. Certainly each actor usually shows great tolerance for the other spouse's oscillations as they seek to achieve commonly shared expectations ("fusion" in the terms of Berger & Kellner, 1964). For example, traditional marriages may simply have an easier microtransition and longer-range development because the expectations are clear and shared. Even when couples have different and divergent expectations for one another, individuals may achieve competency and the dyad may be competent in regard to an expectation of mutual tolerance. However, this form of relationship fails to share much common development because the norms and expectations for the couple's development and stage are not shared. For example, imagine a case where a wife is busy preparing the relationship for having a baby but the husband does not share this goal. Certainly the transition to parenthood will be a difficult developmental transition (see Cowan & Cowan, 2000; Feeney et al., 2001).

Figure 7.2 helps us visualize the additional complexity where two adult, voluntaristic partners are represented. The adults each have expectations. To the extent they are shared expectations about the couple's joint life course and their partner's behavior, the two expectation lines will more or less converge in consensus. The degree of divergence represents the lack of shared expectations and norms. Although every couple may go through periods in the life of their relationship where there are divergences, these may be especially salient immediately after a transition to a new stage or state such as marriage or parenthood. In addition, even if there is relative homogeneity in regard to expectations, the competency graph for either partner or both may be divergent from expectations. An example of this would be where two parents agree to coordinate pickup and drop-off at day care but one of them is always forgetting or is late. In general, such deviations are expected during the oscillations immediately after a transition but less tolerated as the duration from the transition extends across time.

The analysis of expectation and competency behaviors is most complex in dyads (or multimember groups). In adult dyads it involves a measure of the two adult-partner expectation lines and their fit with each other or with a commonly generated averaged line of expectation. Second, it involves measuring the deviations of expectations from the average expectation line as well as the opposite partner's line. And last, it involves the duration since and before a major state transition. Such measures would allow the comparison of partners' expectations across life course transitions as well as within stages. It would also facilitate the measurement of behavioral competency oscillations from the line of shared expectations (averaged) and the degree to which that expectations are shared (variance).[3]

One of the critical tasks for this dyadic theory is to explain the case where expectations are shared in a marital dyad but one spouse's behavior appears incompetent. In cases such as these, it is wise to refer down a level of analysis to the individual level and the nature of role strain and role conflict. If competing demands on the spouse's resources, such as work, are resulting in incompetence in the dyad, such role strain or even conflict would then surface at the dyadic level in terms of incompetence.

There are, of course, many measurement approaches to dyadic interaction, such as the behavioral models used by Gottman (1979). The advantages to my extension of oscillation theory are several. First, this approach uses two common and well-understood social science concepts, normative expectations and behavioral competency, to describe dyadic relationships over time. Second, these concepts and their measurement are well within our current statistical abilities to analyze linear and curvilinear fit. Finally, these concepts fit well with concepts of role transition at the individual level of analysis and, as we shall see in the next section, with the conceptualization of family stage transitions at the group level of analysis.

Family Transitions and Norms

White (1991), Rodgers and White (1993), Bengtson and Allen (1993), and White and Klein (2002) have all offered a relatively consistent picture of transition theory, albeit from slightly different vantage points. White (1991) approached family development as a multilevel theory of the family contextualized by age, cohort, and historical period. Rodgers and White (1993) followed this approach and added theoretical propositions and empirical applications. Bengtson and Allen (1993) took a different perspective on the family from a life course approach using age, period, and cohort but having only a brief discussion of debates on ontogenetic versus sociogenic development. Bengtson and Allen did not discuss development as a critical process, as did the other authors. Finally, White and Klein (2002) argued for the amalgamation of these approaches as I have argued here. All of these treatments have many more commonalities than differences. It is this common approach that I will detail.

The group level of analysis is critical for understanding the family. As White and Klein (2002) have pointed out, however, the family is not like other social groups such as work, voluntary, or play groups. Family relationships last longer than any other relationships we experience. For example, the sibling relationship is usually lifelong. The family is organized by institutional norms tied to kinship structures. The family is the only social group with intergenerational bonds. The family is the only social group that regulates and legitimizes sexual behavior. Some of these differences from other social groups may have in part led Coleman (1990) to characterize these relationships as "primordial."

Defining the family group is somewhat difficult because any analysis must examine the group's formation as well as the group's decay and decline. White (1991) defined the family as an intergenerational group regulated by social norms regarding reproduction, descent, and marriage. The understanding, however, is that the study of family groups may involve dating, cohabitation, and marriage as formative processes. Likewise, family decline might involve the study of transitions such as widowhood. So even though the group is the focus, the *life course analysis* supposes stages that might involve only some members of the family.

This is to emphasize that the family develops over time. Just as an individual at 5 years of age is qualitatively distinct from the same individual at 50 years of age, the family develops, matures, and declines as a social group analogous to the way in which individuals grow and wither. White (1991) points out that we should mean something else besides change when we use the term "development." Following Featherman (1985) and Tuma and Hannan (1984), White defines development as where any specific stage "B" of the family at time 2 is determined by the immediately previous stage "A" the family was in at time 1 and the duration of time the family remained in that prior stage "A." This is a variant on the Markov assumption of conditional probabilities and simply adds the duration in state as a determinant. Furthermore, what is being predicted is the transition to stage "B." Indeed, the definition of development is tied to the notion of predicting transitions.

A simple example will make this less technical. Imagine we have two couples and both are married. We would immediately know that the probability of having a first child is greater for married couples than unmarried. Thus knowing the state (married or unmarried) helps us predict the transition to parenthood. However, if we also knew that one couple had been married for 15 years (duration in state) and the other couple for only 1 year (duration in state), that would change the probabilities of a transition to parenthood. The theory at this level of analysis is concerned with the prediction of state transitions.

As I discussed at the beginning of this chapter, the development of a possibility space for all of the state-to-state transitions (state-space) would give us an analytic tool to discuss possible transitions. However, such a state-space would rely on an academic consensus of the stages or states traversed by families. Although Rodgers and White (1993) delineate a format for achieving this, their solution is cumbersome and difficult. The alternative to the identification of family stages or states seems more workable.

The alternative is to use events as markers for stage transitions. Indeed, when we study transition to marriage we use the wedding day as the transition event and when we study transition to parenthood we use the birth of the child as the marker event. The time since the wedding or birth to the censuring point of the conclusion of the observation (time of the study) gives us the duration in state. With these two elements we can construct a model of stage transitions, but it will be restricted to particular events and not a general and universal analytic model as would be the case with a state-space approach. Nonetheless, event history analysis is the usual way we study both life course and family development transitions. The single biggest difference would be the semi-Markovian assumptions of "development" in the family development approach (see also Allison, 1984; Coleman, 1981; Tuma & Hannan, 1984).

Thus far I have really been discussing analytic and statistical models of the process of development. These are absolutely necessary for achieving theoretical clarity and definitions. It is, however, not an explanation. Rather, the explanation for developmental transitions for the family group once again relies on normative theory.

Each institutional sector, such as polity or education, must have norms that regulate the behavior of individuals and groups acting within that domain. Furthermore, the norms must take into account the changing competencies of individuals as they age and of relationships and families as they spend time in a specific stage. I have already outlined the way in which expectations and behavioral competencies are related at the dyadic level, and that type of analysis could be extended to larger n-adic groups. What I have not accomplished is to explain why transitions occur according to the semi-Markov or Markov assumptions.

The organization of the life course within any institution, such as family, must necessarily bring demands (expectations) into line with capacities (competencies). The way this is achieved is for some norms to be age or stage specific. When several age- or stage-specific norms are linked together in a sequence, the result is a sequencing norm. For example, where I live, adolescents cannot work until 16 years of age, cannot drive until 17, and cannot sign a contract without a cosigning adult until 18 years of age. These are formal age-graded norms that structure the individual's experience and relationships with others. These norms also provide complex constraints by their cross-contingencies, such as at age 16 one cannot take a job that requires driving but at 17 the job may involve driving.

If we apply a similar logic to family norms we find complexes of cross-contingencies that are time dependent, such as *finish your education before having children, get married before you have children,* and *get some job experience before you get married.* The resultant sequencing norm is simply *finish your education, then get a job, then get married, and then have a child.* Now, some of the norms are more salient than others. The norm to get married before having children is more salient than to get a job before marrying. The overall efficacy of a sequential norm is described by the frequency of that event pattern in the population described by the leptokurtosis (strong norm) versus platykurtosis (weak norm) of the distribution. The predictive efficacy of the normative explanation is found in how well the Markov assumption (stage dependency) predicts transitions. For instance, if the preceding sequencing norm were very strong then we would find that the conditional probability for a transition from finishing education to first job is the best predictor compared to other event orderings (White, 1991).

Certainly this normative perspective has been challenged (see White, 1998, for a summary). The argument is that the normative view takes an "oversocialized" perspective regarding actors and that any patterns may simply be patterns based on age alone and not norms. The critical test for such an argument is when age is variable yet behavior is stage or event dependent. For example, almost every life insurance agent knows that parents-to-be are excellent candidates for life insurance because of their anticipated new responsibility and that this is regardless of the age of the new parent. I will return to the critique regarding the "oversocialized" actor perspective at the end of this chapter.

Institutions and Historical Period

One of the most intriguing problems in normative theory is the problem of deviance. This problem is in part intriguing because the general assumption is that conformity to norms is desirable and beneficial. For example, most studies on life course transitions, such as the pioneering studies by Hogan (1978, 1981), have demonstrated that deviance from timing and sequencing norms in early life is related to later life disruptions such as divorce (Hogan, 1981) and later life disruptions in labor force participation (White, 1991). These early studies have been reinforced by later studies establishing similar patterns (Marks & Lambert, 1998). If deviance from timing and sequencing norms has such negative consequences, then why would anyone deviate? It would seem counterproductive to follow any road but the one well traveled.

Several authors (Marini, 1984; White, 1998; White & Klein, 2002) have lodged somewhat different but nonetheless complementary explanations for normative deviance. One argument is simply that the norms are so weak (if they exist at all) that so-called deviance is simply variation (Marini, 1984). Certainly this argument has necessitated the distinction between variation and deviation. Another argument is that people who deviate from the normative path do so because they perceive rewards. For example, medical students spend enormous amounts of time in educational institutions early in their lives but later in life there are economic payoffs to this deviance. Thus the deviance would be seen as tied to economic payoffs not available to others. Undoubtedly this explanation might explain some of the deviance, but not all deviance from timing and sequencing norms necessarily has economic payoffs.

Finally, there is the argument that deviance in one area is tied to conformity in another. That is, when timing and sequencing norms between institutions such as work and family are contradictory or conflicting, conformity to one set of timing and sequencing norms is simultaneously deviance from the timing and sequencing norms in another institution. This "Catch 22"[4] is responsible for most social change. For example, White (1991) explains the rise in cohabitation rates during the 1970s and 1980s as deviance from the sequencing norms of marriage and family but conformity to changing sequencing norms in education and work that push for more education and job experience before marriage, especially for women.

There is little doubt that all three of these arguments bear due consideration. Indeed, these issues have amply been discussed elsewhere (White, 1991, 1998). However, the last argument leads to an area of integration between family development and life course theories that is worthy of some further discussion.

The argument that an actor conforming to the timing and sequencing norms in one institution, such as education, might be deviant from timing and sequencing norms in some other institution, such as family, is especially intriguing as we move to a more diverse and global culture. Certainly every institution in a society must articulate its timing and sequencing norms with other institutions. This cross-institutional articulation is what prevents a tidal wave of expectations at one time point. For example, imagine if you could expect to graduate from university, start your first job, get a mortgage, buy a car, have a baby, experience the death of a parent, and get married all in one year. This indeed would be a tidal wave of expectations, and usually these expectations are spread over a longer duration of time. So cross-institutional articulation of sequencing and timing norms assists social systems, groups, and individuals in timing challenges and sequencing their development in an organized manner.

As cross-institutional timing and sequencing norms fail to articulate with one another, groups and individuals experience contradictory and conflicting expectations. As behavioral conformity is more variant (platykurtic), which behavior represents conformity and which represents deviance is much less clear. A norm that is haphazardly followed by the public and lacks consensus will show a platykurtic distribution. That is, social conformity to the norm is highly variable. A norm that no one follows is not long destined to be a norm. If all of the norms in a social system are platykurtic, then the society itself might be troubled. This is what the early social theorist

Durkheim (1949, 1951) called *anomie* and represents a state of normlessness and lack of normative direction at all levels of analysis.

As all societies move toward a diverse global culture, culture of origin timing and sequencing norms (often considered traditional or ritual) are intermixed with the timing and sequencing norms of the culture of reception. Sometimes these global cultures mix economic, political, and cultural systems that are not completely compatible. For example, one social system might be collectivistic and the other individualistic, one economic system might be "capitalistic" and another "planned." The potential for possible conflicts in timing and sequencing norms and the resulting *anomie* are problematic. This problem, however, represents a period effect in the evolution of the cross-institutional timing and sequencing norms for these societies. The major process here is one of cross-institutional and cross-cultural articulation. The timing and sequencing norms that best articulate between the cultures of origin and reception will undoubtedly allow conformity in both worlds.

It is interesting that these global developments are so readily considered within the framework of transition theory. Certainly there is much more theoretical work to be accomplished here, but the theoretical concepts of the multilevel theory seem to offer several profitable avenues for conceptual and theoretical advances.

Critiques of Transition Theory

There are critiques of many different components of transition theory, but the theory itself is too new to have yet received the full impact of the critic's arrows. In this section I attempt to anticipate the criticisms of this theory rather than return to earlier critiques of family development or life course theories that are no longer relevant.

Certainly some criticism should be reserved for the notion of development as defined by stage and duration dependence. Transition theory seems uneasy with saying the transitions are driven by norms rather than duration and stage dependence, yet the stage and duration dependence is explained by the timing and duration norms.

This critique confuses the mathematical model with the theoretical explication. Certainly the mathematical model suggests that transitions are stage and duration dependent. However, those are the assumptions of a semi-Markov model (White, 1991). These assumptions are only supported by the theoretical propositions regarding timing norms (duration) and sequencing norms (stage dependence). It is important to note that the model is an expression of the theory and not vice versa.

One of the most astounding theoretical advances in microchemistry has been Prigogine's Nobel Prize–winning observation that relatively small perturbations may accumulate to large and significant effects. Certainly the changes in coupling patterns, including cohabitation, could qualify in this regard. Transition theory as it currently stands does not offer sufficient precision for us to understand the micro–macro and macro–micro effects that are so central in the writing of Coleman (1990) and others. Indeed, one could argue that only a few of these effects are elaborated in the theory as it currently is stated. I believe this criticism is well founded.

Another criticism is that cohort, period, and age effects may exist throughout the various levels of analysis yet they are poorly explicated. Certainly the theoretical work by Bengtson and Allen (1993) supports a broader inclusion of these factors, yet the current statement has erred on the side of the normative interpretation and downplayed the importance of history throughout the levels of analysis.

I believe this is also a valid criticism, and the excuse is that age, period, and cohort as concepts interject a level of abstraction that I believe works against the understanding of transition theory. It certainly needs greater inclusion in the theory. At this time, however, there is not much theoretical substance to these concepts except to point out that historical periods, cohort, and age do make a difference to the processes of development and change involved in transitions. White (1991) singled out "age" as being an especially vague concept that may be diversely configured as standing for ontogenetic development, social maturation, age-graded normative behaviors, risk period, and experience. For example, that no 15-year-olds are permitted to lifeguard could be explained by formal norms restricting lifeguarding to only those 16 and older but also to social maturity and ontogenetic development. Certainly age predicts this behavior, but the conceptual interpretation certainly is lacking clarity. Much of the work on age, cohort, and period suffers from similar problems of clarity.

Finally, the general critique of normative theory has been that it takes an extreme and unjustified view of humans as being "oversocialized" (e.g., Marini, 1984; Wrong, 1961). This would be the case if transition theory only used normative conformity to explain transitions. However, the theory explicitly defines effects for deviance from norms and also specifies that in some cases (medical students) the deviation (timing norms) may be associated with positive outcomes (higher lifetime earnings) rather than negative outcomes. White (1991) focuses on deviance (systematic variance) rather than variance as being the major factor determining changes in social norms and hence social change. Likewise, it is argued earlier that platykurtic variation from norms may produce *anomie*. Thus transition theory is far from an "oversocialized" perspective. It does reference creative and idiosyncratic behavior to norms in order to establish the behavior as normative, variant, or deviant.

Conclusion

Transition theory is an amalgamation of a somewhat diverse group of theoretical works that all focus on the study of transitions. At the individual level, Burr, Leigh, et al.'s (1979) work focuses on the variables that promote or impede role transitions. This is a powerful individual-level theory that is relatively clear. At the dyadic relationship level is the extension of Breunlin's oscillation theory. This too is a relatively clear and simple theory that views dyadic interaction as a "call and response" where the dyadic norm composes the "call" and the individual behavioral competency composes the "response." There is a clear linkage with the individual competency using concepts such as role strain from Burr, Leigh, et al.'s discussion of role transitions. The theoretical crossover between levels of analysis is viewed as critical by Coleman (1990), and I concur that such crossovers are absolutely necessary if we are to achieve genuine explanation. At the group level of analysis, transition theory focuses on states or stages and the prediction of family transitions. White (1991), Rodgers and White (1993), and White and Klein (2002) have developed the idea of family stages as a structure of roles and positions. As such, the concept of stages fits well with the discussion of norms and roles at both the dyadic and individual levels. Finally, at the institutional level the focus is on sources of normative change found in cross-institutional sequencing and systematic deviance from existing norms.

Transition theory certainly has a very broad scope, spanning from the individual to global family change, however the actual number of concepts are relatively few. Norms, roles, agreement, variation and deviation, institutions and cross-institutional norms are some of the central notions. Other concepts not included in the current discussion, such as "off-time" and "out of sequence," are well explicated by others (e.g., Falicov, 1988; White, 1991) and directly derive from the concepts presented here. Furthermore, both Rodgers and White (1993) and Bengtson and Allen (1993) attempt the formulation of formal propositions.

Although progress has been made theoretically in regard to this theory, there is a noticeable lack of use of the theory by empirical researchers. This provides an opportunity for students and researchers, but it also gives rise to questions about the ingredients of a theory that make it appealing to empirical researchers. The next section directly addresses such questions.

Notes

1. This example was originally used by John Kemeny (1966) in his excellent discussion of Markov chains.

2. See Yamaguchi (1991) for an excellent discussion of time-varying covariates.

3. For a note on methodological treatments for this problem, see White and Teachman, 2004.

4. Heller, 1961.

PART III

Beyond Theory: Ethics, Ideology, and Metatheory

This section goes beyond what is normally regarded as scientific theory and moves into a discussion of research, ideology, ethics, and metatheory. The rationale for this venture beyond substantive theory is to clarify the differences between these four and develop an understanding of some of the major issues as they pertain to family theory.

Among the critical issues facing family theory is its notable absence from much of the empirical research published in the major academic journals. Chapter 8 analyzes why this "disjunction" between theory and research has developed and why we should be concerned about this as a long-term condition of family studies. This chapter concludes by identifying three dimensions that may be used to organize a metatheoretical classification of family theory. Such metatheory can assist both researchers and theorists to identify significant areas for research and theoretical development.

Chapter 9 examines some of the differences among scientific theory, ideology, and ethics. Indeed, it is often confusing where theory ends and ideology begins, and this chapter is intended to clarify this distinction. At the same time, the difference between ideology with its identification of a prescriptive course of action and ethics also needs to be examined.

Chapter 10 summarizes the journey this book has taken through the forest of ideas that compose history and philosophy of science, theory construction, rational choice, transition theory, research, metatheory, ethics, and ideology. This last chapter closes with a perspective on theories as tools that is meant to make theory less remote and more explicit for researchers. It also resolves the conflicts among postpositivism and science, understanding, and explanation using the arguments that have been followed in this book.

8

Empirical Research
and Theory

Since Lavee and Dollahite (1991) reported a remarkable and regrettable lack of theory used in empirical studies of families, there has been almost no discernible change in this state of affairs. Indeed, this sad state of affairs has also been documented in the area of family therapy research (Hawley & Geske, 2000). This chapter focuses on what I believe are some of the factors creating a disjunction between theory and empirical research, some reasons why it is absolutely necessary to change this disjunction, and finally some suggestions for students and researchers in regard to formulating testable theoretical propositions and interpreting findings.

The Disjunction Between Theory and Research

Lavee and Dollahite (1991) reviewed articles published in the major journals for family research. Since that time, other studies have asked similar questions and come to similar conclusions. For example, Vargus (1999), as I noted earlier in this book, assesses the current state of family theory as follows:

> Marriage and family theorists seem, when considered in relation to classical theory, to be those leading a "wander in the wilderness"—a wilderness rooted in biological categories and no concern for individual processes that transcend those categories. Further, the practitioners are wandering with them, without a Moses. (p. 202)

Vargus's concern is further amplified by Doherty (1999) when he identifies the postmodernist challenges to the idea of "family as a phenomenon" and the critiques of positivist family science (p. 209) as challenges to researchers. And for therapists, Hawley and Geske (2000) report that their study's

> findings raise questions about the role of theory in family therapy research. It may be that *researchers need to take a closer look at what purpose theory serves* [italics added] since a number of studies in this analysis either did not appear to incorporate theory or use it in a way that would be considered traditional "theory" building. Many clinicians today operate from a postpositivist orientation that highlights the uniqueness of each client and they may fail to see the relevance of research that uses theory in a positivist paradigm to evaluate similarities across families instead of focusing on the particular characteristics of each family. (pp. 21–22)

When we examine Hawley and Geske's and Doherty's appraisals in addition to that of Vargus, we find we should be concerned with the direction in which we are headed. We need to revisit the issue of our common goals.

Although there is always room for discussion, I would argue that our major goal is the *production* of knowledge about the family. The concern about this direction of family research *sans* theory depends on a particular view of knowledge. Knowledge in the particular view taken here is defined by the ability to generalize from one context to another (in contrast to the idiographic pursuit of contextually specific information). For example, I have a general understanding of "escalators" regardless of whether the escalator is in a hotel or a shopping center. We all generalize across specific contexts. Indeed, if family researchers and therapists were to abandon the goal of finding general principles applicable across cases (nomothetic laws), what would this say about the future of knowledge in our field?

Many empirical researchers might argue that the use of commonsense hypotheses and popular psychology produces sufficient accounts to help people better their lives and to direct policymakers (see Daly, 2003). Later in this chapter, I will more directly discuss this argument. For the moment, it should suffice to say that such limited goals may not even require empirical research because many of the answers can already be found in the assumptions used to formulate hypotheses. But from the perspective of nomothetic science, the problem is that generalizing from measures or even concepts and hypotheses still lacks the more complete picture that theory affords. Pedhazur and Schmelkin (1991) summarize these many purposes of theory in research by saying that "theory provides the researcher with a 'selective point of view' without which research would be 'the ditty bag of an idiot, filled with bits of pebbles, straws, feathers, and other random hoardings' (Lynd, 1939, p. 183)" (p. 181).

Although the "selective point of view" could be interpreted by sophists as "bias," such an interpretation would miss the point. Rather, the selective point of view afforded by theory allows for focus, consistency, and relative completeness of explanation. At the same time, the selective point of view virtually guarantees that there are or will be competing theories with a different point of view. Because theories are always tentative, the admission that other explanations are possible is implied by the selective nature of theory. At the same time, the fact that the theoretical generalization actually says something sufficiently specific, so that alternative theories are possible and plausible, further implies that scientific theories supply real explanation rather than just sweeping generalizations that cannot be refuted. To put this perspective succinctly, such theories produce "knowledge" from "information."

Necessity of Theory for Credible Science

If the principal purpose that theory serves is to produce knowledge, then the principal purpose of scientific theory is to produce *tentatively held knowledge*. The history of science is like a plain littered with the bones of incorrect and partial theories that were accepted at some point in time. Indeed, this fate awaits most if not all scientific theories. So all scientific theories must assume the probability that rejection, disuse, or modification will be their fate. In this sense, theory is as much process as product. The processes of theory building and modification are the way we advance theory and knowledge.

Previously, in Chapter 3, I discussed the functions of theory listed by White and Klein (2002). The discussion in this book and in Klein and White (1996), although complementary, emphasize distinctly different points of view. In this section, I embark on yet another discussion of the functions of theory but once again from yet another point of view that is no less complementary to the previous two discussions. Here I focus almost completely on the functions of theory for researchers.

The major function theory performs for researchers is to guide and stage empirical research. This function, however, conceals many important dimensions, some of which are easily overlooked. For example, theoretical assumptions such as methodological individualism, holism, levels of analysis, and ontological status of definitions are all important subtexts implied when a researcher uses one theoretical approach versus another. The researcher that adopts commonsense approaches or popular folk psychological approaches fails to understand that these approaches consist of myriad foolish and contradictory assumptions that make them appealing only to the thoughtless. Commonsense approaches provide thinking similar to parents that might punish one child for starting a fight and later wisely say to the children that "it takes two to fight." The articulation between the two levels of analysis and causation is excruciatingly unclear and confused.

The first function of theory for family researchers is to provide conceptual definitions. Most researchers would be well served by general definitions for such terms as "relationships," "communication," and "family." When these terms are used in research they should be viewed as technical terms deserving of "stipulative" rather than "lexical" meaning. All too often, empirical researchers leave technical terms undefined or underdefined and count on the "commonsense" understanding of their audience. The study of cohabitation offers a fine example. In some cases, cohabitation has simply been defined as a couple living together for any length of time. In other cases, time duration such as at least six months is specified. Cohabitation in some countries (e.g., Canada) is equated with common law marriage, whereas in other countries (e.g., the United States) these two are considered distinctly different legal statuses. Cohabitation is often tacitly conceptualized as heterosexual, yet in the absence of marriage it constitutes the major form of domestic arrangement for homosexual partners. There is even more ambiguity about the place of sexual activity in cohabitation, such as if a cohabiting relationship can be platonic or asexual. Finally, over the last 50 years, the meaning of cohabitation in the commonsense world has changed dramatically. This brings up the problem of conceptual equivalence (see Straus, 1969) over periods and cohorts. Indeed, the researcher in this area would be well served by using theories of relationships or even normative theory. They have not been well served by the use of common sense and common culture.

A second function theory serves for the researcher is to supply focus. A particular theory will focus research sufficiently so that competing theories would be eliminated as explanations. Theory focuses and delimits so that disproof may indeed occur. This is such an ingrained part of science that it is enshrined as the null hypothesis. If we adopt commonsense approaches, however, we may end up disproving that one child started the fight although we want to assert the commonsense alternative that it takes two to fight. It is far better to ask theory to push our thinking to deeper levels in regard to both causations and levels of analysis. It may be true that individual A did not start the fight, but that does not imply that causation is at another level of analysis. This is a complex claim and should be treated as such by both theorist and researcher.

A third function for research is to supply relevant mathematical models that are consistent expressions of propositions in theories. Of course, not all theories have mathematical models attached to them; however, the two I have discussed in this book—rational choice and transition theory—each may boast a host of models. Some of these models may be causal (role transitions), and others may be stochastic (Poisson for rational choice and Markov for family stages). Although researchers need not be constrained to only these models, they may use such models as springboards to other consistent models. As researchers move to theoretically specified models, we can see that the days of the singular conceptual hypothesis are limited. Indeed, Pedhazur and Schmelkin (1991) state,

> This view of tests of single hypotheses serving as building blocks for the accumulation of knowledge that will ultimately lead to the construction of theories is, we believe, as sterile as the hope that an accumulation of facts will lead to a meaningful theory. (p. 185)

A fourth function is to provide an intellectual culture. This would be an intellectual culture in which theorists and researchers discuss conceptualization and research opportunities. I want to share an anecdote with you to illustrate this point. A few years ago, I was giving a presentation on theory to esteemed colleagues and graduate students. At the beginning of the presentation, I reminded the audience that they compose today's intellectuals in this area. I was surprised that my use of the word "intellectuals" seemed to evoke shifting in seats and looking to the floor. Subsequently, I tried using the term "intellectuals" with other such audiences only to discover what many of you may already know. We as a culture do not seem comfortable with this nomenclature when it refers to ourselves. I doubt, however, that social science or science can proceed very far if it does not see itself as somewhat removed and at odds with the commonsense and vernacular world. The history of science has taught us that commonsense ideas are very persistent in the lay population. Recall that it wasn't until the 20th century that the Catholic church officially accepted that the sun was not the center of the universe, and even today we still find a few folks who believe in a flat world. Theory helps promote an intellectual culture among researchers and helps encourage them to think beyond the limits of lay conceptions and commonsense interpretations. This function is most critical to the social sciences, where common sense has passed for theory for much too long.

A fifth function is interpretation. After the data are collected and analyzed and reported in the "results" section of a paper or journal article, it is time for interpretation. The most important part of the interpretation is to relate the results to the major theories in an area. It is the interpretation that makes sense of the data. For example, even if data seem to confirm the original model, the interpretation needs to consider places where anomalies exist that might be explained by other theories. In addition, a larger theoretical perspective might be brought to bear by changing levels of analysis and theoretical contexts. For example, the study of divorce is well served by studies of individual marital quality, dyadic interaction, normative theory, and global changes to conjugal family systems. Although it take two to divorce (dyadic), we all realize that changing social norms, barriers to divorce, and alternative attractors, are all implicated. Clearly, to explain divorce requires a conscientiously constructed multilevel theory.

This discussion could continue on to even more functions that theory serves for researchers, but the preceding discussion provides a picture of how this discussion might unfold. It is more productive at this point to ask how we ended up with such a sharp distinction between theory and research. There are several culprits in this regard, and although I will not pretend to be exhaustive I do believe certain of these have had more effect in separating into two camps what should be one marriage.

Probably the single biggest contributor to this separation of theory and research is from funding agencies. Funding agencies have tended to want research funded that would achieve socially acceptable ends and not be an embarrassment. As a result, funding agencies have sometimes focused on research that addresses problems or hypotheses that "everyone" will view as important. Of course scholars are consulted, but after decades of politicians discussing how research is a "golden fleece" of the public purse most granting agencies are cautious. This caution has extended to the desire to have simple and understandable research. Social science theory, in contrast, has become increasingly complex and abstract. Nowhere is this more true than with theoretically driven research.

A second reason why we have a separation is that journals have wanted to have more space for more articles. In an effort to shorten papers it has often been the theoretical parts that are lost. In the physical sciences, the theory is reasonably well developed, and indeed there are esteemed specializations such as "theoretical physics" and "theoretical microchemistry" that have their own conferences and resources. However, the cutting of theory sections in social science journals managed to abruptly halt and discourage theoretical development.

A third reason for the separation is that if we only have to mention or cite the relevant theory in a research paper, we open such references to those who are theoretically glib or superficial. For example, "social capital" is commonly used to justify research, yet this is not a theory but simply a concept. Furthermore, it is a concept that can only be applied to certain levels of analysis. I have seen this concept variously applied to communities and to marriage rather than the individual. This may or may not be justified, but it certainly is not a clear and obvious extension of the concept to these other levels of analysis. Such extensions need to be explained within the broader framework of the theory that accompanies this concept, rather than just cited.

A fourth reason is that scholars, especially in the area of the family, are seldom trained in theory courses. Klein and I did an informal survey of theory courses at the undergraduate and graduate level prior to the writing of the first volume of *Family Theories*. We noted with surprise that although some of the outstanding graduate schools have theory courses, almost an equal number had no such courses. The lack of training leads students—who later become faculty—to have little tolerance for theory when they get funded and published on the basis of common sense, folk wisdom, and popular psychology. The lack of training shows up in regrettable ways. A few years ago I did a paper on Coleman's concept of family structure in the context of rational choice theory. I sent the paper to a major journal publishing family material and received a review back saying that Coleman was not a rational choice theorist! Certainly we cannot expect scholars to stay abreast of theoretical developments when it bears no relation to teaching, publications, or grants.

A fifth reason is the damage attributable to the formal theory construction movement. Scholars received the impression that doing theory was mechanical and rule governed, much like a paint-by-numbers set. The result was that history of science, philosophy of science, and history of theory was deemphasized. The rule-oriented approach also failed to emphasize that theory construction must be creative and insightful. To a certain extent, the view that theory could be constructed mechanically led a generation to assume that theory could be accomplished by statistical techniques such as LISREL. In many cases, the resulting claims for theory were extremely naïve. Moreover, the idea that theory is constructed by computers must be seen as the ultimate anti-intellectualism and the apex of the mechanistic view of theory construction.

Finally, we have entered an age of postmodern thinking where relativism and contextualism can conceal the absence of thought. Terminological obfuscation of what at best could be seen as meaningless statements has found harbor and protection under the terms "theory" and "philosophy." Certainly the most famous example of this was when Alan Sokal, a professor of physics at New York University, wrote an article parodying the language of postmodernists (*Transgressing the Boundaries: Toward a Transformative Hermeneutics of Quantum Gravity*) and submitted it to a postmodern journal where it was positively reviewed and subsequently published. This embarrassment exposed both the peer reviewers and the journal as not being able to detect nonsense when it is dressed in the garb of postmodern obfuscation.[1] But such sad fortune can only happen in an environment that has neglected the intellectual and theoretical training of its young scholars and views academic rewards as for those that are closest to common sense. Overall, then, reclaiming theory into the study of the family is absolutely necessary if we are ever to have a credible science of family. Even more important, regaining theory is the only way we will return to a truly intellectual bearing on the academic compass.

Formulating Testable Propositions and Credible Interpretations

This section deals with suggestions for ways to integrate theory and research. As Burr and Nesselroade (1990) state, "no methodological procedure will substitute for the fundamental necessity of integrating theory and research design" (p. 16). However, my following discussion is much broader than just research design. This discussion entails not only suggestions for integration but also argues that family publication outlets must focus on the production of knowledge. Indeed, there should be two parts to every empirical paper. The first part should come before the research and before design. It should be the tie-in between the research question and theory. The second part should be the interpretation of the findings. These two would be distinctly different: the first is monothematic and the second is multithematic. This point is clarified in the following discussion.

Producing Testable Propositions

There are several routes a researcher may take to produce testable theoretical propositions. Certainly the classic model for producing testable propositions is to deduce a consequence or conclusion from existing propositions. For example, if there are theoretical propositions asserting that *families with high cohesion have greater social stability*, and *members of groups with high social cohesion have lower rates of suicide*, then we could deduce that *members of families with high cohesion have lower suicide rates*.[2] Perhaps this is the way that some philosophers of science and even some family scholars believe that theoretical hypotheses should be derived. Admittedly this is one of the ways; however, most of the researchers I have known do not work in such a linear and one-dimensional manner. Certainly most of the graduate students I have known would find this deductive approach unappealing.

The ways that theoretical propositions may be generated are numerous. To further complicate matters, the process that scholars and students use is often a complicated set of iterations among concepts, measures, other research, and their own interests. I will attempt to capture some of this diversity in the following descriptions. One thing is certain: There is no single prescribed way to generate theoretical hypotheses. It is much more a creative endeavor than a mechanical process.

One way that many researchers generate theoretical propositions is that they focus on a particular conceptual outcome. For example, researchers may focus on child well-being or on marital disruption. The next question that is often asked is in regard to our current knowledge about the causes of child well-being or marital stability. Usually researchers become intrigued by particular vacant areas in our knowledge or by anomalies in the empirical findings. The next stage is to begin to design a study that will address the missing knowledge or anomalies. It is often at this stage that researchers begin to ask what theories might say about this area. It is usually the case that the theories most used by empirical researchers are what could be called minitheories. For example, there might be a minitheory about the number of moves a child experiences during the school years and the child's academic performance (well-being). Moving might be discussed in terms of disruptions in social capital, but a more full-blown application of the rational choice theory is unlikely. Even researchers that conscientiously identify their research with a larger theoretical framework such as rational choice theory tend to use the theory as an orienting device rather than a set of propositions (see, for example, Haveman & Wolfe, 1994). The theoretical propositions that would eventually be tested are, at best, micropropositions.

Another type of approach researchers use to generate theoretical propositions is to formulate research that would test a number of theoretical consequences. The work by Biblarz and Gottainer (2000) offers an excellent example of this type of formulation. Biblarz and Gottainer were concerned with the different microtheories about the effects of family structure on child outcomes. They reviewed five different theoretical models that provide distinct interpretations of the concept of family structure. They are the family structure model, household economic model, evolutionary model, parental fitness model, and marital conflict model. Each of these models provides a different critical test of propositions. For example, if family structure is itself causal, then the structure should make a difference to child outcomes and not how the family got to that structure (e.g., via divorce or death in the case of single-parent structure). If the effect of family structure on child outcomes is actually due to marital conflict, then family structure should not explain variance in child outcomes when marital conflict is present in married and single-parent structures. Such studies as Biblarz and Gottainer go a step beyond the generation of micropropositions because they are analyzing competing theoretical hypotheses. Although the propositions they are generating are micropropositions, these propositions are generated so that they are consistent with the assumptions of larger theoretical frameworks. This generation of micromodels of larger theoretical propositions accompanied by the testing of the competing hypotheses does a great deal for not only sharpening our thinking but also empirical disconfirmation. Even though this is not a purely deductive exercise, it nonetheless goes even further by examining multiple theoretical models.

The last, though not exhaustive, example of generating theoretical proposition derives from a purely inductive approach. Researchers may have a research question in mind and want to use a set of analytic tools in their analysis. For example, researchers, like everyone else, experience fads where the latest methodological tool is seen as creating potential "breakthroughs" for knowledge. In the recent past, such fads have been exemplified by researchers wanting to use structural equation modeling and multilevel modeling. Sometimes this desire to use a technique may even overpower and modify the research question. Although I do not believe that statistical techniques alone can produce theory in some mechanistic manner, I have been impressed by the way that the proper conjunction of statistical technique, appropriate data, critical research questions, and creativity can reap enormous theoretical rewards (e.g., the development of life course theory and the statistical techniques of life table regression initiated by Cox, 1972). For example, Gottman's (1979) research using lagged probabilities to investigate marriage spring to mind, as does Lillard, Brien, and Waite's (1995) use of competing risks in the analysis of cohabitation. Both of these studies were able to move microtheories in these substantive areas in new directions. Gottman (1979) largely buried the *quid pro quo* microtheory of marital interaction, and Lillard et al. (1995) demonstrated that much of the effect of cohabitation on later marital stability is due to selection factors. Neither of these scholars was intensely theoretical, but their work—as all good empirical work—bears great theoretical import.

The picture I am drawing of the production of theoretical propositions by researchers is actually a very simple sketch. Theoretical propositions, or propositions with theoretical import, may emerge from both theoretically conscious research and from research that is more inductively and empirically grounded. To put this succinctly, there are so many ways that researchers produce theoretical propositions from empirical research that one should not offer any glib generalizations. What is apparent, however, is that much of this work remains at the substantive, microtheoretical level and needs to be compiled and integrated into the larger theoretical frameworks.

In addition, there is a distinct difference between research that is a conscientious application of theory and research that is more haphazard in its development of theoretical propositions. The difference resides not in the actual production of propositions so much as the theoretical power of what is produced. Research that begins with a theoretical set of propositions has the great advantage of designing tests so that various hypotheses may be tested and eliminated. For example, the Biblarz and Gottainer (2000) study was able to design tests so that effects of events such as divorce could be isolated from family structure. Such research does not just address one hypothesis, or a uniform collection of hypotheses where if one is false they are all false and all we know is that some hypotheses within the null hypotheses set might be true. Rather, Biblarz and Gottainer systematically examine the major hypotheses and the major alternatives. The set of null hypotheses only contained ones that were not yet developed as theoretical explanations. Of course, such research can only be designed when theory is conscientious and explicit. That is not to say that haphazard empirical work cannot produce theoretical propositions of interest but that such production may be more in the context of discovery than in the context of justification.

The context of discovery (as discussed in Chapter 3), in the present context, refers to the production of theoretical propositions. Within the context of discovery we find qualitative researchers, ethnomethodologists, and phenomenologists as well as quantitative empiricists. Certainly there are many ways to discover propositions. Furthermore, the genetic fallacy is what philosophers of science term the inappropriate judgment of ideas on the basis of how or from whence they originated. In contrast, the context of justification involves the logical coherence, testing, and empirical adequacy of the theory. It is especially this second stage of research where concern with research design should be overpowering. Indeed, the very nature of testing theory entails that the theory be explicit and conscientiously explicated so that such tests maximize the advancement of our thinking.

If we return to the theory-model-data triangle (Chapter 4, Figure 4.3), we find that explicit testing of theoretical propositions is well served by expressing those theories as models. The study of family may not be quite ready to detail theoretical models, although both of the substantive theories covered in the book (rational choice and transition theory) propose models for at least some of the major parts of the theory. Other theories may be further from this type of specification. However, as researchers separate their research into "discovery" and "justification," the emphasis and usefulness of such modeling will undoubtedly rise in popularity. The emphasis on explicit theoretical statements and modeling is, in many ways, tied to changing our reliance on *ex post facto* interpretation as the major use for theory in family studies.

Credible Interpretations

One of the most poorly understood areas of theory is interpretation (see the theory-model-data triangle, Chapter 4, Figure 4.3). Interpretation is also one of the most profound uses of theory. Interpretation is the *ex post facto* explanation of an event or occurrence. Because interpretation is *ex post facto,* there is no necessity to the explanation and any number of other possible interpretations are equally likely. Interpretation falls within the context of justification. A theory must be at a certain level of propositional development before it can be used to interpret diverse events or phenomena. However, the important function of interpretation does not reside so much in testing ideas as in providing a satisfactory *story* of what happened and why it happened. I think of this interpretive *story* as perhaps the most psychologically satisfying part of theory. It is also the aspect of theory that most people incorrectly identify as an "explanation." Its *ex post facto* nature makes it more equivalent to natural history than to predictive explanations.

Near the end of most empirical journal articles is a discussion and conclusion section. Usually in the discussion section of these articles is some interpretation of the results. Of course, if these studies were dealing exclusively with prediction, prospective designs, and experimental controls, all of which were specified by the theory, the results would be interpreted by the theory or its rejection. In much social science research the theory is less well developed and the methods are often survey-correlational designs. As a result, there is significant room for the *ex post facto* and *ad hoc* interpretation of the findings.

The problem we encounter, however, is that many interpretations are a mixture of commonsense assumptions, some theory, and some popular psychology. For example, I recently attended a symposium of family structure where the presenter interpreted findings about single-parent families and child well-being with a mixture of some rational choice theory and some propositions from popular psychology such as "when these single mothers return home they are tired and parenting is a lonely endeavor." Certainly such attributions about loneliness may be true, but the use of such commonsense or popular psychology is then mixed with the theory to interpret behavior. As a result of this mixture, interpretations take on the tone and character of many daytime talk show hosts or hostesses. It furthermore gives social science the additional and unneeded epitaph of just being common sense, folk wisdom, and popular psychology.

Credible interpretations would delete these commonsense and popular psychological notions from interpretation. This might force theorists and researchers alike to reexamine the adequacy of some theories to offer credible stories without recourse to folk wisdom. Indeed, some theories lack one or more of the ingredients necessary for such interpretation. For example, transition theory, as I discussed in Chapter 5, makes the assumption that individuals are motivated to follow the norms; however, there is not an explicit theory of motivation that would tie in with the normative theory. This of course would mean crossing levels of analysis from individual motivation to normative content. The theory doesn't do this. However, there is a danger in that theorists or researchers might be tempted to interpret the missing element of motivation by using folk psychology, such as assuming "of course people want to fit in," or "naturally, people will tend to conform." In such cases, the theory and the research are both poorly served by invoking this *deus ex machina* to salvage and flesh out what is an incomplete theory. Furthermore, it raises the criticism that the social sciences are more social than science. That is, the social sciences just tell us what everybody already knows. (For an alternative view, see Daly, 2003.)

So although interpretation serves an essential function for theory and understanding by providing a plausible story as to how and why something happened, it is also ripe for abuse. When social scientists stop using folk wisdom for interpretations, we will be able to more clearly see the inadequacies in a given theory and to begin to address those inadequacies. Another way to get a picture of the deficiencies of a theory is to use some form of metatheoretical analysis.

Metatheoretical Analysis

One way that researchers and theorists can identify the incomplete or partially formulated areas in a theory is to use metatheoretical analysis (Klein & Jurich, 1993). Metatheoretical analysis can also identify theoretical formulations from other theories that may assist in filling the gap. In the previous example of transition theory, I noted that a theory of motivation was missing from the individual level. Although it is tempting to address such shortcomings using folk wisdom and commonsense concepts, theorists and researchers should really address shortcomings by developing propositions in these areas. Continuing with the example from transition theory, some other theory might offer a formulation of motive that is consistent and coherent with transition theory. For example, one candidate would be Coleman's formulation of rational choice at the individual level and his treatment of the production of norms from the externalities of individual action. Although some of the assumptions might be at odds, this conflict would become conscious and explicit rather than concealed behind generations of folk psychology.

Metatheory is a theory about theories. For example, Turner (1991) used concepts such as the macro–micro distinction and assumptions to produce a metatheoretical classification of theories. Others, such as Martindale (1979), used schemas that included whether theories used mechanistic or organic analogies. Pepper (1942) used the categories of formism, contextualism, mechanistism, and organicism to organize theories.

Each metatheoretical system is organized by emphasizing certain dimensions rather than others. For example, Martindale (1979) argues that underlying each theory is a dominant metaphor that, when identified, allows us to see the coherence of the theory more clearly. This argument is very similar to that made more recently by Lakoff and Johnson (1999). Not all metatheory is necessarily in agreement with this metaphorical stance. For example, Klein and White (1996) proposed that we can identify a large number of critical dimensions to theory, and proceeded to identify what they regard as some of the more salient dimensions for family theories. This more flexible position allows researchers and theorists to emphasize dimensions that are meaningful for their particular purposes.

The Klein and White (1996) approach initially identified three dimensions that have some general usefulness for theorists and researchers. These dimensions are not the only ones that can be used, nor are they necessarily the best for all purposes, but their model does let us demonstrate the way in which these metatheoretical models work. The first dimension Klein and White identify is causation. They point out that when the family behavior is considered, most theories either see causes emanating from within the family group or from the larger society. Causes emanating from within the family group might be due to an especially efficacious individual or family members' interactions. However, macroscopic forces, such as economic changes and normative culture, may affect the family. In general, we can categorize theories by whether they mainly conceptualize family change as endogenous to the family or exogenous to the family.

The second dimension considered in the Klein and White model is time. Theories differ markedly in how they deal with time. For example, exchange and rational choice theories tend to emphasize a very static notion of time. In these static perspectives, an exchange or choice may be made, but it is considered as isolated and distinct and not part of an overall process. When time is considered in such theories, it is simply to consider choices or exchanges at more than one time point. Such an approach just adds a dash of time to the *static* theory in hopes that will do. In contrast, other theories identify time as a process. Such theories are called *dynamic* because they treat time as a property of the process. For example, White (1991) defines family development as stage and duration dependence. Furthermore, this definition of the process is modeled by a continuous-time model called a "semi-Markov" process. Likewise, ecological theories tend to see processes of adaptation and selection as dynamic. So the dimension of time divides theories into those that are predominantly static and those that are dynamic.

The third dimension identified by Klein and White (1996) is the focal level of analysis. Many theories focus on one level of analysis to the exclusion of others. For example, there is little doubt that Coleman's rational choice theory, with its assumption of methodological individualism, is focused primarily on the individual level. At the same time, transition theory is clearly more focused on the effects of norms at several levels and might best be considered a societal or macrolevel theory. Although Klein and White (1996) originally used individual, dyadic, family, and societal levels of analysis, it is a little less cumbersome to simply identify theories as using either methodological individualism or holism.

Table 8.1 shows these dimensions in tabular form with some examples of theories in the body of the table.

Table 8.1 represents some of the major theoretical frameworks discussed in White and Klein (2002). This table is not meant as definitive but as an illustration of how metatheory can be useful. For example, if we desired to "round out" a theory that is exogenous and dynamic, we might pick a complementary category, such as static and individualistic. A finer, more detailed examination would reveal that we might add a theory of motivation to normative theories or vice versa. The initial use of such metatheoretical models is simply to alert researchers and theorists as to which theories might cover material that would be useful in other theories that neglect these areas. It is

Table 8.1   Three-Dimensional Metatheory of Family Theories

| Level of Analysis | Causation | | | |
| | Endogenous | | Exogenous | |
	Static Time	*Dynamic*	*Static*	*Dynamic*
Individualism	Exchange & rational choice	Symbolic interaction	Role theory	Feminism
Holism		Systems theory	Conflict	Ecological and transition theory

always necessary, of course, to move to detailed examination of various formulations of theories and to create increasingly detailed metatheoretical models to add the requisite detail.

Metatheory also provides a way of taking stock of theoretical progress and weaknesses in the diversity of theorizing. For example, viewing Table 8.1 it is fairly obvious that no theories appear in some categories. For example, the holistic-endogenous-static cell is empty. That would be a theory that sees the family as causal but does not allow dynamics to occur. The reason this cell is empty is that it would almost be contradictory for such a theory to be proposed.

Table 8.1 represents a relatively subjective and somewhat arbitrary set of judgments. Indeed, there is a need for the development of methods that could be commonly adopted to generate such dimensions. In the absence of such agreement on methods, metatheory continues to be useful to elucidate how individual scholars and teams of scholars view the theoretical landscape of their substantive area.

Conclusion

This chapter has focused on some of the problems in the articulation of and cooperation between theory and research. It is tempting to take the current disjunction between theory and research as more significant than it is. I would argue that although the disjunction is important, empirical researchers are quite capable of producing modest low-level theory about particular phenomena. Furthermore, theorists are equally capable of reviewing the masses of empirical studies and generating more general propositions. What is truly missing from the picture is the conscientious testing of theoretical propositions that would refine, reform, and refute theoretical propositions. Part of the missing element is that the testing and modeling of theory would propel empirical research to become increasingly sophisticated in terms of research design so that multiple theoretical models could be tested. While the current situation will do, it is less than optimal. Optimism would support the argument that the next generation of researchers and theorists may be better at addressing these issues than the current generation. I believe there is every reason for optimism.

Notes

1. For the full debate, see www.physics.nyu.edu/faculty/sokal or Koertge, 1998.
2. This is assuming that these relations are monotonically linear and transitive.

9

Theory and Human Values

Contextualism and relativism in theory, as found in many postmodern statements, is often though not exclusively associated with the call for researchers to put their values into science (Allen, 2000; White & Marshall, 2001). For many of us, this cry to put values back into our science and research raises thorny problems—such as whose values, and the issue of bias and credibility (Harding, 1991). The problem is not that science was ever value free, a claim even Weber (1949) dismissed, but that the values now being advocated would take us further from the production of knowledge rather than closer. I think real progress is only achieved when scholars research what they find interesting or fun or of value. It is essential, however, that we shouldn't confuse the values or goals in the context of discovery with those in the context of justification, and I believe that is exactly the current state of the discussion.

Broadly conceived, the context of discovery concerns the production of propositions and the context of justification concerns the testing of propositions. In previous chapters (e.g., Chapter 3), it was admitted that new propositions could evolve out of testing of other propositions so that the line between these two "contexts" is not absolute. However, the distinction between these "contexts" is most useful in regard to sorting out the thorny issues of theory, ideology, and values.

A natural place to begin the discussion about values is first with the notion of "values" and second with a discussion of the critical values that propel scientific theory. When we talk about values it is important to realize that we are focusing on the sliding scale of valuation of objects, ideas, and beliefs. How valuable these ideas and beliefs are to us may be a function of situation, world view, religion, or any number of other variables. Basically, our valuation is equivalent to the importance or salience of the ideas and beliefs to us. For many of us, our values need not be consistent with one another nor do we demand they represent a coherent system of valuation. They only need to be a ranking of one idea or belief as more important or more preferred than another.

Theory always contains values (Knorr-Cetina, 1981, 1999; Longino, 1990, 2002). When we theorize about something, we select our subject over other subjects. Although this might not be solely an expression of values, it just as easily could be an expression of values. Indeed, the very definition of theory, as a set of systematically connected general propositions used to explain phenomena, emphasizes that we value this type of knowledge rather than idiographic and particularistic descriptions. Emphasizing that propositions are systematically connected demonstrates a valuing of logic and coherence. Certainly we could provide justification for these values but we would, in the final analysis, justify these values by even higher-order values. We could argue that without laws of noncontradiction we couldn't make sense of anything and "making sense" is a value. We could further argue that generalizations are efficient and parsimonious. However, such attempts at justification lead eventually to infinite regress of one reason after another until we arrive at primitive or core values.

It might be easier to understand the relation of values to theory by turning the preceding discussion around. Ultimately, we favor theory because we value generalizations and coherence and explanation. This is as much a world view as it is a methodology. However, most scientists are trained in this world view and system of values. From a symbolic interaction perspective, those who are willing to play the game must share the rules and those who play must abide by the rules of the game. But the rules regarding scientific theory are methodological rules tied to the major goal of science, which is explanation.

Epistemic Values

Explanation may be the major goal of science, but anyone could argue that other more moral goals such as the "betterment" of humanity should be the major goals of science. Indeed, the goal of explanation would yield one type of science and the goal of human betterment would yield a vastly different type of science. The issue is not that one goal has greater intrinsic value but that in regard to explanation the solution is via methodological agreement, or what Allchin (1998) calls "epistemic values."

Epistemic values are values regarding the nature and production of knowledge. Such values can be contrasted with cultural or normative values that affirm a valued good in itself. Epistemic values are values that simultaneously are about the process of producing scientific knowledge and are justified by the goal of science: explanation. When explanation is understood as a "covering law" model, some of the values are largely the subject of instrumental and methodological debate. There is, however, a core of epistemic values.

The core of epistemic values for science has to do with the process. This process has been described by Merton (1973) as characterized by values on skepticism, universalism, open communication, and evidence. Allchin (1998) adds that "honesty" in research and reporting must be considered a prime value in science. So although some canons of methodology in science are debatable, core values of honesty, skepticism, and universalism are essential if scientific theories are to provide "explanation."

At a somewhat broader level, the epistemic values also ensure a social function for the greater society. This function is to provide the social system with credible evidence. Obviously, credible and reliable evidence has to be valued within the larger culture and society. As we know from our brief historical review, this value on credible evidence has often been sacrificed to other values and beliefs such as religion (Galileo's recant of heliocentrism) and political beliefs (eugenics in Nazi Germany). Indeed, the worry expressed by Gross and Levitt (1994) that postmodernist relativism is returning our culture to the "dark ages," where superstition and supernaturalism are viewed as being as valid as scientific claims, is testament to the view that cultural values ebb and flow in their support of credible knowledge.

Human Betterment and Theory

In contrast, the goal of human betterment is quite a different sort of goal. For example, we could argue for material betterment or spiritual betterment (see Bubolz & Sontag, 1993). We could argue about what is "better." Indeed, we would find these arguments would lead us into two areas in the philosophy of ethics, meta-ethics and normative ethics (see Hospers, 1967). I believe we would also find that the values about "betterment" would focus on the meaning of "good" or "right" conduct as a property of goodness. The discussions of explanation, however, would say a "good" explanation is one that satisfies the consensually developed methodological criteria and not the moral or ethical criteria.

Despite having said this, I would argue that good theory and propositions, methodologically speaking, might come from any area *including* the moral area of discourse. To believe otherwise would be to commit the "genetic fallacy" of judging propositions by their origin. Thus the context of discovery is quite open to the development of value-laden theory, ideology,[1] and belief. As a consequence, however, the context of justification becomes even more important because it is the area that determines the empirical and logical adequacy of these propositions.

It is exactly the context of justification, the evaluation of the empirical testing, and logical coherence of a theory that determine if the theory is a "good" explanation as measured by the consensual "epistemic" values and standards of the community of scientists. This is to posit that the evaluation of "good" is not a statement of moral or esthetic good, but a statement of "fit" with the standards of science in exactly the same way that we would describe a "good" high jump or a "good" job. So science values the goal of explanation and the methodological principles to judge the achievement of those goals. This goal is consensual and therefore can be changed and modified. It should be clear by this point in the argument, however, that in order for theories to be evaluated, the methodology of the context of justification must remain coherent and universal.

This is not to say that the rules in the context of justification do not undergo change and modification. Changes in the criteria for the context of justification will change as technical, methodological, and theoretical changes occur. Certainly changing the consensus of the community of scholars in any discipline is a slow and phlegmatic process. But one thing should be clear. The statements that scientists judge in the context of justification are statements such as "It is raining" or "Rebecca is combing her hair." Such statements are qualitatively distinct from moral discourse, where statements such as "Rebecca *should* comb her hair" compose the subject at hand. The changes in the criteria for justification deal with correct methods and techniques, not with right and wrong.

Ideology always contains values; however, the values in ideology are tied to different types of outcomes rather than explanation. Most ideologies not only state the desired goal or outcome but describe the current state of affairs and what is needed as a process or program of action to achieve the desired outcome. For example, liberal feminism describes the current state of affairs as "patriarchy," the method of change is legislation and equality rights, and the desired outcome is gender equality. However, when feminists argue that the outcome of "good" theory must be to liberate and empower women (e.g., Gordon, 1979; Osmond & Thorne, 1993), one wonders if this value might possibly come into conflict with credible science and which value would be supreme. Likewise, Marx viewed the current status as class struggle, the process of change was dialectical materialism, and the outcome was communism.

Although many ideologies propose that action is explained by the goal or outcome and hence could be viewed as teleological, ideologies are quite capable of offering theoretical propositions about the processes and the interpretation of the current state of affairs without becoming teleological. For example, we can examine sources of class conflict as they relate to social change without viewing the social change as necessarily attached to the final goal of communism, nor do scientists need to become Marxist to use these propositions regarding social change. As such, ideology can be a valuable source of propositions for theories of social change.

Ethics always contains values. The study of ethical values is often divided into meta-ethics, normative ethics, and applied ethics (Hospers, 1967). Although there are theories of ethics (usually known as metatheory), these theories are very distinct from scientific theories. The goal of ethical theory (metatheory and normative) is to establish what is "good" behavior and what is "bad" behavior. The complexity of these moral discriminations is intriguing. For example, if we help feed someone today, are we contributing to the person's long-range dependency and lack of independence? Is independence always a good, or can some forms be bad? Is there a universal prescriptive law (such as the Golden Rule or Kant's categorical imperative) that can be applied to moral judgments in all areas? As interesting as such questions may be, they clearly are not questions resolved by science. As scientists we might provide credible information and knowledge that would assist in developing arguments, but the final resolution is a question of adequate scientific facts and of human values and morals.

Producing arguments in favor of values or moral positions is, I think, outside what one can expect science to do. Philosophy, ideology, and religion all produce value positions. This is not to say that the context of discovery is value free, because it is not. Furthermore, the consensually defined context of justification will contain social values inherent in any historical period. Nonetheless, the goal of science is to produce knowledge and not moral discourse. As such, we can demand of social scientists that they hold the highest standards possible at any point in our social development to facilitate the production of credible knowledge.

Application and Social "Good"

The place that values, ideology, and scientific knowledge all come together is in application or treatment. If the principal goal of science is explanation, one of its principal uses is in achieving social goals. For example, we use social scientific knowledge to try to curb child abuse or to develop stronger marriages. However, it is important to distinguish between good knowledge (a methodological question) and good action (a moral or ideological action).

A contemporary example may make this clearer. The current political administration in the United States has recently announced a program aimed at keeping marriages together. The value that is at stake is eliminating harm to children and adults. Marital breakdown is seen as harmful to children and as affecting the health of adults. Furthermore, the economic savings could be considerable. Now, this is a matter of values. Who would not want to alleviate suffering and promote health in a population as well as save public money?

Science comes into this when we ask if it is the marital breakdown that hurts children or the parental conflict, and likewise, if it is the marital breakdown or the reduction of resources after the breakdown (Amato, 2000). For example, if marriages that have high conflict are kept together, does that still reduce the harm to the children? It is when we get to cause and effect that we expect responsible and credible answers from science. We would not want these answers to be based on whether the scientist is a Republican or a Democrat, a feminist or a Communist. In other words, we want good, credible science (methodology) so that we can do good acts (ideology and morality). Indeed, good intentions informed by less than credible information and theory are a waste of resources and potentially a contributor to immoral acts.

Note

1. A systematic body of concepts and goals that constitute a sociopolitical program.

10

Conclusion: Theories as
Tools for Studying Families

What has been achieved in this book? Are we any closer to understanding how we produce credible knowledge and the way in which theories of family are advancing our knowledge? I think the answer is that a great deal has been achieved. In order to understand how far we have come, it is useful to briefly review the journey.

Chapter 1 introduced a definition of theory and discussed why we need theories about *families* rather than theories about the more generic *social group*. In Chapter 2, we reviewed the history of family theory. It was in this second chapter that we encountered the theory constructionists of the 1960s and 1970s. Although this movement resulted in some theoretical advances in some areas (see Chapter 7), it also had the consequence of making theory and theorizing a mechanical process, a process similar to paint by numbers. There was scant emphasis on creativity and insight. Indeed, this mechanistic view led some researchers to even claim that mathematical models such as structural equation modeling could produce theory. Not only were such claims unjustified, but they were potentially damaging in that some of that generation were led to conclude that theory is nothing more than rampant empirical inductionism aided by a mathematical model. As a consequence, we entered the 1990s and the new millennium with little consensus on directions for family theory or even methods for "doing" family theory. Whether this is referred to by Cheal (1991) as a "parology" of theory or cited as the threat of postmodernism to the development of theory (White, 1997) makes little difference at this point. What is important is that family theory appears confused and only vaguely directed toward the goal of producing knowledge.

The third chapter actually addresses Kuhn's (1970) general premise about science and scientific theory. This chapter is unlike so many discussions of Kuhn's arguments in that it neither directly addresses each of Kuhn's arguments nor moves to address what some still champion as the most compelling argument, "incommensurability" (e.g., Longino, 2002). Rather, Chapter 3 approaches this subject from a much more fundamental concern. Kuhn's history of science was selective and focused on the last 300 years. Even more upsetting is the assumption Kuhn seemed to make, that chemistry and physics provide the best models for the development of science. This assumption implied that all sciences progressed in the same way and that only the prescientific social sciences had failed to move into this monolithic and monotonic progression. Of course, such monotonic views of economic and social development were rejected by social scientists in the 1950s, but somehow such views were still current in the history of science espoused by Kuhn. This third chapter simply challenges this position by presenting a broader perspective on science; a perspective that includes the taxonomic advances of human prehistory along with the advances in the 19th century in geography and biology. Indeed, a broader perspective on science frees up our perspective on theory because we no longer feel the need to demonstrate our "science" by mathematical models alone. This frees us up to think about our theory.

Chapter 4 continues this quest to unravel some assumptions of history and philosophy of science that have so bound thinking about theory. Some of this "unraveling" is simply accomplished by making important distinctions such as "context of discovery" and "context of justification" (Kaplan, 1964). Such distinctions help us gain some organization and classification of arguments. But the major theme in Chapter 4 is that much of what we do in science is best understood as a series of mappings from a familiar domain to a less familiar range. In other words, much of what we do in science can properly be understood as metaphor (e.g., Black, 1962; Lakoff & Johnson, 1980, 1999). For some this statement might seem to reduce the importance or significance of theory. I would argue, however, that this is far from the case. It is much easier to see what theory does for us when we talk about it as metaphor. This is not to say that the discussion of metaphors or the many forms of metaphor is a simple matter. But seeing theory as metaphor helps us readily understand what an explanation is and therefore what a theory does for us.

Chapter 5 details the purposes and functions that theory serves in the social sciences. These are discussed using the lens of metaphor to show how these functions actually work. The types of theory are discussed, in part, to prepare the ground for introducing the two substantive theories in the chapters to follow.

Chapter 6 presents the first of two substantive theories of the family. Rational choice theory in the hands of one of its most well-known and competent sociological proponents, Coleman, reflects the great advances made in this area throughout the 1980s at the University of Chicago. Becker's 1990 Nobel Prize was in part awarded for his work extending microeconomic theory into previously emotional areas such as family (*Treatise on the Family*). Coleman's (1990) treatment of rational choice demonstrated how benefits that can only be acquired by group action can be explained from a standpoint of methodological individualism. Furthermore, Coleman's discussion of social capital in regard to the family is one of the most useful theoretical and formal approaches to explaining child outcomes. Finally, Coleman's discussion of the limits of rational choice by what he terms "primordial" relationships is one of the most thought-provoking reflections on the scope and boundaries of this theory.

Chapter 7 presents a very different type of theory. Whereas much of rational choice could be seen as static and dominated by the assumption of methodological individualism, transition theory is dynamic and practices methodological holism. As such, it provides a wonderful and bold counterpoint to rational choice. Furthermore, whereas rational choice is largely a motivational theory, transition theory is normative. Transition theory has been formally developed as both propositions and models by White (1991), Rodgers and White (1993), Bengtson and Allen (1993), and White and Klein (2002). The theory is a composite of various normative theories focusing on different levels of analysis. Each of these levels is linked to the other levels through the concept of norms. This theory traverses family-related behavior from role transitions to macrosocial change. It incorporates time as both event histories in real time and as period and cohort analyses.

These two theories do not only provide clear and distinct comparisons in regard to motivation, levels of analysis, and assumptions. The important part of the picture provided in this section might be easily missed. The point is that these two theories represent tools for researchers. Neither is a set of "true beliefs," but each of these theories provides researchers with relatively consistent and coherent metaphors to explain phenomena. This point is perhaps best made in Chapter 8.

Chapter 8 is concerned with the disjunction between empirical research and theory in the area of the family. Although this separation is a concern, it does not mean that empirical researchers alone cannot produce theoretical propositions. It is just that the propositions produced in this manner tend to be at a low level of generality and are not integrated into areas of knowledge other than the specific area from which they were generated. In Chapter 8 I lay out several arguments as to what theory can do for the empirical researcher and the field of inquiry. At the conclusion of this chapter is a suggestion for how to use metatheory to identify the ways in which theories might complement one another. For example, rational choice provides an account of the production of norms that might be useful at some levels of transition theory. The overview here is again that theories are tools for researchers and theorists.

Finally, Chapter 9 clarifies the role of the scientist in relation to value systems such as ideology, religion, and morals. Science and scientists are not value free or even value neutral, but the type of values expressed in science are qualitatively different from those in other areas such as moral discourse. The values in science are epistemic values—values that focus on good methodology for the outcome of credible knowledge—rather than values about outcomes such as the betterment of mankind or the achievement of equality. However, I argue that for any moral action to have the desired effect, it must be informed by credible information and knowledge. Producing such knowledge is the goal of science.

Theories as Tools for Understanding

Throughout this book, I have argued in various ways that theory is different from belief. I have also argued that theory is not "the Truth" but is simply a tentative proposition we hold until a more useful proposition is devised. And in this final section I have introduced the metaphor that theory is a tool. This position may seem familiar to those readers familiar with the pragmatism of Peirce (1905; see also Apel, 1981) or the instrumentalism of Dewey (1929). I am less confident in the inclusion of Rorty (1982) in this camp, as is the eminent epistemologist Haack (1993, 1998). Rather than confound those who are not familiar with this position, and to make sure I properly identify the position, I will spend a few of the closing pages of this book describing this account of theory.

A tool is a physical implement with a purpose contained in its design. A screwdriver is designed to fit certain types of screws (i.e., slot or Phillips). Although the purpose of a screwdriver is clearly to drive screws, that is not to say that any user cannot innovate and use the tool in ways for which it was not expressly designed. Even though these other uses may not be the primary focus, the tool may nonetheless function for opening a paint can, as a pry bar, and as a stir stick. The only limitation on the ways we can use the tool is our imagination and the actual physical construction of the tool. Of course, the tool (screwdriver) must always serve its original purpose, because if it ceases to be able to drive screws, it ceases to be a screwdriver. A scientific theory that ceases to explain cannot claim that it is a theory.

Theories are nonetheless like tools. They do not contain the truth, nor is the user's belief in the theory's truth a requisite for its use. Theories are coherent clusters of ideas that explain phenomena. A good theory is one that explains phenomena and hence produces knowledge. However, as all tools need replacing with time, so do scientific theories. At some point, theories do not explain anomalies or new discoveries and some other group of ideas does so more convincingly. At such points the theory is replaced. That is not to say that these theories do not continue to function in other capacities, such as illustrating incorrect directions science has stumbled along as, for example, with the chemistry theories of phlogiston and ether.

Although the principal purpose of theory is to produce knowledge, theories as tools may also be used in innovative ways. A scientific theory that is further developed to assist in family therapy might provide sound academic explanations. Likewise, an academic theory might provide guidance to practitioners. The design of the theory, however, is to explain a phenomenon, and the resulting innovation is serendipitous but not necessarily a matter of conscious design—much like the screwdriver is not consciously designed to pry paint cans open.

Whenever I go to my local tool store, some clerk is always trying to sell me a newly designed tool that is "three tools in one" or "does it all." Despite my wariness about such claims, I have been an optimistic supporter, only to be later disappointed with these wonder tools and to return to the basic tools. This experience leads me to reflect unfavorably on attempts to unify all of family theory. Each theory has assumptions and concepts that construct its intellectual shape as a tool. Sometimes these may be used in a complementary fashion such as when I turn a screwdriver with a pair of pliers. This does not mean that from that point on I can use the two tools in conjunction. Indeed, often the pliers would just be in the way of the functioning of the screwdriver. I think this analogy holds for theory, though I am certainly willing to listen to arguments about prospects for a single unified grand theory of the family.

Finally, the "theory as tool" metaphor can only be stretched so far. At some point each of these classes, tools and theories, have unique elements that defy a complete mapping of one to the other. That is when the metaphor of theory as tool breaks down. Thus, as with most ways of understanding, this metaphor serves us well in only some and not all situations. But it is my opinion that at the current junction in family theory this metaphor will serve us well for some time to come.

The Equivocation Between Explanation and Understanding

It is tempting to say that two roads lie in front of us. One road is the road of traditional science as applied to the study of individuals and social groups such as the family and emphasizing nomothetic explanation. The other road, well trodden over the last four decades by phenomenologists, critical theorists, critical feminists, and deconstructionists, emphasizes the qualitative nature of understanding. Many scholars see the two roads in sharp contrast to one another and argue that students and scholars must choose one or the other. However, choosing one over the other, in my view, would be a disaster for theory and for the social sciences. Such a choice would also be inconsistent with the arguments in this book.

One of the major points in this book is in regard to Kaplan's distinction between the context of discovery and the context of justification. The "genetic fallacy" in the context of discovery is to judge ideas on the basis of how they were generated. There is no way to judge an idea on the basis of its genesis. Furthermore, if ideas help us understand phenomena, they then are functioning as useful *post hoc* metaphors. However, it is the task of the canons of scientific justification, both logical coherence and empirical adequacy, to establish a theory as knowledge. In the context of justification, we find that the "ideas" do predict and explain.

The point is that both of these contexts are necessary for science. There should be little doubt that the context of discovery is enriched by diversity of methods, approaches, and thinking. In family theory, this diversity includes ideology, qualitative research, case studies, literature, and even poetry. For example, personal retrospectives, such as those offered by Marks (2000), provide insights into privilege and education in the United States in the 1960s that might initiate theories about cohort effects to explain intergenerational changes in SAT scores. Indeed, the diversity of ideas we find in the context of discovery is very rich.

Sometimes the richness and understanding found in the context of discovery is used to make claims about the context of justification. For example, O'Connor and O' Neill (2000) state,

There are several aspects of qualitative methodologies that lend themselves to research with emancipatory goals and purposes. First, qualitative methodologies tend to move beyond a positivist frame of reference which advocates that there is only one, "true" reality. Instead, the notion of multiple realities is introduced. This concept opens the space for hearing the voices of others because it recognizes that in order to fully understand a particular phenomenon or process, ascertaining the perspectives of those who have experienced it is essential. (p. 1)

Indeed "ascertaining the perspectives of those who experienced it is essential" for understanding but not for evidence or assertions that are needed in court, or for evidence required to convince bureaucrats to develop programs, or for social scientists to produce general theory. In the context of discovery, we do not dictate the methods that are used to produce theoretical propositions. But in the context of justification, the claims that are held to be "knowledge" should have been demonstrated to be logically and empirically credible.

The feminist philosopher Duran (1998) urges other feminists not to forsake scientific and credible research because it was exactly such research that documented family violence and spousal abuse. To leave this to a relativistic diversity of perspectives epitomized by "I am right and you're right" would be a grave error. Indeed, it is the evidence, the credible data, the legally admissible data, that shows there is child abuse or spousal abuse. Duran (1998) warns that if feminism is not scientific then feminists better well be in control of power because the other road would mean that "truth" is simply established by political power. We should not give up on science as producing evidence and data that are credible with other scientists and with the public. We would not want social programs costing thousands if not millions of taxpayers' dollars justified by one or two anecdotal cases. The scientist's fear of calls for the abandonment of scientific methods has been well expressed by Gross and Levitt (1994) as a fear of a return to the "dark ages" of superstition. I don't seriously believe this is a likely outcome, but the argument for the role of credible evidence launched by such diverse scholars as Duran and Gross and Levitt does suggest we need to be vigilant in the defense of scientific epistemic values.

I believe the social sciences, study of the family, and development of family theory would be well served by the viewpoint that research conducted in the context of discovery may lead to greater understanding, better metaphors, and the production of interesting and novel propositions. These are all tasks that theory and science needs. It is also important that understanding not be confused with explanation. Clearly, I can understand a poem, but to say I predict it is utter nonsense. There is, however, a vital role for measurement and prediction in the arena of justification. Social science knowledge is clearly grounded in the context of justification and accountability. But we should not mistake that both of these "contexts" are dealing with ideas, albeit in different ways. We should be vigilant to ensure that the goal of the production of credible knowledge is shared, for then these two contexts are optimally complementary.

In closing, I am reminded of the flattering portrait of academics in family studies painted by Klein and White (1996):

> If we look at the history of science, it is not a particular research finding or project that survives the test of time, nor even the reputations of people who produce them. Only basic ideas and theories survive over time. For most scholars, these ideas are what initially compelled them to join the academic enterprise and, indeed, it is this life of ideas that still furnishes the most significant but intangible rewards for many of us. (p. 270)

Let us attempt to make this portrait an accurate one. It is up to us to ensure that the life of ideas continues to be vigorously encouraged and enjoyed by the next generation of students and scholars.

References

Adams, B., & Steinmetz, S. (1993). Family theory and methods in the classics. In P. Boss, W. Doherty, R. LaRossa, W. Schumm, & S. Steinmetz (Eds.), *Sourcebook of family theories and methods: A contextual approach* (pp. 71–94). New York: Plenum.

Aldous, J. (1996). *Family careers: Rethinking the developmental perspective.* Thousand Oaks, CA: Sage.

Aldous, J. (1970). Strategies for developing family theory. *Journal of Marriage and the Family, 32,* 250–257.

Allchin, D. (1998). Values in science and in science education. In B. J. Fraser & K. G. Tobin (Eds.), *International handbook of science education.* Dordrecht, Netherlands: Kluwer Academic.

Allen, K. (2000). A conscious and inclusive family studies. *Journal of Marriage and the Family, 62,* 4–17.

Allison, P. (1984). *Event history analysis: Regression for longitudinal event data.* Beverly Hills, CA: Sage.

Amato, P. R. (2000). The consequences of divorce for adults and children. *Journal of Marriage and the Family, 62,* 1269–1287.

Apel, K.-O. (1981). *Charles Sanders Peirce: From pragmatism to pragmaticism* (J. M. Krois, Trans.). Amherst: University of Massachusetts Press.

Becker, G. (1981). *A treatise on the family.* Cambridge, MA: Belknap.

Bengtson, V. L., & Allen, K. R. (1993). The life course perspective applied to families over time. In P. Boss, W. Doherty, R. LaRossa, W. Schumm, & S. Steinmetz (Eds.), *Sourcebook of family theories and methods: A contextual approach* (pp. 469–499). New York: Plenum.

Benton, T., & Craig, I. (2001). Philosophy of social science: The philosophical foundations of social thought. New York: Palgrave.

Berger, P., & Kellner, H. (1964). Marriage and the construction of reality. *Diogenes, 46,* 1–25.

Bianchi, S., & Robinson, J. (1997). What did you do today? Children's use of time, family composition and the acquisition of human capital. *Journal of Marriage and the Family, 59,* 332–344.

Biblarz, T. J., & Gottainer, G. (2000). Family structure and children's success: A comparison of widowed and divorced single-mother families. *Journal of Marriage and the Family, 62*, 533–548.

Black, M. (1962). *Models and metaphors: Studies in language and philosophy.* Ithaca, NY: Cornell University Press.

Blalock, H., Jr. (1969). *Theory construction.* Englewood Cliffs, NJ: Prentice Hall.

Blalock, H., Jr. (1994). Why have we failed to systemize reality's complexities? In J. Hage, (Ed.), *Formal theory in sociology: Opportunity or pitfall?* (pp. 130–141). Albany: State University of New York Press.

Blood, R. O., & Wolfe, D. M. (1960). *Husbands and wives.* New York: The Free Press.

Blumer, H. (1962). Society as symbolic interaction. In A. M. Rose (Ed.), *Human behavior and social processes* (pp. 179–192). Boston: Houghton Mifflin.

Blumer, H. (1969). *Symbolic interactionism: Perspective and method.* Englewood Cliffs, NJ: Prentice Hall.

Booth, A., Carver, K., & Granger, D. A. (2000). Biosocial perspectives on the family. *Journal of Marriage and the Family, 62*, 1018–1034.

Boss, P., Doherty, W., LaRossa, R., Schumm, W., & Steinmetz, S. (Eds.). (1993). *Sourcebook of family theories and methods: A contextual approach.* New York: Plenum.

Bossard, J., & Boll, E. (1950). *Ritual in family living.* Philadelphia: University of Pennsylvania Press.

Bourdieu, P. (1986). Forms of capital. In J. Richardson (Ed.), *Handbook of theory and research for the sociology of education* (pp. 241–260). Westport, CT: Greenwood.

Braithwaite, R. B. (1953). *Scientific explanation: A study of the function, probability and law in science.* Cambridge, UK: Cambridge University Press.

Breunlin, D. C. (1988). Oscillation theory and family development. In C. Falicov (Ed.), *Family transitions.* New York: Guilford.

Bronfenbrenner, U. (1979). *The ecology of human development.* Cambridge, MA: Harvard University Press.

Bronfenbrenner, U. (1989). Ecological systems theory. In R. Vasta (Ed.), *Annals of child development* (Vol. 6, pp. 187–249). Greenwich, CT: JAI.

Bubolz, M., & Sontag, S. (1993). Human ecology theory. In P. Boss, W. Doherty, R. LaRossa, W. Schumm, & S. Steinmetz (Eds.), *Sourcebook of family theories and methods: A contextual approach* (pp. 419–448). New York: Plenum Press.

Buchler, J. (Ed.). (1955). *Philosophical writings of Peirce.* New York: Dover.

Bulcroft, R., & White, J. M. (1997). Family research methods and levels of analysis. *Family Science Review, 10*, 2–19.

Burgess, E. W. (1926). The family as a unity of interacting personalities. *Family, 7*, 3–9.

Burr, J. A., & Nesselroade, J. R. (1990). Change measurement. In A. von Eye (Ed.), *Statistical methods in longitudinal research* (Vol. I, pp. 3–34). London: Academic Press.

Burr, W. R. (1973). *Theory construction and the sociology of the family.* New York: Wiley.

Burr, W. R., Hill, R., Nye, F. I., & Reiss, I. (Eds.). (1979). *Contemporary theories about the family* (2 vols.). New York: The Free Press.

Burr, W. R., Leigh, G., Day, R., & Constantine, J. (1979). Symbolic interaction and the family. In W. R. Burr, R. Hill, F. I. Nye, & I. Reiss (Eds.), *Contemporary theories about the family* (Vol. 2, pp. 42–111). New York: The Free Press.

Carnap, R. (1966). *Philosophical foundations of physics.* New York: Basic Books.

Carnap, R. (1974). *An introduction to philosophy of science.* New York: Basic Books.

Carter, E., & McGoldrick, M. (Eds.). (1980). *The changing family cycle: A framework for family therapy.* New York: Gardner.

Carter, E., & McGoldrick, M. (Eds.). (1988). *The changing family cycle: A framework for family therapy* (2nd ed.). New York: Gardner.

Carter, E., & McGoldrick, M. (Eds.). (1999). *The expanded family life cycle: Individual, family and social perspectives* (3rd ed.). Boston: Allyn & Bacon.

Caspi, A., Wright, B., Moffit, T., & Silva, P. (1998). Early failure in the labor market: Childhood and adolescent predictors of unemployment in the transition to adulthood. *American Sociological Review, 63,* 424–451.

Cheal, D. (1991). *Family and the state of theory.* Toronto, ON: University of Toronto Press.

Chomsky, N. (1965). Aspects of the theory of syntax. Cambridge: MIT Press.

Christensen, H. (1964). Development of the family field of study. In H. Christensen (Ed.), *Handbook of marriage and the family* (pp. 3–32). Chicago: Rand McNally.

Coleman, J. S. (1981). *Longitudinal data analysis.* New York: Basic Books.

Coleman, J. S. (1988). Social capital in the creation of human capital. *American Journal of Sociology, 94,* S95–S120.

Coleman, J. S. (1990). *Foundations of social theory.* Cambridge, MA: Belknap.

Cowan, P. A., & Cowan, C. P. (2000). *When partners become parents: The big life change for couples.* New York: Erlbaum.

Cox, D. R. (1972). Regression models and life tables (with discussion). *Journal of the Royal Statistical Society, Series B, 34,* 187–220.

Daly, K. (2003). Family theory versus the theories we live by. *Journal of Marriage and the Family, 65,* 771–784.

Davies, P. (1995). *About time: Einstein's unfinished revolution.* New York: Simon & Schuster.

Derrida, J. (1976). *Of grammatology* (G. Spivak, Trans.). Baltimore: Johns Hopkins University Press.

Dewey, J. (1929). *Experience and nature.* LaSalle, IL: Open Court.

Doherty, W. J. (1999). Postmodernism and family theory. In M. Sussman, S. Steinmetz, & G. Peterson (Eds.), *Handbook of marriage and the family* (2nd ed., pp. 205–217). New York: Plenum.

Doherty, W., Boss, P., LaRossa, R., Schumm, W., & Steinmetz, S. (1993). Family theories and methods: A contextual approach. In P. Boss, W. Doherty, R. LaRossa, W. Schumm, & S. Steinmetz (Eds.), *Sourcebook of family theories and methods: A contextual approach* (pp. 3–30). New York: Plenum.

Duran, J. (1998). *Philosophies of science/feminist theories.* Boulder, CO: Westview Press.

Durkheim, E. (1949). *The division of labour in society.* Glencoe, IL: The Free Press.

Durkheim, E. (1951). *Suicide.* Glencoe, IL: The Free Press.

Elder, G., Jr. (1974). *Children of the great depression: Social change in life experience.* Chicago: University of Chicago Press.

Elder, G., Jr., Modell, J., & Parke, R. (Eds.). (1993). *Children in time and place: Developmental and historical insights.* New York: Cambridge University Press.

Emerson, R. (1976). Social exchange theory. In A. Inkles, J. Coleman, & N. Smelser (Eds.), *Annual review of sociology* (Vol. 2, pp. 335–362). Palo Alto, CA: Annual Reviews.

Engels, F. (1946). *The origin of the family, private property and the state.* New York: International Publishers. (Original work published 1884)

Epstein, N. B., & Santa Barbara, J. (1975). Conflict behavior in clinical couples: Interpersonal perceptions and stable outcomes. *Family Process, 14,* 51–66.

Falicov, C. (Ed.). (1988). *Family transitions.* New York: Guilford.

Featherman, D. (1985). Individual development and aging as a population process. In J. Nesselroade & A. Von Eye (Eds.), *Individual development and social change: Exploratory analysis* (pp. 213–241). New York: Academic Press.

Feeney, J. A., Hohaus, L., Noller, P., & Alexander, R. (2001). *Becoming parents: Exploring the bonds between mothers, fathers, & their infants.* Cambridge, UK: Cambridge University Press.

Feyerabend, P. (1975). *Against method: Outline of an anarchistic theory of knowledge.* London: New Left Books.

Gadamer, H. (1982). *Reason in the age of science.* Cambridge: MIT Press.

Gerth, H., & Mills, C. W. (Trans. & Eds.). (1958). *From Max Weber.* New York: Oxford University Press.

Goode, W. (1963). *World revolution and family patterns.* New York: The Free Press.

Goode, W., Hopkins, E., & McClure, H. (1971). *Social systems and family patterns: A propositional inventory.* Indianapolis, IN: Bobs-Merrill.

Gordon, L. (1979). The struggle for reproductive freedom: Three stages of feminism. In Z. Eisenstein (Ed.), *Capitalist patriarchy and the case for socialist feminism* (pp. 107–136). New York: Monthly Review Press.

Gottman, J. M. (1979). *Marital interaction: Experimental investigations.* New York: Academic Press.

Gottman, J. M., & Notarius, C. I. (2000). Decade review: Observing marital interaction. *Journal of Marriage and the Family, 62,* 927–947.

Gould, S. J. (2002). *The structure of evolutionary theory.* Cambridge, MA: Harvard University Press.

Greenfield, S. (1961). Industrialization and the family in sociological theory. *American Journal of Sociology, 67,* 312–322.

Gross, P., & Levitt, R. (1994). *Higher superstition: The academic left and its quarrel with science.* Baltimore: Johns Hopkins University Press.

Gubrium, J., & Holstein, J. (1993). Phenomenology, ethnomethodology, and family discourse. In P. Boss, W. Doherty, R. LaRossa, W. Schumm, & S. Steinmetz (Eds.), *Sourcebook of family theories and methods: A contextual approach* (pp. 651–672). New York: Plenum.

Haack, S. (1993). *Evidence and inquiry.* Cambridge, MA: Blackwell.

Haack, S. (1998). *Manifesto of a passionate moderate: Unfashionable essays.* Chicago: University of Chicago Press.

Habermas, J. (1971). *Knowledge and human interests* (J. Shapiro, Trans.). Boston: Beacon Press.

Hage, J. (1972). *Techniques and problems of theory construction.* New York: Wiley.

Hage, J. (Ed.). (1994). *Formal theory in sociology: Opportunity or pitfall?* Albany: State University of New York Press.

Harding, S. (1991). *Whose science? Whose knowledge?* Ithaca, NY: Cornell University Press.

Hatcher, D. (1991). Can critical thinking survive the postmodern challenge? *Inquiry: Critical Thinking Across the Disciplines, 7,* 8–17.

Haveman, R., & Wolfe, B. (1994). *Succeeding generations.* New York: Russell Sage.

Hawley, D. R., & Geske, S. (2000). The use of theory in family therapy research: A content analysis of family therapy journals. *Journal of Marital and Family Therapy, 26,* 17–22.

Hellemans, A., & Bunch, B. (1988). *The timetables of science.* New York: Simon & Schuster.

Heller, J. (1961). *Catch 22.* New York: Dell.

Hempel, C. G. (1952). *Fundamentals of concept formation in empirical science.* Chicago: University of Chicago Press.

Hempel, C. (1966). *Philosophy of natural science.* Englewood Cliffs, NJ: Prentice Hall.

Hetherington, E. M. (1999). Social capital and the development of youth from nondivorced, divorced and remarried families. In A. Collins & L. Brett (Eds.), *Relationships as developmental contexts. The Minnesota symposia on child psychology* (Vol. 30, pp. 177–209). Mahwah, NJ: Lawrence Erlbaum Associates.

Hill, R. (1949). *Families under stress.* New York: Harper & Brothers.

Hill, R., & Hansen, D. (1960). The identification of conceptual frameworks utilized in family study. *Marriage and Family Living, 22,* 299–311.

Hill, R., Katz, A., & Simpson, R. (1957). An inventory of research in marriage and family behavior: A statement of objectives and progress. *Marriage and Family Living, 19,* 89–92.

Hill, R., & Rodgers, R. H. (1964). The developmental approach. In H. Christensen (Ed.), *Handbook of marriage and the family* (pp. 171–211). Chicago: Rand McNally.

Hogan, D. (1978). The variable order of events in the life course. *American Sociological Review, 43,* 573–586.

Hogan, D. (1981). *Transitions and social change: The early lives of American men.* New York: Academic Press.

Holman, T. B., & Burr, W. R. (1980). Beyond the beyond: The growth of the family theories in the 1970s. *Journal of Marriage and the Family, 42,* 729–742.

Homans, G. C. (1950). *The human group.* New York: Harcourt, Brace & World.

Homans, G. C. (1967). *The nature of social science.* New York: Harcourt, Brace & World.

Hospers, J. (1967). *An introduction to philosophical analysis* (2nd ed.). Englewood Cliffs, NJ: Prentice Hall.

Kahneman, D., Slovic, P., & Tversky, A. (1982). *Judgment under uncertainty; heuristics and biases.* Cambridge, UK: Cambridge University Press.

Kahneman, D., & Tversky, A. (1979). Prospect theory: An analysis of decision under risk. *Econometrica, 47,* 263–289.

Kahneman, D., & Tversky, A. (1983). Can irrationality be intelligently discussed? *Behavioral and Brain Sciences, 6,* 509–510.

Kahneman, D., & Tversky, A. (1984). Choices, values, and frames. *American Psychologist, 39,* 341–350.

Kaplan, A. (1964). *The conduct of inquiry.* San Francisco: Chandler.

Kemeny, J. (1966). *Introduction to finite mathematics* (2nd ed.). Englewood Cliffs, NJ: Prentice Hall.

Klein, D. M., & Janning, M. Y. (1997). Philosophies of family scientists. *Family Perspective, 30,* 483–502.

Klein, D. M., & Jurich, J. A. (1993). Metatheory and family studies. In P. G. Boss, W. Doherty, R. LaRossa, W. R. Schumm, & S. K. Steinmetz (Eds.), *Sourcebook of family theories and methods: A contextual approach* (pp. 31–67). New York: Plenum.

Klein, D. M., & White, J. M. (1996). *Family theories: An introduction.* Thousand Oaks, CA: Sage.

Knapp, S. J. (1997). Knowledge claims in the family field: A hermeneutical alternative to the representational model. *Family Perspective, 30,* 369–428.

Knorr-Cetina, K. (1981). *The manufacture of knowledge.* Oxford, UK: Pergamon.

Knorr-Cetina, K. (1999). *Epistemic cultures: How the sciences make knowledge.* Cambridge, MA: Harvard University Press.

Koertge, N. (Ed.). (1998). *A house built on sand: Exposing postmodernist myths about science.* Oxford, UK: Oxford University Press.

Kuhn, T. (1962). *The structure of scientific revolutions.* Chicago: University of Chicago Press.

Kuhn, T. (1970). *The structure of scientific revolutions* (2nd ed.). Chicago: University of Chicago Press.

Kuhn, T. (1996). *The structure of scientific revolutions* (3rd ed.). Chicago: University of Chicago Press.

Lakoff, G., & Johnson, M. (1980). *The metaphors we live by.* Chicago: University of Chicago Press.

Lakoff, G., & Johnson, M. (1999). *Philosophy in the flesh.* New York: Basic Books.

Latour, B. (1999). *Pandora's hope: Essays on the reality of science studies.* Cambridge, MA: Harvard University Press.

Lavee, Y., & Dollahite, D. (1991). The linkage between theory and research in family science. *Journal of Marriage and the Family, 53,* 361–373.

Leik, R. K., & Meeker, B. F. (1975). *Mathematical sociology.* Englewood Cliffs, NJ: Prentice Hall.

Levinger, G. (1977). *Close relationships*. Amherst: University of Massachusetts Press.

Levi-Strauss, C. (1966). *The savage mind*. London: Weidenfeld & Nicolson.

Levi-Strauss, C. (1969). *The elementary structures of kinship*. Boston: Beacon.

Lewis, R., & Spanier, G. (1979). Theorizing about the quality and stability of marriage. In W. R. Burr, R. Hill, F. I. Nye, & I. Reiss (Eds.), *Contemporary theories about the family* (Vol. 2, pp. 1–41). New York: The Free Press.

Lillard, L. A., Brien, M., & Waite, L. (1995). Premarital cohabitation and subsequent marital dissolution: A matter of self-selection? *Demography, 32*, 437–457.

Lillegard, N. (2003). Philosophy of social science. In J. Fieser (Ed.), *Internet Encyclopedia of Philosophy*. Retrieved September 2003 from www.utm.edu/research/iep/

Longino, H. E. (1990). *Science as social knowledge: Values and objectivity in scientific inquiry*. Princeton, NJ: Princeton University Press.

Longino, H. E. (2002). *The fate of knowledge*. Princeton, NJ: Princeton University Press.

Lundberg, G. (1942). *Social Research*. New York: Longmans and Green.

Lupri, E. (1969). Contemporary authority patterns in the West German family: A study in cross-national validation. *Journal of Marriage and the Family, 31*, 134–144.

Magrabi, F. M., & Marshall, W. H. (1965). Family developmental tasks: A research model. *Journal of Marriage and the Family, 27*, 454–461.

Malinowski, B. (1932). *Argonauts of the western Pacific*. London: Routledge.

Malthus, T. (1872). *An essay on the principle of population* (7th ed.). London: Reeves & Turner. (Original work published 1798)

Marini, M. M. (1984). Age and sequencing norms in the transition to adulthood. *Social Forces, 63*, 229–244.

Marjoribanks, K., & Kwok, Y. (1998). Family capital and Hong Kong adolescents' academic achievement. *Psychological Reports, 83*, 99–105.

Marks, N. F., & Lambert, J. D. (1998). Marital status continuity and change among young and midlife adults. *Journal of Family Issues, 19*, 652–686.

Marks, S. (2000). Teasing out the lessons of the 1960s: Family diversity and family privilege. *Journal of Marriage and the Family, 62*, 609–622.

Martindale, D. (1979). Ideologies, paradigms, and theories. In W. Snizek, E. Fuhrman, & M. Miller (Eds.), *Contemporary issues in theory and research: A metasociological perspective* (pp. 7–24). Westport, CT: Greenwood.

McGinnis, R. (1965). *Mathematical foundations for social analysis*. Indianapolis, IN: Bobbs-Merrill.

McLain, R., & Weigert, A. (1979). Toward a phenomenological sociology of family: A programmatic essay. In W. R. Burr, R. Hill, F. I. Nye, & I. Reiss (Eds.), *Contemporary theories about the family* (Vol. 2, pp. 160–205). New York: The Free Press.

Mead, G. H. (1934). *Mind, self and society* (C. Morris, Introduction and Ed.). Chicago: University of Chicago Press.

Merton, R. (1973). The normative structure of science. In R. K. Merton, *The sociology of science: Theoretical and empirical investigations* (pp. 267–278). Chicago: University of Chicago Press.

Norris, C. (1989). Philosophy, theory and the "Contest of Faculties": Saving deconstruction from the pragmatists. In Rajnath (Ed.), *Deconstruction: A critique* (pp. 67–82). London: Macmillan.

Nye, F. I. (1979). Choice, exchange, and the family. In W. R. Burr, R. Hill, F. I. Nye, & I. Reiss (Eds.), *Contemporary theories about the family* (Vol. 2, pp. 1–41). New York: The Free Press.

Nye, F. I., & Berardo, F. (1981). *Emerging conceptual frameworks in family analysis*. New York: Praeger. (Original work published 1966)

O'Connor, D. L., & O'Neill, B. J. (2000). *Toward social justice: Teaching qualitative research*. Paper presented at the joint conference of the International Federation of Social Workers and the International Association of Schools of Social Work, Montreal, Quebec, Canada.

Osmond, M., & Thorne, B. (1993). Feminist theories: The construction of gender in families and society. In P. G. Boss, W. Doherty, R. LaRossa, W. Schumm, & S. Steinmetz (Eds.), *Sourcebook of family theories and methods: A contextual approach* (pp. 591–622). New York: Plenum.

Parsons, T. (1943). The kinship system of the contemporary United States. *American Anthropologist, 45*, 22–28.

Parsons, T. (1959). The social structure of the family. In R. Anshen (Ed.), *The family: Its function and destiny*. New York: Harper and Brothers.

Parsons, T., & Bales, R. (1955). *Family, socialization and interaction process*. New York: The Free Press.

Parsons, T., & Shils, E. (1952). Values, motives and systems of action. In T. Parsons & E. Shils (Ed.), *Toward a general theory of action*. Cambridge, MA: Harvard University Press.

Pedhazur, E. J., & Schmelkin, L. P. (1991). *Measurement, design and analysis: An integrated approach*. Hillsdale, NJ: Lawrence Ehrlbaum Associates.

Peirce, C. S. (1905). What pragmatism is. *Monist, 5*, 411–436.

Peirce, C. S. (1955). *Philosophical writings of Peirce* (J. Buchler, Ed.). New York: Dover.

Peirce, C. S. (1958). The fixation of belief. In P. Weiner (Ed.), *Charles S. Peirce, Selected Writings* (pp. 114–136). New York: Dover. (Reprinted from *Popular Science Monthly* (1877), 12:1–15)

Pepper, S. C. (1942). *World hypotheses*. Berkeley: University of California Press.

Popper, K. (1959). *The logic of scientific discovery*. New York: Basic Books.

Potter, G. (1999). *The philosophy of social science: New perspectives*. Essex, UK: Pearson Education.

Prigogine, I., & Stengers, I. (1984). *Order out of chaos*. New York: Bantam

Reichenbach, H. (1958). *The philosophy of space and time*. New York: Dover.

Rodgers, R. H. (1973). *Family interaction and transaction: The developmental approach*. Englewood Cliffs, NJ: Prentice Hall.

Rodgers, R. H., & White, J. M. (1993). Family development theory. In P. G. Boss, W. Doherty, R. LaRossa, W. Schumm, & S. Steinmetz (Eds.), *Sourcebook of family theories and methods: A contextual approach* (pp. 225–254). New York: Plenum.

Rodman, H. (1967). Marital power in France, Greece, Yugoslavia and the United States. *Journal of Marriage and the Family, 29,* 320–324.

Rorty, R. (1979). *Philosophy and the mirror of nature.* Princeton, NJ: Princeton University Press.

Rorty, R. (1982). *Consequences of pragmatism.* Minneapolis: University of Minnesota Press.

Rudner, R. S. (1966). *Philosophy of social science.* Englewood Cliffs, NJ: Prentice Hall.

Sabatelli, R. M., & Shehan, C. L. (1993). Exchange and resource theories. In P. G. Boss, W. Doherty, R. LaRossa, W. Schumm, & S. Steinmetz (Eds.), *Sourcebook of family theories and methods: A contextual approach* (pp. 385–411). New York: Plenum.

Safilios-Rothschild, C. (1967). A comparison of power structure and marital satisfaction in urban Greek and French families. *Journal of Marriage and the Family, 29,* 345–352.

Santa Barbara, J., & Epstein, N. B. (1974). Conflict behavior in clinical families: Preasymptomatic interactions and stable outcomes. *Behavioral Science, 19,* 100–110.

Schusky, E. L. (1965). *Manual for kinship analysis.* New York: Holt, Rinehart and Winston.

Sprey, J. (1979). Theoretical practice in family studies. In J. Sprey (Ed.), *Fashioning family theory: New approaches* (pp. 9–33). Newbury Park, CA: Sage.

Sprey, J. (1999). Theorizing in family studies: Discovering process. *Journal of Marriage and the Family, 62,* 18–31.

Stinchcombe, A. (1968). *Constructing social theories.* New York: Harcourt, Brace & World.

Straus, M. (1969). Phenomenal identity and conceptual equivalence of measurement in cross-national research. *Journal of Marriage and the Family, 31,* 233–239.

Strauss, A., & Corbin, J. (1997). *Grounded theory in practice.* Thousand Oaks, CA: Sage.

Suppe, F. (1977). *The structure of scientific theories* (2nd ed.). Urbana: University of Illinois Press.

Suppes, P. (1960). *Axiomatic set theory.* Princeton, NJ: Van Nostrand.

Suppes, P. (1984). *Probabilistic metaphysics.* Oxford, UK: Blackwell.

Teachman, J., & Crowder, K. (2002). Multilevel models in family research: Some conceptual and methodological issues. *Journal of Marriage and the Family, 64,* 280–294.

Teachman, J., Paasch, K., & Carver, K. (1997). Social capital and the generation of human capital. *Social Forces, 75,* 1343–1359.

Thibaut, J. W., & Kelley, H. H. (1959). *The social psychology of groups.* New York: Wiley.

Thomas, D. L., & Wilcox, J. E. (1987). The rise of family theory: A historical and critical analysis. In M. B. Sussman & S. K. Steinmetz (Eds.), *Handbook of marriage and the family* (pp. 81–102). New York: Plenum.

Thompson, L., & Walker, A. (1982). The dyad as the unit of analysis: Conceptual and methodological issues. *Journal of Marriage and the Family, 44,* 889–900.

Tönnies, F. (1957). *Community and society: Gemeinschaft und Gesellschaft* (G. P. Loomis, Trans.). East Lansing: Michigan State University Press. (Original work published 1887)

Tuma, N., & Hannan, M. (1984). *Social dynamics.* New York: Academic Press.

Turner, J. (1991). *The structure of sociological theory* (5th ed.). Belmont, CA: Wadsworth.

Turner, J. (1994). The failure of sociology to institutionalize cumulative theorizing. In J. Hage (Ed.), *Formal theory in sociology: Opportunity or pitfall?* (pp. 41–51). Albany: State University of New York Press.

Turner, J. (1998). *The structure of sociological theory* (6th ed.). Belmont, CA: Wadsworth.

Turner, J. (2001). *Handbook of sociological theory.* New York: Plenum.

Tversky, A. (1972). Elimination by aspects—Theory of choice. *Psychological Review, 79,* 281–290.

Tversky, A., & Kahneman, D. (1974). Judgment under uncertainty: Heuristics and biases. *Science, 185,* 1124–1131.

Tversky, A., & Kahneman, D. (1981). The framing of decisions and the psychology of choice. *Science, 211,* 453–458.

Tversky, A., & Kahneman, D. (1988). Rational choice and the framing of decisions. In D. E. Bell, H. Raiffa, & A. Tversky (Eds.), *Decision making: Descriptive, normative, and prescriptive interactions* (pp. 167–192). Cambridge, UK: Cambridge University Press.

Vargus, B. S. (1999). Classical social theory and family studies: The triumph of reactionary thought in contemporary family studies. In M. Sussman, S. Steinmetz, & G. Peterson (Eds.), *Handbook of Marriage and the Family* (2nd ed.) (pp. 179–204). New York: Plenum.

Weber, M. (1949). *The methodology of the social sciences* (E. Shils & H. Finch, Trans. & Ed.). New York: The Free Press.

White, J. M. (1991). *Dynamics of family development: The theory of family development.* New York: Guilford.

White, J. M. (1997). Family theory, science, and the problem of certainty. *Family Perspectives, 30,* 445–454.

White, J. M. (1998). The normative interpretation of life course event histories. *Marriage and Family Review, 3/4,* 211–235.

White, J. M., & Klein, D. M. (2002). *Family theories* (2nd ed.). Thousand Oaks, CA: Sage.

White, J. M., & Marshall, S. (2001). Consciously inclusive family research: Can we get there from here? *Journal of Marriage and the Family, 63,* 895–898.

White, J. M., & Mason, L. K. (1999a). Post-positivism and positivism: A dialogue. *Family Science Review, 12,* 1–21.

White, J. M., & Mason, L. K. (1999b). Reconstructing the positivistic "strawman." *Family Science Review, 12,* 44–48.

White, J. M., & Teachman, J. D. (2005). Comment on "Multilevel methods in family research." In V. Bengtson et al. (Eds.), *Sourcebook of family theory and research.* Thousand Oaks, CA: Sage.

Winch, P. (1958). *The idea of a social science and its relation to philosophy.* London: Routledge & Kegan Paul.

Wittgenstein, L. (1956). *Remarks on the foundation of mathematics.* Oxford, UK: Blackwell.

Wrong, D. (1961). The oversocialized conception of man in modern sociology. *American Review of Sociology, 26,* 183–193.

Yamaguchi, K. (1991). *Event history analysis.* Newbury Park, CA: Sage.

Zelditch, M., Jr. (1956). Role differentiation in the nuclear family: A comparative study. In T. Parsons & R. Bales (Eds.), *Family, socialization and interactional process* (pp. 307–352). New York: The Free Press.

Zetterberg, H. (1963). *On theory and verification in sociology.* Totowa, NJ: Bedminster.

Zimmerman, C. C. (1947). *Family and civilization.* New York: Harper.

Author Index

Subject Index

individual, 124–128
microtransitions, 131
role, 124–128
stage, 123
stage, events as markers for, 135
state-to-state, 135
See also Transition theory
Transition state-space, 118
Transition theory, 1, 91–92, 115–142
age, period, cohort, and, 140
behavior-expectation oscillations
   and, 128–134
critiques of, 139–141
dyads and, 128–134
family transitions and norms, 134–137
institutions and historical
   perspective, 137–139
See also Transition
Treatise on the Family, A (Becker),
   96, 169
Trobriand kinship, 124
Two-sciences perspective, 83

Understanding, equivocation between
   explanation and, 172–174
Urban VIII (Pope), 37
Utilitarian theories, 83
Utility, maximization of, 111

Validity, changing criteria for, 80
Values:
   epistemic, theory and, 162–163
   ethics and, 165
   ideology and, 164
Variables, dependent, 70
Variation, deviance vs., 137, 140
Venn diagram, 58
Verstehen, 39, 83

Wallace, Alfred, 38
Wife, employment of, 19
World Ethnographic Sample, 16
World War II, family at end of, 14–15

Zealotry, problem of, 114

About the Author

James M. White is known internationally for his work in the area of family theory. His first book, *Dynamics of Family Development*, developed a new approach to family development and generated interest both in the United States (1991) and abroad (Japan, 1994). His second book, with David M. Klein, surveys the major extant theories used for studying the family and is now it its second edition. He has also coauthored *Families in Canada* (third edition, 2004). He has been a keen supporter of the Theory Construction and Research Methodology Workshop (TCRM) hosted by the National Council on Family Relations and has presented many papers to this group. Besides his interest in researching family theory and development, he is also interested in marital interaction, family structure, and cohabitation. He is the author of numerous journal articles appearing both in sociology journals and such journals as the *Journal of Family Issues*, the *Journal of Social and Personal Relationships*, and the *Journal of Marriage and Family*. He has authored chapters for books, including the chapter he coauthored with R. H. Rodgers on family development in the *Sourcebook of Family Theories and Methods: A Contextual Approach* (1993). He has served as referee for numerous journals in family relations and public health and is an associate editor for the *Canadian Journal of Public Health*, the *Journal of Comparative Family Studies* and *The International Encyclopedia of Family Relationships*. He is past president of the Northwest Council on Family Relations, whose membership includes academics, practitioners, and therapists from the states and provinces of the Pacific Northwest. He is a professor in the School of Social Work and Family Studies at the University of British Columbia and resides with his wife and three daughters in Vancouver, Canada.